More Stories by Japanese Women Writers

An Anthology

Edited by

Kyoko Selden and Noriko Mizuta

An East Gate Book

M.E.Sharpe
Armonk, New York
London, England

An East Gate Book
Consulting Editor: Doug Merwin

Selection, introduction, and editorial material copyright 2011 by Kyoko Selden and Noriko Mizuta.

All rights reserved. No part of this book may be reproduced in any form without written permission from the publisher, M.E. Sharpe, Inc., 80 Business Park Drive, Armonk, New York 10504.

The EuroSlavic and Transroman fonts used to create this work are © 1986–2010 Payne Loving Trust. EuroSlavic and Transroman are available from Linguist's Software, Inc., www.linguistsoftware.com, P.O. Box 580, Edmonds, WA 98020-0580 USA, tel (425) 775-1130.

Library of Congress Cataloging-in-Publication Data

More stories by Japanese women writers : an anthology / edited by Kyoko Selden and Noriko Mizuta.
 p. cm.
"An East Gate Book."
ISBN 978-0-7656-2733-9 (cloth : alk. paper)—ISBN 978-0-7656-2734-6 (pbk. : alk. paper)
1. Japanese fiction—Women authors. 2. Japanese fiction—1868– 3. Japanese fiction—Women authors—Bio-bibliography. I. Selden, Kyoko Iriye, 1936– II. Mizuta, Noriko.

PL770.55.W64M67 2010
895.6′3440809287—dc22   2010021695

Printed in the United States of America

The paper used in this publication meets the minimum requirements of American National Standard for Information Sciences Permanence of Paper for Printed Library Materials, ANSI Z 39.48-1984.

∞

IBT (c) 10   9   8   7   6   5   4   3   2   1
IBT (p) 10   9   8   7   6   5   4   3   2   1

Contents

Introduction
Kyoko Selden and Noriko Mizuta   v

1. **This Child**
   Higuchi Ichiyō (Translated by Michael K. Bourdaghs)   3

2. **Her Daily Life**
   Tamura Toshiko (Translated by Kyoko Selden)   9

3. **The Song the Owl God Himself Sang: "Silver Droplets Fall Fall All Around"**
   Chiri Yukie (Translated by Kyoko Selden)   26

4. **Miss Cricket**
   Ozaki Midori (Translated by Seiji M. Lippit)   35

5. **Thorn**
   Mori Mari (Translated by Angela Yiu)   45

6. **Masks of Whatchamacallit**
   Hayashi Kyōko (Translated by Kyoko Selden)   52

7. **Water's Edge**
   Tsushima Yūko (Translated by Gillia Kinjo and Susan Bouterey)   76

8. **Cherry Blossom Train**
   Saegusa Kazuko (Translated by Alisa Freedman and Kyoko Selden)   86

9. **The Strange Story of a Pumpkin**
   Kurahashi Yumiko (Translated by Kyoko Selden)   96

10. **Mama Drinks Her Tea**
    Ogino Anna (Translated by Vyjayanthi Ratnam Selinger)   102

11. **Transit**
    Ogawa Yōko (Translated by Alisa Freedman)   127

12. **The Tidal Hour**
    Yū Miri (Translated by Robert Steen)   139

13. **The Tale of Wind and Water**
    Sakiyama Tami (Translated by Kyoko Selden) — 158

14. **Stars Scintillating in My Eyes**
    Tawada Yōko (Translated by Kyoko Selden) — 176

15. **Fiction Within Fiction: "Shōno Yoriko, Fiction"**
    Shōno Yoriko (Translated by Kyoko Selden) — 187

16. **You People's Love Is Near Death**
    Kawakami Mieko (Translated by Kyoko Selden) — 213

About the Authors — 223
About the Editors and Translators — 245

Introduction

Kyoko Selden and Noriko Mizuta

More Stories by Japanese Women Writers: An Anthology presents translations of sixteen stories by Japanese women writers spanning more than a century. It complements our earlier collection, *Japanese Women Writers: Twentieth Century Short Fiction* (1991), itself an enlarged edition of *Stories by Contemporary Japanese Women Writers* (1982). The present volume introduces additional important authors, themes, and perspectives not represented in earlier volumes.

The original *Japanese Women Writers* featured fourteen authors and fourteen stories dating from 1934 to 1987. Our objective in that collection was to illuminate the place of women writers in the historical development of modern Japan and their contribution to its literature. The selected stories revealed the changing consciousness, perspectives, and styles of women writers in the course of a tumultuous era of war followed by occupation, democratization, and rapid growth.

The present volume contains selections from a wider span of years, 1895 to 2008, including four from before 1934 and six from after 1987. They are by authors from across the archipelago—Hokkaido, Tokyo, Yokohama, Ise, Kobe, Osaka, Okayama, Kōchi, Nagasaki, and Okinawa—and across the class, regional, and ethnic spectrum. Their literary styles are diverse, including formal and informal, standard and local dialect. Their themes are equally varied, including ethnicity, pregnancy, abortion, maternity, single womanhood and single motherhood, troubled marital relations, conflict between work and family, fragmented identities, affection between father and daughter, but also the legacy of the atomic bomb, tensions between mainland Japanese and Okinawans, and conflicts between orthodoxy and heresy. Some of the authors experiment with modern written or spoken styles at a time when archaic styles were still common. Others incorporate dialect or create space for an ethnic language to assert its presence against the standard language.

Some privilege rhetoric or imagery above plot, and a few inject new life into archaic expressions.

The literary styles, voices, and language of the authors featured in this collection are strikingly diverse. Higuchi Ichiyō (1872–1896), at a time when authors still wrote in premodern Japanese, invented ways to vividly capture the colloquial language of her time, especially that of children and young women. Yū Miri (b. 1968) also skillfully captures the speech of contemporary youth. Chiri Yukie (1903–1922) used her literary skills to render old Ainu verses into contemporary Japanese. Tamura Toshiko (1884–1945) characteristically wrote in a persistent, argumentative style to give expression to discontented women and depict conflicts between women and men. Ozaki Midori (1896–1971) pursued human psychology introspectively, as does Kawakami Mieko (b. 1976) in her fiction, which often seeks to ascertain existence through physical perception. Mori Mari (1903–1987) and Ogawa Yōko (b. 1962) employ styles rich in imagery, Mori as a tool for creating a romantic and often sensuous atmosphere, and Ogawa as a vehicle for developing character and plot. Kurahashi Yumiko (1935–2005) and Saegusa Kazuko (1929–2003) utilized classical or non-Japanese themes in their work, often for symbolic, allegorical, or satirical purposes. Hayashi Kyōko (b. 1930) employs a restrained style to portray war experiences with the greatest possible precision. Like Chiri Yukie, Tawada Yōko (b. 1960) and Sakiyama Tami (b.1954) are bilingual and employ their layered linguistic experiences as writing strategies, Tawada working between Japanese and German and Sakiyama between Ryukyuan and Japanese. Tsushima Yūko (b. 1947) typically combines the languages of reality, dream, and illusion, often using different characters to tell the same story in their different voices. Shōno Yoriko (b. 1956) and Ogino Anna (b. 1956) write colloquially without apparent restraint, Shōno with tenacity, even aggressiveness, and Ogino with artistic flair.

In the early days of the Meiji period (1868–1912), written Japanese retained the Edo period (1600–1868) convention of employing diverse premodern written styles, including literary Japanese based on Heian Japanese, *kanbun* (writing using exclusively Chinese characters modeled after classical Chinese and read in premodern Japanese), and *sōrōbun* (epistolary writing, also used for official documents in the Edo period). By the late nineteenth century, however, these styles had come to be seen as obsolete, and at a time when a standard vernacular was developing in Tokyo, efforts were made to bring written Japanese closer to spoken Japanese. This was known as the *genbun itchi* (unification of spoken and written languages) movement. The *genbun itchi* style was adopted in primary school textbooks in 1903, and by 1922 the pages of the *Asahi shimbun* were largely in the vernacular. The author-translator Futabatei Shimei's novel *Ukigumo* (Drifting Clouds [1887–89]), which he wrote in his early twenties, is known as the first work of fiction written in the vernacular.

Women's writing, which already figured prominently in the *Man'yōshū*, the earliest extant poetic anthology, rose to extraordinary levels during the Heian period (794–1185) with such prose works as *The Tale of Genji* and *The Pillow Book*, as well as major poetic diaries, and was marked by many rich moments throughout the Kamakura, Muromachi, and Edo periods. It gained fresh vitality in the Meiji period, spurred by the pursuit of modernization and the human rights movement, which heightened women's self-awareness and desire for expression and made available new channels for education and publication.

When Higuchi Ichiyō started writing stories, the established convention, *kyōka* (semivernacular comic poetry) aside, was for women to write in *gikobun*, a pseudoclassical style modeled after the classical language of the old days, that is, in the style of Heian tales, memoirs, diaries, and travelogues. Ichiyō (her preferred, single pen name) wrote in the February 1, 1895 entry of her posthumously published diary that the celebrated women writers of the Heian were no divinely endowed geniuses; they were the same as Meiji women like herself, and the reason no modern fiction by women had recently appeared was because no one tried to write, not because women were unable to write. Writing in Heian Japanese, she said, could never capture the lives of the Meiji period. "When we write about today's life, how would we be able to portray it with the language of the mid-Heian?" Ichiyō was famously moving toward an approach employing the living language of the time, one that would shape the future of women's—and men's—writing in the Meiji period.

Ichiyō's writing combined literary Japanese in narrative passages with the lively spoken language of her time and locale, which she used for dialogues and internal monologues, in ways reminiscent of late-Edo popular fiction. The styles merge seamlessly, retaining the traditional unpunctuated story-writing convention of not setting off dialogue from narrative lines by means of line changes or quotation marks. In some stories written shortly before her early death, the majority of the text consists of direct quotations, with narrative statements merely providing links between spoken passages. "This Child," a young woman's monologue and the first story in the present collection, is written entirely in the vernacular, with the use of modern spoken Japanese polite endings *desu*, *-masu* and their variants in narrative passages. Ichiyō's other fiction appeared in publications meant for both men and women: literary magazines like *Bungakkai* (Literary World), *Bungei kurabu* (Literary Club), and *Shin-bundan* (New Literary Circles), popular magazines *Taiyō* (The Sun) and *Kokumin no tomo* (Companion to the People), and the *Mainichi* and *Yomiuri* newspapers. But "This Child," as the Ichiyō specialist Seki Reiko points out, was published in *Nihon no katei* (Japanese Homes), a monthly magazine for young married women. This venue must have made Ichiyō particularly consider the readability and the ease of conveying her message. Appearing eight years after Futabatei's *Drifting Clouds*, "This Child," also a work by an author in her early twenties, marks the birth of modern Japanese literature written in the vernacular by women. Ichiyō was also the first modern professional female writer in the sense of supporting herself with her pen.[1]

In "This Child," the main character's assertion of the female identity, criticism of her reticent husband, and her initial resentment of the birth of her child are resolved into self-criticism and appreciation of family life through love of her infant son. In other stories, Ichiyō handles such themes as a wife's affliction on discovering her husband's infidelity, the decision of a discontented wife to leave her husband, and a wife who chooses to continue to see her lover from before her marriage. In the last, she addresses a woman's spiritual freedom in an age when marriage was primarily a matter of families rather than of individual choice.

Chiri Yukie, writing in the Taishō period (1912–1926), and Sakiyama Tami, writing since the 1970s, are also pioneers; the former as an Ainu who brought selections of Ainu oral tradition into mainstream Japanese literature, and the latter as an Okinawan who has created a style of Japanese literature enriched by Ryukyuan language and cultural elements.

The Ainu, an indigenous people, historically lived in northern Honshu, Hokkaido, the Kuril Islands, and Sakhalin Island. In the Edo period, the Matsumae domain at the southern tip of Hokkaido, then called Ezochi, was inhabited and ruled by Japanese, while the rest of the island was inhabited by the Ainu. Hokkaido was brought under Japanese control in 1869 in what many regard as the first expansive step in the forging of an empire that would eventually extend across East and Southeast Asia and beyond. The Meiji government's assimilation policies subjected the Ainu, their way of life, and their culture to intense pressure. The Ainu had to adopt Japanese or Japanese-style names. Ainu children attended primary schools where they were allowed to speak only Japanese. With the state promoting the migration of ethnic Japanese to the Hokkaido frontier, the Ainu quickly became a small minority in their homeland, and Ainu land was seized and transferred to Japanese settlers.

Historically, the Ainu had no written language, although Ainu is now commonly written with a set of katakana that has been expanded to accommodate its pronunciation.[2] Chiri Yukie, a young Ainu who died of heart disease at age nineteen, with the encouragement of the linguist Kindaichi Kyōsuke transcribed into roman letters portions of Ainu oral literature and translated it into standard Japanese. In doing so, she navigated between Ainu and roman letters and between the literary language of Ainu oral tradition, passed on to her by her grandmother and other Ainu bards, and the modern Japanese written language.

Japanese interest in Ainu language and culture goes back at least several centuries. The explorer Matsumiya Kanzan included in a memoir of his journey to Matsumae (1736) an Ainu-Japanese word list. The travel diary (1791) of the folklorist Sugae Masumi contains a wealth of Ainu expressions. Matsuura Takeshirō (1818–1888) also used some Ainu expressions in recording the lives of contemporary Ainu individuals. The missionary John Batchelor compiled *An Ainu-English-Japanese Dictionary* (1889), and the ethnologist Bronisław Piłsudski compiled *Materials for the Study of the Ainu Language and Folklore* (1912). Piłsudski also made voice recordings on wax cylinders during his second stay in Sakhalin in 1902–3. The rich oral tradition of the Ainu, however, had never been systematically transcribed or translated into Japanese until the late Meiji, when Kindaichi began his work with the assistance of Ainu bards; nor was it systematically tape-recorded until the Ainu ethnologist Kayano Shigeru began recording in 1960, at a time when much had already been lost.

Chiri Yukie was the first to transcribe and translate into Japanese from the oral tradition. Her translation of thirteen songs of gods, including the owl song that appears in this volume, is widely known for its poetic beauty and folkloric richness.

At least as early as the sixteenth century Ryukyuans had adopted the Japanese writing system of hiragana and Chinese characters,[3] the earliest extant example aside from stone inscriptions being the *Omoro sōshi* (Anthology of Omoro Songs [1531–1623]), a compilation of court and regional songs. From 1879, when the Ryukyu kingdom was abolished and the islands were incorporated within Japan as Okinawa prefecture, the Ryukyuan languages were suppressed through Japanese public education, as had been the case with Ainu speech. While Ryukyuan virtually disappeared in written literature (with the exception of some poetry and songs), Okinawan writings in Japanese have been part of Japanese literature since the early twentieth century. Unlike Ainu, spoken Ryukyuan has partially remained as a living language, in part because Ryukyuan is closely related to Japanese, in contrast to Ainu, which has no apparent genealogical relationship to any other existing languages. In addition, with a Ryukyuan population of some 500,000 by the 1850s, with a much smaller influx of Japanese to the Ryukyus, and with some Ryukyuans living in remote islands where their languages were less directly threatened, Ryukyuan languages survived Japanese assimilation policies somewhat longer.

The postwar Okinawan author Sakiyama Tami grew up in a village of settlers on Iriomote Island, where the Miyako language was spoken at home, other Ryukyuan tongues were spoken in the neighborhood, and standard Japanese was spoken and written at school. She later became familiar with a version of Okinawan (the primary Ryukyuan language spoken on the main island) mixed with standard Japanese. Drawing on the tension between Japanese and Ryukyuan as a source of literary energy, her fiction incorporates old *shimakotoba* (island speech), now largely going out of use, revitalizing it as a tool for conveying the unique voices of island people as well as her own discomfort about, and resistance against, standardized, "proper" Japanese. In this way, she imbues her characters with special vividness, particularly those who seem to hear voices from the past.

While Higuchi Ichiyō presented spoken Japanese dialogue in the context of the medium of literary Japanese, Sakiyama embeds *shimakotoba* in dialogue in texts written in standard Japanese. Because *shimakotoba* is largely incomprehensible to most general readers of Japanese, she employs a few devices, including one that other Okinawan authors have also used: partially giving Chinese characters to *shimakotoba* and adding *shimakotoba* pronunciation in *rubi* (a katakana pronunciation guide added alongside the Chinese characters). For example, in writing about "tales," she uses the corresponding character 譚 (*tan*) and adds the *shimakotoba* word *panasu*, a word corresponding to the Japanese *hanashi*. In some cases, however, she simply forces the reader to guess at the meaning. She has titled one book in *shimakotoba* alone, written in hiragana with neither characters nor *rubi* to help: *Yuratiku yuritiku* (Swaying, Swinging [2003]). From the sound *yur-* and its repetition, the reader infers that the title refers to a repeated swaying motion. Sakiyama's strategy is to shake readers out of a comfort zone that takes standard Japanese for granted and into fresh consciousness.

Chiri Yukie and Sakiyama Tami are divided by nearly a century and the length of the Japanese archipelago, but they equally highlight their respective original languages. Whereas Chiri first laid claim to Ainu literary significance by bringing it into the mainstream, where it could be appreciated by Japanese readers, Sakiyama challenges the monopoly held by the Japanese language.

Tawada Yōko has long resided in Germany and publishes in both German and Japanese. She delights in exploring the tension between languages. When, already familiar with German as well as Russian, she began living in Germany in 1982, she adopted the persona of a bemused foreign observer of both the German and Japanese languages. She likes to create deliberate distance from words, reducing them to mere sounds or the smallest units of meaning and freely allowing them to evoke unrelated images. For example, she finds alienation in the German word *Heftklammerentferner* (staple remover) because of the verb *entfernen* (to distance) and location in the word *Wort* (word) because of the noun *Ort* (place). She delightedly discovers the Japanese word *bin* (bottle) in *Ich bin* (I am) and *sumire* (violet) in *tsumire* (a gefilte fish–like ingredient in the Japanese dish *oden*). The Japanese word *ani* (older brother) may suggest *oni* (demon), turning a narrator's train of thought in an unexpected direction. Tawada deploys this sort of playful awareness of language as a thinking and writing strategy and a source of humor. She writes while engaging in dialogue with foreign words that have their own intractable personalities. This, as she indicates in an essay in *Katakoto no uwagoto* (Prattling in Delirium [1999]), helps create a space beyond herself. Likewise, she prefers to treat her mother tongue as something possessing its own independent personality.

Dialogue between foreigners naturally gives rise to fuzzy understanding, misconceptions, or total lack of communication. Tawada ingeniously deploys such (mis)communication in her fiction, for example in her novella "Kakato o nakushite" (1991, translated as "Missing Heels" [1998]), in which a bewildered immigrant woman experiences linguistic and cultural disorientation. The poetic prose tetralogy selected for this volume combines Hamburg as a location and Japanese as a medium—the Japanese evoking a certain premodern flavor—introducing strange people in the Ottensen district near the main Hamburg station, the wharf, Hamburg University, and the vicinity of the Sternschanze station. Tawada's rendering of the proper name Sternschanze into Hoshigata Hōrui-eki (星形堡塁駅, Star-Shaped Fort Station), an unfamiliar expression in Japanese, illustrates how she whimsically takes a fresh look at words: first deliberately distancing them and then interpreting them literally to create linguistic awareness. The title of her 2003 collection of essays, *Ekusofonī* (Exophony), subtitled *Bogo no soto e deru tabi* (Journeys Out of the Mother Tongue), is characteristic.

Like Higuchi Ichiyō, the Taishō writer Tamura Toshiko addressed the discontent of young wives, but with greater daring. Having left the tutelage of the stylistically ornate traditional author Kōda Rohan, she wrote candidly in the then well-established *genbun itchi* style about male-female conflict. In her fiction, men demand obedience, decline to respond to reason with reason, burst with jealousy and vengeance, or resort to physical violence. Her women despise men or are repulsed by them, assert their own personalities, attempt to reason if at times unreasonably, refuse to feel bad or apologize when caught in illicit love affairs, deliberately provoke men to violence, or question why women have to have children and take on maternal responsibilities. They assert themselves, display strength, and do not hesitate to defy conventions defining female behavior. In one story, Tamura sympathetically treats the theme of *bekkyo kekkon* (marriage in separation), in which two married people live independent lives apart. These stories are also notable for their introduction of powerful, even shocking, images: the young woman who, the morning after her first night with a man, stabs a goldfish's eye with a pin when the fish smell reminds her of the male smell; a bat that, in imagination, sucks the blood of a young girl performer in a small playhouse; whispers of resentment, cursing life, heard from a rainy public cemetery across a street; a dream about a female mummy with rouged lips lying under a male mummy.

Tamura eloquently portrays women trapped between professional pursuits and family obligations, fidelity and illicit love, the female ego and male expectations, and, as in the piece selected in this collection, the desire to be a superwoman and the practical limits on what one woman can do.

As Tamura had rejected the old literary style to develop her own, Ozaki Midori likewise challenged social conventions to pursue literature. The publication of "Mufūtai kara" (From the Doldrums) in the journal *Shinchō* in 1920, while Ozaki was enrolled in what is today's Japan Women's University, raised the hackles of the school authorities at a time when the Meiji principle of training young women to become *ryōsai kenbo* (good wives and wise mothers) still prevailed in educational circles. Drawing attention to oneself by publishing in a major literary periodical was deemed contrary to the modesty and purity expected of female students. Ozaki chose to leave the college after less than a year of attendance.

She stayed in Tokyo most of the next dozen years and continued to write, mostly for magazines for women readers like *Fujin kōron* (Women's Central Review) and *Nyonin geijutsu* (Women's Art). In 1932, her older brother took her back to her hometown in Tottori prefecture, thwarting her plan to marry a younger man with little income. This, together with drug addiction, resulted in a total break from writing for the rest of her life.

As the title of the full-length novel *Daishichikan-kai hōkō* (Wandering Through the Realm of the Seventh Sense [1931], published in book form in 1933) suggests, Ozaki explored unusual, surreal human perceptions. In contrast to Tamura Toshiko's fiction laden with concrete descriptions of marital problems, Ozaki's central characters often have little connection to the real world; rather they swim through strangely surreal worlds of seasons, fragrances, ideas, and books, as in the case of "Miss Cricket," included in this volume.

After many years of near oblivion, Ozaki has been reevaluated as a modernist and a feminist. Her native Tottori prefecture has hosted an annual forum on Ozaki since 2001. In 2005 the female director Hamano Sachi brought out the film *Daishichikan-kai hōkō: Ozaki Midori o sagashite* (Wandering Through the Realm of the Seventh Sense: In Search of Ozaki Midori). William Tyler's collection *Modanizumu: Modernist Fiction from Japan, 1913–1938* (2008) includes Ozaki's "Shijin no kutsu" (Shoes Fit for a Poet). The editor and critic Matsuoka Seigō views Ozaki as a forerunner of the late Shōwa and early Heisei version of *shōjo shōsetsu* (light fiction for girls usually written by female authors), which often features a disoriented, insecure young woman in a world that is itself far from being secure.

In like manner, others find in Mori Mari the source of *yaoi shōsetsu* (female-oriented fiction or visual fiction, typically by female authors, about romantic male-male relationships that are characteristic of the *shōnen-ai* (boys' platonic love) genre.

Mori Mari, daughter of the great Meiji–Taishō author Mori Ōgai, was a translator of French literature and a theater critic. She had a late literary debut, at age fifty-four, with a collection of literary essays, or rather autobiographical fiction, called *Chichi no bōshi* (My Father's Hat). In the piece included in this volume from that collection, she reminisces about the father-daughter relationship during the years between her marriage at age sixteen and his death three years later while she was in Europe with her husband. The relationship was at that time devoid of the childhood intimacy that had securely connected her to him prior to her marriage. Rich as these reminiscences are in concrete details pertaining to streets, shops, traffic, people's facial expressions, and words, they also convey the faraway feeling with which she recalls, thirty-three years after his death, the touch, for example, of his gloved hand in the purple evening dusk at cherry-blossom time.

Her nonautobiographical fiction introduces a range of romantic characters, including a girl with innocently destructive childlike charm, a slender and tightly muscled young man with beautiful eyes dreamy yet cold, a boy in profile casting an upward Narcissus-like glance, a French-Japanese man with a hint of decadence, and an Italian-Japanese sadist and heroin addict. She locates such characters in a chamber of nectar in a garden gone to seed, a room behind a thick mahogany door on which the devil's face is sculpted, among gray clouds over lingering twilight, and a chilly, damp wind blowing through the woods, perhaps heralding a storm. The characters are embedded in stories of intense father-daughter affection, male relationships, possessiveness, love, and death. It is a world of romanticism, exoticism, and beauty that is passionate, languid, corrupt, or doomed.

Mori Mari's romanticism is conveyed through a highly stylized, sometimes slightly archaic, Japanese. Her punctuation marks freely follow narrative rhythms rather than grammatical rules. She writes, for example, "kanashii shibo dake ga, katamatta node, atta" (the fact was that a sad longing alone gelled), or "sono akai kage wa Reo no ushiro ni chiisaku natte, itta" (its red form, I found, gradually grew smaller behind Leo), with an unconventional rhythmic break between the grammatical units *node atta* and *natte itta*, with attention to *atta* (so it was) and *itta* (so it gradually happened) as denoting a special awareness of time. Her ornate use of Chinese characters, after the fashion of a convention enjoyed by Meiji authors, also heightens the romantic aura. She writes, in characters, *ikenie* (生贄, live offering), *nikuyoku* (肉欲, carnal desire), and *danshoku* (男色, male homosexuality), with French-derived katakana glosses added alongside: *victime*, *volupté*, and *sodomie*. Her fondness for multistroke characters, as in *kanran* (橄欖, olive), *enji* (臙脂, dark red), *matsuwaru* (纏る, to entwine), and *karakau* (揶揄う, to tease), and favoring of Chinese-derived representations of foreign loan words like *yōhai* (洋盃, "Western wine cup," glass), *shin'i* (襯衣, "intimate robe," undershirt), and *hyōka* (氷菓, "ice sweets," ice cream) also enhance the rich texture of her pages.

Tsushima Yūko shares with Mori Mari the condition of being associated with a well-known novelist father. Unlike Mori, Tsushima never knew her father, Dazai Osamu, who participated in a watery double suicide when she was an infant. But her deep-felt connection to Dazai is evident in her fiction, which often explores single mother–child relations in fatherless families. Water is a central theme in her story in this volume as it is in "Suifu" (Underwater Capital [1980]), about a single mother with a small child and about her mother, who, having lost her husband to the water god's lure, dwells on memories and visions of water. The "capital" alludes at once to the toy castle in the child's fish tank and to the legend of the immortal dragon palace, of which Dazai Osamu has his own version in his *Otogi zōshi* (Old Tales [1945]). Another recurring theme in Tsushima's work concerns her older brother, who had Down syndrome and died when she was thirteen, along with her own son, whom she lost when he was nine. She celebrates her brother as a pure-hearted, loving child who knows nothing of resentment or jealousy, and she finds solace in evoking dreams about, and writing of, her lost son. A character modeled after Dazai Osamu, who speaks heavily accented Tōhoku dialect amid the family of Yamanashi dialect speakers, plays an important role in *Hi no yama: Yamazaru-ki* (Mountain of Fire: An Account of a Wild Monkey [1998]), an ambitious fictional chronicle of the three-generation Meiji to Heisei history of the family on the maternal side of a woman (a projection of the author) who, before her death, transmits her uncle's memoir to his grandson. The family originally lived in Kōfu, in Yamanashi prefecture, near the once volcanic Mount Fuji, while some younger members end up in Tokyo, Nashville, New York, and Paris. The novel revolves around multiple voices, the long memoir interspersed with other characters' monologues, diaries, essays, notes, letters, and phone conversations. *Amari ni yabanna* (All Too Savage [2008]) also uses multiple voices, to portray in this instance the failed marriage of a woman living in Taipei for five years starting in 1930, the year of the Wushe Incident, when mountain people in central Taiwan rose in an abortive rebellion.[4] It interweaves her numerous letters, mostly addressed to her fiancé and later husband, with her diary, third-person narratives, the thoughts of her middle-aged niece (another projection of the author), who visits Taiwan seventy years later in quest of a spiritual communion with the aunt, as well as the two women's dialogues with Taiwanese and aboriginal individuals. In both novels, the young niece loses her child, but particularly in the latter work, she profoundly empathizes with her aunt, who had experienced a stillbirth, a miscarriage, and the death of an infant, amid conflicts between her "savage" femininity and her husband's lack of understanding reinforced by his mother's domination. There is an obvious parallel between the Kōfu-born aunt, who grew up surrounded by mountains, and the mountain tribes of Taiwan, and between her husband or mother-in-law and Japan's colonial rule.

From junior high school through college, Tsushima attended Shirayuri, a Catholic missionary school in Tokyo that traces its genealogy from the Convent of Saint-Paul de Chartres in seventeenth-century France. A precocious reader from childhood, during her college days she read widely among Japanese and non-Japanese authors, including Dostoyevsky, Joyce, Virginia Woolf, Faulkner, and Tanizaki Jun'ichirō. She also developed interests in Ainu and aboriginal Taiwanese cultures. While teaching Japanese literature in Paris in 1991–92, she included the Ainu oral tradition in the curriculum. One result is the 1996 publication of a French translation, with her graduate students and with the cooperation of the 2008 Nobel Literature laureate Jean-Marie Gustave Le Clézio, of Chiri Yukie's anthology, including the song translated in this volume. Tsushima's interest in Taiwanese aboriginal folklore is well demonstrated in *All Too Savage*.

For Hayashi Kyōko (b. 1930), Shanghai was the departure point that nourished the objective eye characterizing her fiction. Her core literary theme, however, is the atomic bomb, which brought instant death to many and protracted severe physical and psychological effects over a lifetime and beyond for many more, including the author. Since the bombing, she has constantly sought mental and physical peace, "sometimes in my mother, at other times in my husband, and at still other times in my child's clear eyes." But such comfort being momentary, she wrote in 1999, there was no choice but to live face-to-face with August 9. She has traced her own experiences, recorded the deaths and illnesses of friends and teachers, and examined both Japanese and American scientific writings. In Haruna Mikio's *Hibakusha in the U.S.A.* (1985) and Jay M. Gould's *The Enemy Within: The High Cost of Living Near Nuclear Reactors* (1996), she finds evidence of her and other *hibakusha*'s sense that, after recovery from external symptoms of the A-bomb disease, radioactive toxin remains in the body and then, suddenly, surfaces after unknown incubation periods or creates health problems in the second generation.

Like Sakiyama Tami, she too grew up with linguistic diversity: standard Japanese, Shanghainese, and later the Nagasaki dialect. In her Shanghai stories, especially those collected in *Missheru no kuchibeni* (Michelle Lipstick [1980]), the Shanghai dialect lends vividness to street scenes presented through the gaze of a child, while her A-bomb stories are enriched with Nagasaki dialect. But above all, Hayashi's writing is distinguished by a cold gaze at war scenes and a detached writing style, with fluid shifts between Shanghai, Nagasaki, and Los Alamos, and between past and present.

The title of the story included in this volume, "Masks of Whatchamacallit," refers to strange-faced clay figurines sold in a store visited by the narrator and her survivor friend. Made by a physically handicapped young man, they look up toward heaven, mouths gaping. The figurines provide a compelling symbol of the agony of war culminating in the A-bomb that inaugurated the nuclear age. The use of polite standard Japanese, with extra *desu* and *-masu* sentence endings in the speech of the narrator's husband, effectively underlines his aloofness, prejudice, and lack of support at the time his *hibakusha* wife was pregnant.

Other authors included in this volume also engage historical and political issues: Tsushima Yūko writes about the air raids in Tokyo and Kōfu, about the relations of Japanese with Taiwanese and aborigines; Saegusa Kazuko about children born of Special Attack Corps members and village women; Kurahashi Yumiko about the postwar student movement and its challenge to the imperial system; and Ogawa Yōko about the Holocaust. But among these authors, Hayashi is the writer who most persistently addresses large historical issues through her literature, specifically, colonialism and the bomb, war and peace, and relations between Chinese and Japanese as well as between Americans and Japanese. One Shanghai story is included in our earlier volume of stories by women writers. A Nagasaki story by the same author related to the atomic bomb merits a place in this collection.

Saegusa Kazuko and Kurahashi Yumiko are roughly Hayashi's contemporaries. Saegusa was sixteen and living in Kobe when the war ended. Like Hayashi Kyōko, she was mobilized as a student worker. Kurahashi was ten years old when Kōchi city, where she grew up, was bombed just one month before the end of the war. While Hayashi strictly chronicles the events she observed or researched, Saegusa and Kurahashi frequently explore the surreal.

Saegusa's interest in Japanese literature and history, especially Noh, led her to Greek drama and its tragic heroines. Many of her works explore womanhood, maternity, and ancient matriarchy. While positing that mythical matriarchy was chaotic and thus eventually gave rise to a male-centered order, she experiments with puncturing that male order and bringing back matriarchal elements. She also considers the possibilities of female authority in the present day, given opportunities for women to achieve social and economic independence. For Saegusa, a woman who seeks pure love should not have a child; and if a woman relates to a man in order to have a child, he being a mere instrument in the process, she should not seek love.

In the traditional Noh play *Utō* (Rhinoceros auklet, a bird known for parental affection), a bird hunter descends to hell, where he is tortured by monster birds. His hunting method had been to mimic the parental call of the *utō* and locate the well-hidden fledgling by its answering call. In a playwright's play within the novel version in Saegusa's *Hōkai kokuchi* (Annunciation of Disintegration [1985]), the hunter is not only tortured in hell as in the original drama but also becomes an *utō* in his next life. When he calls to his son, the child replies, and monster birds from hell then attack the child. A rising playwright in the same novel bases his own drama on Aeschylus's *Oresteia*, in which Agamemnon's son Orestes kills the usurper Aegisthus and the queen, Clytemnestra. This younger playwright, the hired surrogate father of a child, eventually marries its mother. In his version, Aegisthus, rather than Agamemnon, is Orestes's biological father. Yet Orestes claims Agamemnon, who loved him, as his real father and, in avenging Agamemnon's death, ends by becoming both a patricide and a matricide. Saegusa thus raises the possibility of a child choosing his father, regardless of who the natural father is, as well as the possibility for a surrogate father to claim fatherhood against the natural father.

Kurahashi Yumiko also derives inspiration from Greek drama and Noh, and from existentialist and other types of European literature. She creatively twists and reworks the diction and conception of her sources, often juxtaposing themes from diverse traditions, Roman and Chinese as well as Greek and Japanese. Preferring to stir the imagination through logic rather than through appeals to emotion, she uses objective, parody-laden, satirical approaches. In particular, she satirizes political and religious missionaries presuming to revolutionize society, belittles male prejudices that present women as alien to abstract concepts and ideologies, and parodies the patriarchal imperial system in which the emperor is the symbol of the nation. Her early pieces include cool-headed, stylistically developed satires of ideologically driven groups such as a student activist group or a political party. Her serious engagement with language and style is already evident in her debut work from her student days, a young woman's monologue addressed to her boyfriend. While her themes and vehicles continued to expand to include historical fiction, picaresque novels, and fairy tales, what remains central to her writing is her insistence on how, in what style and voice, to present the target of her critical examination. The story included in this volume caricatures, in Senecan fashion, a vacuous pumpkin-faced politician and the political system that allows him to remain in office.

Kurahashi persists in using the traditional Japanese *kana* spelling system (as had Kawabata Yasunari, Mishima Yukio, and Maruya Saiichi), which was officially replaced in 1946 by the current, simplified system.[5] Although publisher preferences prevailed in most cases, this is one indication of her respect for presentation.

Like Tsushima Yūko, Ogino Anna received a French Catholic education, although just briefly, at Futaba School in Fukuoka, founded by the Soeurs de l'Enfant Jésus, transferring after two years to the American Reformed Church missionary school (Ferris) in Yokohama. A voracious reader interested in Boccaccio and the Marquis de Sade as a seventh and eighth grader, she eventually became familiar with Japanese popular culture as well. She was especially fond of *rakugo*, introduced to her by her Hyōgo-born artist mother. Apprenticed later to the *rakugo* master Kingentei Bashō, Ogino performs under the professional name of Kingentei Konna (punning on her name Anna, with wordplay between *anna*, "that sort of," and *konna*, "this sort of"). Ogino also regularly participates in amateur street performances. She is known for her freedom and versatility of writing in a style that is rich in puns and the abundant use of Kansai dialect. The exuberance of intellect and humor characterizes her ingenious and often parodic use of historical figures like the Dutch painters Pieter Brueghel the Elder and Hieronymus Bosch, Betty Blue in the French film of that title, the American actress Marilyn Monroe, as well as Kawabata Yasunari and other modern Japanese authors. A particularly good example of her approach is the surrealistic character Hieronymus, so named after Hieronymus Bosch's painting of a grotesque plant in *John the Baptist in the Wilderness*, who speaks Kansai dialect in the first-person narrator's dream, another being a cockroach named Athanasius in the same story, also a Kansai dialect speaker.

Ogino's literary debut piece, included in this volume, humorously titled "Uchi no okan ga ocha o nomu" (Mamma Drinks Her Tea) in the seven-five syllabic pattern,[6] displays her characteristic linguistic playfulness even as it is laden with nostalgia and pathos, as her Kansai-speaking mother tells stories of her bucolic childhood and the narrator, in standard Japanese, recalls her Paris days.

Shōno Yoriko, Ogino's contemporary, eloquently handles themes of single womanhood and social prejudice, addresses feminist issues, embraces indigenous local myths predating the official early eighth century mythology, pre-Edo Buddhist-Shintoist syncretism, while contesting conventional literary and social ideas. She repeatedly questions orthodoxy and upholds heresies and the multiplicity of identity. Likewise, rather than sharply distinguishing between the genders, she recognizes the man within the woman. She is an outspoken protagonist in the literary disputes referred to as *junbungaku ronsō* (debate over "pure" literary fiction), where she defends literary fiction against a concept of popular fiction that sells, entertains, and is thus valued by her critics. She denounces the equation of the literary value of fiction with its market value as a commodity.

As she challenges convention in general, she also challenges conventional writing styles. She freely mixes written and spoken, formal and extremely informal styles. In some cases, like Mori Mari, Shōno chooses rhythmic punctuation over grammatical punctuation. But unlike Mori, who overpunctuated, she underpunctuates long-winded speech patterns or threads of thought.

Shōno finds an affinity between herself and Mori Mari despite differences in style and approach, Shōno with her hard-hitting criticisms of preconceptions and stereotypes and Mori with her aestheticism and rich imagery. What they share is the spirit of rejecting conventions and celebrating inventiveness. Shōno admires Mori enough to have written a full-length novel about her, or rather, about her ghost, and to name some of her cats drawing on the exotic names of Mori's characters.

Ogawa Yōko has more than once explained how she constructs her stories: for her, fiction begins not with plots but with places or scenes, then characters. Once she can concretely visualize situations made of the locale and characters, the story develops naturally. In other words, images precede plots.

The place may be a hospital room, a museum of keepsakes, a collector's house, a craft studio, a villa in the woods, an apartment house in Germany, a greenhouse in Prague connected to a cave, a lobby in the Hong Kong airport, or a tiny hideout in the basement of an old house on an unknown island. Ogawa vividly portrays the details of each locale with attention to light and shadow, sound and image, stillness and motion.

Against such backgrounds are characters with stories: a former failed child-contest entrant, a mathematician with memory problems, a precision-minded harpsichord builder, a specimen maker with a locked specimen collection room, a perfumer who seals his past into his perfumes, a young man without a tongue, an old Russian immigrant to Japan who poses as a Romanov court survivor, islanders fated to progressively lose their memory and others who retain their memory and are subject to "a memory hunt" by the secret police. Many of the characters embody fragility: a raised arm that cannot be lowered, sudden or gradual loss of things familiar, suppressed identity, self-induced shattered dreams, aphasia, dwarfism, obsessive-compulsive neurosis, a sense of void, and images of falling and vanishing. These fragile, often eccentric characters interact with close individuals like a caring sister, an affectionate niece or nephew, a lover, or kind neighbors—for the most part compassionate people, except some mothers, who appear as oppressors, and in one case a younger sister with complex feelings about her older sister's pregnancy.

This sympathetic handling of characters is combined with a sense of the elusive, transient, or intangible—"not a clear sensation worthy of being called a smell, but something like a hint that crosses the deep corner just for a second" or "comfortable silence in which the air flowed like a rivulet at the bottom of the eardrum." With empathy for fading things and human decay, references to a hollow, void, and dark cave abound in her fiction.

Unlike Hayashi Kyōko, Saegusa Kazuko, and Kurahashi Yumiko, who experienced war, Ogawa is a postwar author. But she relates to the war through Anne Frank, whose diary she encountered as a junior high school student. In addition to stories like the one included in this volume, in which the narrator's grandfather is a French-Jewish Holocaust survivor, she has written a book-length travelogue about her visit to Amsterdam, where she saw places and individuals associated with Anne Frank.

Yū Miri, Korean by citizenship but a lifelong Japanese resident, is an essayist, playwright, and actress besides being a prolific writer of fiction. Her fiction explores complex family relations involving separation, divorce, parent-child conflicts, love, death, and, as in the case of "The Tidal Hour," included in this collection, young people's delicately inflected psychology. In this story the often listless, anxious, and irritable main character from a difficult family background bullies a quiet transfer student who has her own troubles. The title suggests both the tide of puberty and the waxing and waning of the main character's mental tide, the low tide exposing a rough seabed and the rising tide threatening to drown her.

In her autobiographical fiction, Yū openly portrays her personal experiences. The tetralogy consisting of *Inochi* (Life [2000]), *Ikiru* (To Live [2001]), *Tamashii* (Soul [2001]), and *Koe* (Voice [2002]) details her relationship with a man she once lived with and later lost to cancer, as well as the birth of a child conceived with a married man who eventually left her. *Yū Miri fukō no zenkiroku* (The Complete Record of Yū Miri's Unhappiness [2007]) is another example of her candid reflections as a writer, woman, and single mother. In contrast with an earlier generation of ethnic Korean writers in Japan, she does not specifically focus on ethnicity but rather, even when the characters in her fiction are such Koreans, handles her themes as universal issues.

Similar to Tamura Toshiko, Yū Miri, Ogino Anna, and Tawada Yōko in their nonwriting artistic pursuits, Kawakami Mieko also performs professionally. A successful singer before embarking on her career as a fiction writer, she remains a recognized songwriter and poet. In her fiction, she explores inner consciousness, questioning and ascertaining self-identity by, for example, creating a character who experiences existence exclusively through a back tooth, thus reducing identity to that dental substance and playing with the idea of the loss of identity along with the loss of that tooth. In the piece included in this volume, "You People's Love Is Near Death," Kawakami highlights the alienation and isolation of an individual amid a bustling throng.

Kawakami makes abundant use of the Osaka dialect, colloquialisms, puns, onomatopoeia, sentence fragments, long sentences and paragraphs, liberated from the novelistic discipline of coherence and grammatical correctness. While reflecting the stylistic preferences of the e-mail and cell-phone generations, Kawakami makes conscious efforts to write in a language accessible to young readers of *keitai-shōsetsu* (cell-phone fiction, i.e., twenty-first-century stories published initially through cell phones). At the same time, Kawakami's long sentences and paragraphs can also be seen as a return to the premodern narrative styles that preceded the standardization of punctuation and paragraphing. Higuchi Ichiyō, writing in the Meiji period, still resonated with the run-on narrative styles of earlier times. This volume begins with Higuchi Ichiyō and ends with Kawakami Mieko. Interestingly, Higuchi is one author who influenced Kawakami.

Like Tawada Yōko and Yū Miri, Kawakami Mieko maintains an official Web site, illustrating how young authors today communicate directly with their audience beyond via their published works. Unlike Tawada, whose site provides formal information about her publications and other literary and performative activities, Yū and Kawakami blog their casual thoughts and personal observations. Kawakami calls her site, which is particularly colloquial, *Junsui hisei hihan* (Critique of Pure Pathos), punning on *Junsui risei hihan* (Critique of Pure Reason) and reflecting her interest in philosophy.

* * *

Recognition of *joryū bungaku* (female literature) as a separate and legitimate school of literature with a long, brilliant tradition, and the existence of educated women readers, contributed to the flourishing of women's literature in the Meiji period. Over the course of a century, and particularly following the Occupation, women became better integrated into all sectors of life. This, and above all the achievements of women writers, gradually ended the need for separating women from mainstream literature. Breaking with the expectation that female-school writers would confine their work within boundaries considered appropriate for them as inheritors of the age-old female tradition of poems, tales, personal essays, memoirs, and diaries from the Nara and Heian periods, women addressed such sociopolitical issues as war, peace, the atomic bomb, empire, ethnicity, and revolution. They also explored theoretical and aesthetic issues.

Still, until the 1980s or so, women writers were frequently referred to as *joryū sakka* (female-school authors) and were viewed as separate from mainstream male authors. Since the 1982 publication of *Japanese Women Writers*, however, there have been further changes in the literary climate for women. The term *joryū bungaku* itself is now outdated. When the women authors (Ueno Chizuko, Tomioka Taeko, and Ogura Chikako), in *Danryū bungakuron* (On Male-School Literature [1992]) coined the term "male-school literature," they were provocatively challenging the assumption that there was "literature" and, secondary or subordinate to it, there was "female-school literature," which was something to be appreciated primarily by those harboring a feminine sensibility. The term *josei sakka* (women writers), in balance with *dansei sakka* (male writers), common nowadays, implies no such sharp break between the work of male and female authors.

Joryū Bungakusha-kai (Association of Female-School Writers) dissolved in 2007, with Tsushima Yūko as the last president. Founded in 1936 by Uno Chiyo, Hayashi Fumiko, and other women writers for the purpose of "deepening mutual friendship as well as preparing for mutual critique and literary discipline," it began awarding literary prizes in 1946 (nine authors in our two volumes are recipients). The association once served as an important pillar supporting women writers, but that era has now passed.

The biannual Akutagawa Prize for new authors (founded in 1935) was first awarded to a woman in 1938, followed by two in the forties, four in the sixties, five in the seventies. The number subsequently increased to seven in the eighties, ten in the nineties, and eight in the first decade of the current millennium. The Tanizaki Jun'ichirō Prize, first awarded in 1965 and given to outstanding established authors, went to four women out of nine recipients in the nineties and four out of eight in the years 2000 to 2009. Seven of fourteen winners of the Itō Sei Literary Prize between 1995 and 2009 were women. These ratios are higher than those of leading international prizes, including the Pulitzer, Booker, and Nobel literature prizes: seven out of twenty in the period 1990 to 2009, six out of nineteen in 1990 to 2008, and four out of nineteen in 1990 to 2008, respectively, were women. In Japan, where new authors usually start by publishing short fiction in coterie literary magazines, winning literary prizes is a crucial path to appearances in prestigious literary journals or books and recognition as an established writer. In addition to gains in such spheres as business, science, intellectual life, and government, women have achieved particular distinction and recognition in literature.[7]

Multivolume compilations have appeared in recent years illuminating the place of women writers in modern Japanese literature. The *Josei sakka shirīzu* (Women Writers Series, twenty-four vols. [1998–99]), editorially supervised by Ōba Minako and three other women authors, collects sixty-one major authors, from Nogami Yaeko to Tawada Yōko in the first twenty-two volumes, with an additional volume of seventeen writers classified as important minor authors and another of tanka, haiku, and modern poetry. *Tēma de yomitoku Nihon no bungaku: Josei sakka no kokoromi* (Theme by Theme Interpretations of Japanese Literature: Attempts by Women Writers, 2 vols. [2004]), edited by Saegusa Kazuko, Tsushima Yūko, and six other women and editorially supervised by Ōba Minako, is a collaboration of forty-one women writers, seven of whom are represented in this volume, and two in the earlier volume. The publication of *Josei haiku no sekai* (The World of Female Haiku, ed. Kadokawa Gakugei Shuppan, 6 vols. [2008]), critical essays on women haiku poets mostly by women haiku poets, draws attention to women's contributions in the realm of poetry.

This collection echoes these developments as it makes available women writers' distinctive perspectives, voices, and diverse linguistic and stylistic approaches.

We thank Michael K. Bourdaghs, Susan Bouterey, Alisa Freedman, Gillian Kinjo, Seiji M. Lippit, Vyjayanthi Ratnam Selinger, Robert Steen, and Angela Yiu for their translations. Miya Mizuta, Lili Selden, and Yumi Selden lent generous, informed editorial assistance. In particular, Miya Mizuta carefully edited the majority of the stories over the years. Marc Peter Keane read the introduction and offered helpful comments. Michael D. Ashby rendered invaluable assistance through thoughtful editing of the entire text. Mao Kido, and especially Kayo Shinozaki, assisted in securing copyright permissions and seeing this volume to publication. Doug Merwin, our original editor for *Japanese Women Writers*, Patricia Kolb, Makiko Parsons, and Angela Piliouras, of M.E. Sharpe, provided professional advice over the years. To all these friends we express deep gratitude.

Kyoko Selden
Noriko Mizuta

Notes

1. The family circumstances, including her older brother's death in 1888 followed by her father's death in 1889, made Ichiyō responsible as head of the family for the livelihood of her mother, her younger sister, and herself. Writing therefore became a means of earning a living rather than a pursuit for personal fulfillment or informal circulation.

2. The *Ainu Times*, a quarterly published since 1997 by the Ainu Pen Club and the only newspaper published in Ainu, prints articles in expanded katakana, sprinkled with Chinese characters for Japanese loan words, side by side with a romanized text for each article. (Japanese translations appear one issue behind.) Its goal is to restore Ainu to daily life, to convey today's events and thoughts, not to record an oral tradition as in earlier attempts.

3. Katakana was seldom used.

4. The Wushe Incident was the largest and last aboriginal rebellion against the Japanese colonial forces. A fight with a Japanese patrolman triggered an assault by some 1,200 Atayal tribal members on a school athletic festival attended by many Japanese, killing (by Japanese count) 215 Japanese and 2 Taiwanese, and wounding others. The Japanese retaliated with overwhelming force, and the fifty-day incident led to the deaths and suicides of 700 Atayal. In addition 500 Atayal surrendered, of whom 200 were later killed by pro-Japanese Atayal.

5. The postwar language reforms included "phoneticization" and simplification of the *kana* spelling system (i.e., the hiragana and katakana syllabary symbols). For example, *tefu* (てふ), *chiayu* (ちやう), and *chou* (ちょう) in the traditional system, all pronounced *chō* in modern Japanese, were unified to *chou*; and the old *kana wi* (ゐ) and *we* (ゑ) were eliminated. Novelists Kawabata Yasunari, Mishima Yukio, and Maruya Saiichi, among others, continued to write in the traditional system.

6. The seven-five syllabic pattern is one of the most basic patterns in Japanese poetry. It can, as in this case, produce a bouncing rhythm.

7. Indicative of women's activities in some of these areas, in 2004, among numerous female company presidents, the first female airline company president took command of an aircraft rental company called Airtransse. In the 1990s, two women scientists successively chaired the Physical Society of Japan. In 2006, the ratio of women university and college presidents was 16.7 percent at public institutions, 7.5 percent at private institutions, and 2.3 percent at national institutions; the ratio of women professors was 14.5 percent, 11.7 percent, and 6.4 percent, respectively (Science Portal, October 18, 2006, http://scienceportal.jp/news/daily/0610/0610181.html). The 2009 Lower House election resulted in 54 women representatives out of 480 and 42 women Upper House representatives out of 242. Moreover, between 2000 and 2009, there were 6 female prefectural governors serving at different times; in 2005, of the 256,668 doctors working at hospitals or clinics, 42,040 were women. Cf. www.gender.go.jp/danjo-kaigi/siryo/ka27-2.pdf

More Stories by Japanese Women Writers

An Anthology

1
This Child

Higuchi Ichiyō

If I were to speak up and say that my child is adorable, surely everyone would enjoy a good laugh. They would laugh because there is no one who thinks her own child uncomely, and it is comical for one to carry on as if only she possessed a splendid jewel. And so I will refrain from putting into words such an ostentatious thought, yet in my heart it is not even a matter of adorable or uncomely—I must restrain myself from bringing my hands together and offering up a prayer of thanksgiving!

    This child could be called my personal guardian angel. Yes, he wears an adorable smile on his face and he passes the time in carefree play; still I cannot possibly describe the immensity of everything his carefree, smiling face has taught me. Certainly, the many books I read in school and the things my teachers taught have helped me, and when I am in the thick of events I often look back on them and think, "Yes, that was so," or "This was just so"; yet none of those things can equal the way this child's smiling face can immediately, before my eyes, stop my rushing feet dead in their tracks or calm my hysterical heart. Unlike a great scholar's loud, brainy exhortations, the face of this child when he is asleep, innocently resting on his pillow, both hands drawn up toward his shoulders, causes my eyes to fill with tears that well up from the bottom of my heart, and in spite of my stubborn self-pride, I become unable to make my usual boasts about how I don't much like children.

    He uttered his first cries in this world late last year, as the year's end approached. When I think of it now, I find it shameful, but since at that point I still felt lost, as though I were drifting through space, when I first saw this red face, I thought, "Oh, why did you have to be born healthy? If only you had died, I could have returned to my parents' home as soon as I had recuper-

---

    "Kono ko" (1895). Translated from *Nihon no Katei* magazine (1895) by Michael K. Bourdaghs. Translation copyright 2011 by Michael K. Bourdaghs.

ated and not have to spend another minute at this husband's side. Why did you have to be born so healthy? I hate it! I hate everything! Now must I be chained to this marriage come what may and live for all ages in this darkness without even a glimmering of hope?" In this spiteful way, I pitied myself. Though people congratulated me, I myself felt not the slightest happiness. I could only think it sad that my life was gradually going to grow more and more unbearable.

Try putting another person in the position I was in then—no matter how well resigned she had been to her fate, she too would find this world tiresome and uninteresting. Without a doubt, yes, I am certain she could not stop the words from escaping her lips; brazen hearted me would not be the only one to exclaim, "Brutal! Cruel! How can heaven allow this?" I was certain I had done not even the slightest wrong, nor made any mistakes—all our clashes had arisen out from my husband's heart alone. I hated him with a fury. Furthermore, I resented my own father (actually, my stepfather, an uncle to whom I ought to have felt grateful) because he had purposely picked out this sort of husband, turning my entire life into agony. I most resented the gods or whoever it was that had decided my fate, like tossing the blind off a cliff—me, who in the first place had never done any wrong, who had obediently gone off to be married as she was told. I decided that the world was a loathsome place.

An indomitable spirit is a good thing. Without it, one cannot overcome difficulties. If you have a spineless, gentle disposition, there will always be some who will say you are like a sea slug. But there are also times and circumstances when it simply will not do to display an indomitable spirit. I suppose it would be fine if one could understand the particulars of a situation and keep one's strong-spirited nature bound up inside. From the perspective of someone watching, my sort of unconcealed opposition to any yielding must have appeared disgraceful. My husband must have felt even more keenly than I did about him that his wife was unworthy. Even so, at that time I was unable to reflect on myself, much less to guess what was in the heart of my husband. When he displayed an unhappy face, it instantly offended me, and the slightest rebuke from him set off a blazing annoyance. Although I would not dare to rebut his words, for a time I would fall silent and would eat nothing. I would also often burst into anger at the maidservants, and more than a few times I left the bedding out and spent the whole day lying supine on it. I am a crybaby, and for all my stubbornness, I cried my eyes out, biting the hem of my quilt. Mine were tears of utter bitterness, bitter tears brought on by my own stubborn spirit, with neither rhyme nor reason.

When I first came here as his bride three years ago, we were quite friendly for a time, and neither of us had any complaints. But growing used to each other is both a good thing and a bad thing, for both our selfish wills came out. Any number of whims and desires bubbled up to the surface, causing all sorts of grumbling, and furthermore, because I am by nature impertinent, against my better judgment I even went so far as to complain about those things my husband did away from home. "You always conceal things from me, and never tell me even the slightest bit about things going on outside our house. Your heart is miles away from me!" I said spitefully. "I do not treat you like a stranger. Don't I tell you everything?" he answered, laughing off my complaint. But I could plainly see he was hiding something, and my heart could not bear it. When you become suspicious about one thing, you begin to question ten or twenty others. Morning and night, I began to think, "What? Another lie!" Everything somehow became strangely jumbled in my mind, and I could not come to any resolution. When I look back now, I am certain that he was concealing things. But, after all, I was a woman, a chatterbox, and he wasn't about to speak to me about his work and such. Surely, even now he is hiding a great many things. I accept and believe that to be a certainty, yet now I feel no bitterness. I know that refusing to discuss such matters is my husband's strong point, and that his refusal to take heed of my tears and my anger was owing to my husband's fine character. If by any chance he would have spoken of his official business to the frivolous woman I was then, what silly things I might have done! Even with that not being the case, a great many people, plaintiffs and defendants both, used our servants to relay dubious gifts to my hands, along with messages that they were in great distress over such and such a circumstance and that the judge's decision was a matter of life and death to them. That I did not accept any of the gifts was not some just refusal by the proper wife of Justice Yamaguchi Noboru. To the contrary, it was because, engrossed in our domestic quarrels, I had no space in my heart to even think of broaching such topics with my husband. Rather than taking up such matters with him and receiving meaningless hackneyed answers in return, simply remaining silent I thought was by far the smarter course. In this way, fortunately, I was able to escape the stain of having accepted bribes. Still, the distance between my husband and me only grew, the clouds between us thickened, and we became two who could no longer understand each other's hearts. When I think of it now, I realize that this all stemmed from the way I treated him, and there is no doubt that I handled things badly. The reason my husband's heart wandered astray was that my own heart had departed from its proper path, and now I shed unending tears of regret.

At the very worst point in our relationship, when we had utterly turned our backs on each other, I didn't ask and he didn't tell me where he was going when he stepped out. If, during his absence, a message arrived for him from somewhere, no matter how urgent the matter, I never cut open the seal. Instead, I sent the messenger away with a note acknowledging receipt, as if some blockhead, rather than a dutiful wife, was watching the house during the master's absence, and I indifferently tossed the message somewhere. When he returned, my husband was of course furious. He at first scolded and admonished me, he remonstrated, and then attempted to console me, but the roots of my obstinacy were sunk too deep. Using the words "You hide things from me!" as a shield, I descended into a sulk where a few kind words could no longer move me, and then my husband would get disgusted. It is fine when a house reverberates with quarrelsome words, but when it reaches the point of silent mutual hatred, when the house becomes nothing more than a roof, ceiling, and four walls, it is colder and more desolate than a night spent with the evanescent dew in a field. It is a mystery that the tears I shed in those days did not freeze.

When you think about it, people are self-centered creatures. During good times, they remember nothing, and only in trying and unpleasant times do they dwell on the past or on the future they are facing—on how very promising, outstanding, and satisfying it was or will be. As a person thinks such things, the present becomes more and more hateful, and she wants somehow to escape from it, to cut away these fetters. Without fail, she thinks that if she could only be freed from this, how beautiful and good would be the place at which she could arrive. Because of this, I too was lost in dreams such as this—I was certain that it was not my destiny to end up in such misfortune; in the days before I married, when I still lived the life of the adopted daughter of the Komuro family, how many people kindly made arrangements for me and arranged introductions to potential suitors (among whom were the distinguished navy man Ushioda and the fair-complexioned Dr. Hosoi, whom I nearly married). To then be married off to this taciturn husband must have been some sort of temporary mistake. Simply to carry on with this mistake and to pass a worthless life was wretched, I thought. I made no attempt to rectify my own warped heart, but instead looked with hostility upon the people who had arranged these matters.

With so irrational a wife, one who treated him coldly, no husband could be so fine as to treat her with kindness. When my husband returned home from his office, I went out to greet him, according to the rules of conduct, yet when I met him I spoke not one heartfelt word, but instead I put on the blunt airs of one ready to say, if you mean to be angry, go ahead and be angry, do anything you please—until my husband could no longer bear it and suddenly rose to his feet and left the house. His destination was always the same: some red lantern in the licensed quarter, or a tiny assignation room at some rendezvous teahouse. This angered me and intensified my bitterness, but to tell the truth, it was I who had poorly pleased him. He went off to seek such amusements because he could not bear the unhappiness in our home. In this way, I drove him to profligacy. My husband became a noted man-about-town outside our house.

My husband was not like the pampered son of some wealthy family, floating off into ecstasy while being flattered by geishas; his heart was not in it. Instead, you could say he was only doing it to check his temper, as a sort of diversion, and when he drank sake, he did not become pleasantly intoxicated; instead his face would grow pale and blue veins would appear on his forehead.

When he returned home, his speaking voice was hard-hearted and loud, and he would fly off the handle and scold the maidservants on the slightest pretext. Although he did not scold me, he would glare angrily at my face with his grouchiness (of which my gentle husband now has none) and his terrifying, horrid expression, and with me at his side also seething in anger, our servants couldn't bear it. Generally, we changed maidservants about twice a month. On each occasion, more of our belongings would disappear, so that the destruction and filching of our property was enormous. I lamented to myself, "Why is it that only unfeeling people gather around me? Is the whole world such an unfeeling mass? When people draw near me, do they all purposely labor to annoy me? Whether I look right or left, I see not a single trustworthy face. It's horrible!" I abandoned myself to despair and made no attempt to treat those I met with due civility. When my husband's colleagues came to pay a call, I wouldn't lift a finger to serve them until he specifically ordered me to do so, and even then I sent only the maidservants into the parlor, making some excuse about a headache or a bad tooth, I carried on with my selfish conduct regardless of whether or not we had visitors. I didn't even respond when he called for me! I wonder how people looked on me; some may have gone so far as to judge me with words such as "No doubt, Yamaguchi married himself into a hundred years' blight!" or "His wife is the most despicable woman!"

Around that time, if my husband had said he would divorce me, I would have taken leave of him without giving it a second thought, and shutting my eyes to my own wrongdoing, I would have concocted some nonsensical reason such as, "If the gods have decided to make me such an ill-fated, pitiful wretch, then I can do nothing about it. Do what you will; I will follow my own dictates, and if things should turn out badly, then they will turn out badly. If they should turn out well, it will be a godsend." I shudder now when I think what would have become of me. Thankfully, my husband did not take the drastic step of serving me with notice of divorce, and for some reason decided to keep me around. I don't know whether he thought that, instead of simply divorcing me in a fit of mounting anger, he could better torment me by forcing me to remain forever in this cage. But now, when I have no bitterness, and especially none toward my husband, I know that the reason today's pleasures are pleasing, the reason I have come to understand things, is that he made me suffer so—it became possible only by my passing through that experience. When I think of these things, I realize that not one person did me any harm—not even Haya, the serving maid who walked about hurriedly and pertly, revealing my faults to the world; nor even Katsu, the cook who served no purpose other than to talk back to me. I ought to refer to them all as my benefactors. Now I am surrounded with only good maids, and I hear their compliments (even if they may be lies) about how no mistress treats her maids better than I do. If this is so, it is because I realized that the maids' poor service was a reflection of my own heart. There is no villain in this world who torments people without any reason, and even the gods do not send misery down on people who from head to toe contain not one whit of wickedness. The reason I can say this is that even someone like me, who handled everything around her unwisely, who was a good-for-nothing with no redeeming feature, yet whose heart remained stainless: even one such as I could be granted something as adorable and beautiful as this boy.

When I was about to give birth to this boy, I was still enveloped in a fog. It didn't appear that this fog would lift easily even after the birth. But for some reason, when he raised his first cry at birth, my body was filled with adoration and love, and though I bemoaned my fate, if someone had made to take him away, I would have abandoned my obstinacy and not allowed anyone to touch him—he belonged to me and no one else—and I would have smothered him in hugs.

That my husband and I think the same way was first shown to me by this child. I would hug the child, I would kiss his cheeks and say, "Baby is not Dada's, Baby is Mama's alone. Even if Mama goes off somewhere, Mama won't leave Baby behind. Baby is mine, mine!" The baby smiled, as if he somehow understood, and I thought that this cheerful adorable boy was not at all like his cruel-hearted father. I had decided that the child was mine, but when my husband returned home from somewhere with an unhappy expression, he would sit down at the baby's pillow side, and with an unsteady hand he would hold up a pinwheel or shake a rattle, and, rubbing his dark face as though he were afraid he might weep, my husband would say, "In all our house, only Baby cheers me." As I watched this, worrying that the baby might cry or be afraid, I found that the baby smiled and grinned at my husband in the same way he had at me. One time, my husband, twirling his beard between his fingers, said, "Do you think this child is adorable?" "Of course," I answered. "In that case, you're adorable too," he said, a pleasantry entirely out of his usual character. He laughed in a loud voice, and his face at that moment bore an undeniable resemblance to this child's features. He was adorable; how could I have spent all this time hating my husband? If I treat him well, he treats me well. They say that children are sometimes the wisest teachers; I have been taught everything about life by this child, a boy who has yet to speak his first words!

2

Her Daily Life

Tamura Toshiko

I

She was twenty-one years old when she married Nitta.

After they came to know each other by chance at a certain place, Nitta began to fall in love with her. Masako too was in love with the man. He wished to marry her, but around that time Masako was feeling doubts about marriage because of apprehensions not uncommon among intelligent, modern young women who were capable of thinking about their ego. It was not that she was afraid of marriage; rather, she was thinking too hard about her postmarital self. Misgivings about how she would be treated by the man after marriage, in particular, made the young Masako turn an inquiring eye toward all sorts of married lives in society.

There, all she found were cases of humiliation of women, about which she could only feel indignant. She noticed a thick chain that wound around each woman's waist. Masako saw nothing but the pale, ghostly faces of those who had completely lost themselves. One woman was so busy washing baby diapers all day from morning to night that she panted unhealthily when pumping a mere bucket of water. Another was the man's absolute servant. In each case, the woman's heart was compressed by her husband or children, and the blood of all those living women, which should course freshly through the veins, was made muddy and sour like sewer water. They had no leisure to think reflectively about such things as pure love. They knew nothing else but to busily direct attention toward their children with the kinds of vulgar, instinctive love that dogs and cats lavish on the young they bore. Moreover, women had no leisure to think about their responsibility for their homes. Even for their

---

"Kanojo no seikatsu" (1917). From Tamura Toshiko, *Tamura Toshiko sakuhinshū* (Tokyo: Origin Shuppan Sentā, 1988), vol. II. Translated by Kyoko Selden. Translation copyright 2011 by Kyoko Selden.

housework they felt no responsibility. They merely laid hands unconsciously, as if in a daze, on chores that pressed on them. Indeed, miscellaneous duties were heaped like a mountain before family women. The tattered clothes of men's lifetime piled up day after day before women without a moment's pause. Daily chores endlessly continued hour after hour with hardly any boundaries. Thus, women were too exhausted to discover the greatest meaning called responsibility in their lives. Like a doll on a float that advances in swimming motions as it is pulled from the front and pushed from the back, women, with their souls totally closed, passed one blind day after another as their doll-like bodies were pushed from the back and pulled from the front.

Masako shuddered when she thought of such daily lives of women. No matter what, she thought, she would refuse to accept such a life. She wanted to keep herself alive. She must not seek a married life that might make her lose her soul before the man's ego. She was determined to live by herself to the end, while honoring her existence. She must not fall into the trap of marriage in quest of a servile pretext called love. In order to stably maintain herself in terms of a material life too, she worked toward a profession. While gaining a livelihood by means of uninspired writing, Masako also continued to pursue her desire for self-enhancement. But when she chanced to encounter Nitta, the young Masako fell in love.

Nitta asked her again and again to marry. He wanted to possess the entirety of the woman he loved. But Masako did not respond to that for a while. Agonizing over how to unify love that came unexpectedly and marriage, at one point this intelligent woman wondered if she must discard love for the sake of principle. And when she realized that it was after all an unnatural course, Masako agonized all the more.

"Somehow or other, I wish to live freely," Masako said to Nitta. "I want to keep my love free and natural. I don't wish to be obliged by love to marry. Wouldn't it be possible for you and me to live freely in love forever, while avoiding marriage?" To him, her words sounded like the sheer fantasy of a maiden who did not yet know physical love. He found her seriousness rather humorous. He confessed to Masako with what passion he desired her physically. She blushed at his unmasked words but could not feel contempt for this man's desire. She thought it natural. Still, she could not bring herself to want to marry. In the man's intention to ask for marriage rather than in the emotion with which he sought carnal love, she found cowardliness and ugliness. To give herself to her lover was a matter of Masako's eternal freedom, but to agree to marry was to have her entire life closed off by the man. That the man pressed her to marry, she thought, was the same as encircling her with an iron chain in order to deprive her of freedom all her life.

"Marry I will not," she said. Nitta told her that that idea was wrong.

"I have a feeling that you regard me in the same way as you do ordinary men in the world. I believe I have a rather newer understanding of women. I don't think of you at all as my inferior. I think of you as one to share equal rights with me. I respect your independent spirit. Needless to say, we should not construct the typical husband-wife relationship. In every point you are my partner, and I am your friend. I will recognize your freedom more than before, and help you open up the path you are trying to follow. To let you live freely also means to let myself live freely. I am not merely asking for your hand as a housewife. In having you as my wife and at the same time wanting you to respect yourself as a woman with a soul is my ideal of marriage. That I think is true marriage. And it is also sacred marriage. If such a marriage cannot be hoped for, I would sooner not ask you to marry," Nitta spoke earnestly.

Masako was extremely pleased by his words, which she thought were truly understanding of women. They conveyed profound understanding not just of her but of women broadly; and hearing her lover talk this way, she could only think his human scale large and his sentiments lofty. That was, as Nitta said, true marriage. The man offered to recognize her freedom. And he offered to respect her intention and her art. It was impossible for her not to believe those words. Her lover was a new man. Living with this new man's new understanding, she believed, would make her the happiest woman in the world.

They married. Nominally as his wife, she was to spend mornings and evenings at Nitta's house. They decided that they would live in separate rooms. They forbade each other to casually enter each other's room. Masako studied in her room. As she felt it humiliating to be fed by her husband, she did not forget to produce things, however slight they might be, by her own strength. Nitta was a philosopher and critic of modern times. He too shut himself in his room, engrossed in writing and reading.

They needed a maidservant. It was hardly possible for Masako alone to handle all the chores, including cleaning, washing, and cooking. In particular, therein would originate the process of her becoming a housekeeper and letting her ideas rot. Both Masako and Nitta feared it. To him too it was painful to have her allocate portions of her important study hours to housework. So they decided to have a maidservant. One young woman after another entered his house, but they could not find a single ideal maid.

Every one of them was unclean. Their work was disorderly, irregular, and slovenly. Unless ordered, their slow brains remained rusty, refusing to move. They misunderstood the meaning of loyalty, which they thought meant doing things exactly as told. They left everything undone unless told. Taking the initiative to do unrequested chores, they felt, was presumptuous. It was utterly impossible to find an ideal woman who would mirror in her brain the housekeeper side of Masako's thoughts and silently perform accordingly.

Masako instantly became exhausted. She was tired from ordering and tired from teaching. The nuisance of repeating, in her study, the order of housework to the maidservant sapped her nerves. The manners and movements of the ignorant maidservant irritated the intelligent woman. Rather than dealing with such a servant all day, Masako thought handling housekeeping by herself would be far less onerous and even enable her to secure some of her time as her own. The maid casually entered Masako's study, where her husband could not come in at will, and unsparingly disturbed her calm thoughts by consulting, "What shall I do with that? What shall I do with this?"

In the end Masako stopped having a maid. She picked up the habit of clearly separating her housekeeping time from her study time and occupying her brain only with things in the kitchen during the time she was there.

It was easy. Nitta was also thinking about sharing housekeeping chores. He thought it a duty he had toward the one who had equal rights. When she came out to the kitchen, he did so. While she cut vegetables, he turned on the gas. When she washed soiled utensils, he scrupulously wiped them with a cloth. They cleaned the house together. They even felt they could enjoy meals better that way. Rather than experiencing the nuisance of having an ignorant maidservant in the house, sharing the housework was refreshing and helpful in making Masako calm. Physical work proved agreeable because it switched off a part of her brain tired from thinking. With her slender arms, she energetically swept outside the rather spacious house. When wearing a white apron and cutting vegetables with a sharp knife, she sometimes found a certain elegance in the act.

"It's unexpectedly better to have housekeeping chores. My mind has come to work very delicately, as if my nerves were always on a cogwheel. I'm so glad to find this sharpness in myself," said Masako. She was diligent.

But this did not last long, either. Miscellaneous chores she could not process began accumulating. His shirts to be laundered, socks to be mended—even such things required her minute attention. When chores were put in order, the order collapsed instantly. Each time a guest visited, she had to rise from her chair. Serving tea or serving coffee seemed a trifling thing, and yet it derailed her day by slicing into her hours. Although Nitta at first felt sorry about this and tried to handle those chores by himself, as the woman thought about her time so the man could not help but think of his time. Like her, he participated in housework. He made efforts to help with the woman's everyday duties. How much of his work time was taken away by these insignificant odd jobs he did not know. When in his study, he could not refrain from thinking of this. Before he realized it, he started neglecting housework. In particular, he had the serious responsibility for the life the two shared. He was in a situation to have to work harder than before in order to make a living. The facts of their daily life compelled him to handle new male duties and responsibilities toward society. The more conscious he became of this, quite spontaneously, his conduct started showing his evaluation of his work as important and large, and the housework, like washing his own shirts and helping to boil vegetables, as extremely light. He no longer was attentive enough to leave his desk and hasten to the kitchen on hearing a sound from there. Masako's housekeeping chores gradually increased. It came to the point where housework was a matter she coped with. Chores, chaotic like garbage, tormented and agonized her.

Falling into confusion she no longer knew how to handle, Masako sometimes neglected cleaning the house. But the moment she slackened, love and understanding for the man's work made her feel she could not keep still. The wish to let him feel as happy as possible urged her to work. Being an intelligent woman, her heart functioned with delicate care as she worked around him. No matter when, she could not leave that meticulous attention. At each moment, Nitta's emotions and feelings were vividly reflected in her mind. She was unable to forget her good intentions of helping him keep his composure by being as attentive as possible.

The man tended to be absent from home. Having many connections outside, he went out every day. Masako had stopped going out at all. Aside from shopping in the neighborhood, she now felt extremely lazy about dressing up and going out. That was because she could not stay without paying attention to housework. Almost neurotically she concentrated on handling and finishing housework, and securing time for her own study as much as possible, if only one hour longer. After being home weeks in a row, sleeping and waking from night to day, sometimes she gazed vacantly at the clear sky. Recalling the free, happy mood from the days when she used to make trips by herself, she was occasionally tempted by the color of the sky. She instantly checked the impulse, however.

"Traveling stirs no interest in me now."

II

Masako could not at all settle into her own studying. Keeping to her room, she thought about her present life. At times she felt that even love between husband and wife felt oppressive. Noticing that she was unwittingly trying to always locate herself within Nitta's feelings, she could not resist feeling repugnance about the servility of her sentiment.

No matter how she looked at it, her life was subordinate to the man's. This was the undeniable fact of their life together. Nitta, who recognized the woman's freedom and swore that he would keep open the way she wished to live, was not unaware that after all their present life was depriving the woman of her freedom.

Masako once was high-spirited, with a sharp sense of art, full of joie de vivre. Seeing her now dispirited and pale, keeping to her room all day long, Nitta was overwhelmed with pity. While wishing to free Masako as much as possible from the troublesome housework, the effort soon began to exhaust him. While watching the touching attempt of the woman, who, with a certain amount of patience and faith, tried her best to handle the housework, there was nothing he could do but reassure himself over her heroic faith and turn his face away.

"Are you managing to study?"

"Yes, I am."

Hearing this answer, all Nitta could do was silently feel relieved. When finding by his side his wife who did everything for him with good intentions and compassion, Nitta was very happy. More than when she was withdrawn to her room and engrossed in her own work, Nitta felt deeper love for Masako when she faced him with wifely feelings. That his wife wished to have more time to be in her room even at the cost of this loving thought was, to him, desolate and painful. He did not, however, confess that to her. He was ashamed of it, thinking it an insult to his ideological friend. He blamed himself, thinking it servile to demand such feelings from her. Even so, he could not deny that she appeared beautiful and lovely when she was handling housework with wifely gentleness, active mind, and minute attention. It was certainly sad for Nitta that Masako would become a complete housewife for him, but, for example when feeling tired, it was painful for him to see Masako's face likewise deeply troubled from serious thinking.

Masako knew all this. She knew everything Nitta was feeling about her. A sudden expression of joy, indicative of his fondness of the moments when she was a good wife, emerged from time to time on his face without his knowledge and surprised her. The more she became aware of it, the more she felt disappointed by her life. And yet her love for Nitta did not let her go against his momentary demand when he wanted her as his good wife. She felt that, motivated by a wish to be a good wife in response to his satisfaction, coquetry had inadvertently pervaded the bottom of her heart. For her it was the first step of dreadful compromise.

She felt so much pain that she made conscious efforts to interpret with great precision, and truly understand, her daily life. Her circumstances that forced her to handle housekeeping despite her inability, her love for her husband, her understanding of his work—and, most important, her art, along with the pain of seeing her life gradually oppressed by marriage—she thought of these things as if mathematically calculating one thing after another, jotted them down, and critiqued them. She had reached a point where going to the kitchen overwhelmed her with pain, and she felt she could hardly continue this kind of work. Not only that; the more she devoted herself to housekeeping, the harder her intelligent mind worked to prevent her from being inconsiderate about anything whatsoever. In particular, becoming even more sensitive to the management of the man's clothing and the meals she served him, she was unable to ignore any negligence in those areas. Masako was often more tortured than helped by her own intelligence.

In order to escape from the confusion stemming from that contradiction, she thought a number of times about returning to a single life. If she were alone, her faithful, kind mother at home would handle all the housework that was part of Masako's current burden. Masako would not have to worry about her clothing. No detail of cooking or laundry would trouble her. She would be able to work freely in a position like the one Nitta occupied. Masako could not refrain from longing for her past life when she was alone and had her sovereign rights. She pondered returning to her single life.

"Our love is genuine. Just because our lives become separate, our mutual love will not turn out to be unfortunate. Rather, we will be able to separate ourselves from troubling things that lead our hearts to confusion, and instead continue our studies calmly."

This was how she tried to think. However, it was just a matter of theory. After living together, if only half a year, the idea of parting was profoundly painful. Unable to make the effort it would require, she thought and thought again. "The entirety of your present life is love," she mentally addressed herself. "There is nothing but love. To lead a full life simply as this love guides you will be what is natural for your current life." When this new thought filled her brain, Masako felt, as if coming to her senses, that she was able to clearly grasp a proper creed for her life. It was nothing novel, but she repeated in her heart that a life of love was beautiful, pure, and happy. She thought she should not let go of it and tried to firmly hold it with her soul. She was ready to try to deduce the meaning of her future life solely from such love.

She had once thought her feelings servile when much time went to coiffing and making up for the man, but she felt at peace now that she thought her love for the man made her adorn herself. When thinking that doing housework too was one of the manifestations of sincerity toward the man, she also felt at peace. Viewing housework as hardship was precisely what was cowardly. She should sort out steps of her work clearly and in the greatest detail in order to manage it all. Doing so represented her strong self. She would carry out her housework perfectly and without delay, and beyond that she would gradually open up her own path of life. She would on the one hand tend to her duty as a wife, and, on the other, would diligently seek the way for living as a woman who possesses a soul. That would prevent any contradiction in her life. Fulfillment of her love should be able to proceed with a certain harmony between the two parallel lines. So thought Masako.

This conclusion helped her collect her confused senses to some extent. After pleasurably taking care of housework, she was able to turn to her work in her study with a composed, relaxed attitude. A certain kind of delight even lurked in that relaxed mind of hers. She was also able to try to please Nitta's feelings in a very natural way. The two gradually came to enjoy loving each other as a married couple. In the husband's strong embrace, the wife felt totally meek without any hint of selfishness, and this she felt was extremely beautiful. Unlike mere friendship, which was unstable—she had used this expression with the intention to connect their lives as partners—the man's love as a husband was healthy with the kind of strength that made her adore him. On occasion she felt enchanted by that powerful love. When feeling so, unawares she sweetly flattered his feelings. Masako no longer thought her coquetry subservient. In the way that intuitive desire, which the male and female genders naturally possess, revealed itself in their bodies with a delicate difference in strength, Masako could not but feel an even greater charm.

III

Two years passed as they spent days and months together. Their life was happy for a while. Clinging to her creed of love, Masako repeatedly brushed away all feelings of discontent and inadequacy.

That creed of love soon threatened to slip away from one hand. Aside from loving each other, at times the two of them ran against life's facts about which they had to fight. Although she quickly repented after each quarrel, a vague sense of humiliation followed each time and remained in her chest. With bitter thoughts, she gazed at the trace of that insult in herself.

Naturally, Masako had not neglected her work in her room. After long months gaining experience she became capable of efficiently handling housework and was able to turn to her own work with greater enthusiasm.

Around that time her artist comrades from before her marriage, all males, resumed visiting her frequently. They were sincere, understanding young people who respected her fine talent and superior art and whom she treated as spiritual friends. When paying a visit, those friends enjoyed talking with Masako more than with Nitta. She too was ready to welcome them with pleasure, as before, those who understood her art well. Having been buried in her housework, away from society for some while, she could not but feel excited once again when seeing them. Without exception, their eyes gleamed with a yearning for art. Looking at that gleam alone made her feel waves of joy in her chest. The words of those friends who were burning with new ambitions, which had reached her after a long while, never ceased to create a strong, ringing echo in her heart. She felt almost like dancing with joy, hand in hand with those young friends, in the large sky of yearning for art—thoroughly tasting the joy, she felt intoxicated when parting with them.

Afterward, when she poured all her yearnings for art on Nitta and expected him to powerfully calm her excitement, she felt disappointed as if everything had instantly turned dark. It was because he had never looked so spiteful and cold. Looking as if at the height of displeasure, he was sunk into a strange reticence. When the piercing silence of the man, who nearly seemed to be crushing with his teeth all manner of pains, whipped at her chest that had been full of yearning and pathos, Masako was simply miserable. Suppressing her panting, oppressed breathing, she could only ask quietly why he looked so displeased. On such an occasion, Nitta answered,

"I suppose you don't have to associate with such friends."

"Why should I not associate with them?"

"I can't say exactly why, but it is painful for me that you associate with those people."

"How can I believe you said such a thing?"

Taken aback by the words, so lacking in understanding, she looked at him in silence.

"You don't take me seriously at all," she said quietly after a while.

"Those people are my most valued friends," she added. "Why should I not associate with them? I think it odd. I have no right to object like that about your friends. The same applies to you too. How can you raise such an objection?"

"It's not an objection. It's unpleasant to me that you talk with those young people."

"How ignorant you are. How self-debasing. You are insulting me. You don't recognize my freedom, do you?"

Masako further reviled him. She said nothing was so mistaken as his attitude.

"Are you telling me to be isolated? Are you telling me to remain alone? Can I not have friends?"

Masako was so sad she burst into tears. To her Nitta seemed utterly cruel. He looked like a man with the heart of a rock, with neither sympathy nor understanding. She was filled with hatred for him.

"I am mistaken. But I can't do anything about it," Nitta said. He could do nothing about his ugly, ignorant jealousy. He could not even begin to think of setting free the path of her life.

"Even if you lose one hundred friends," he explained, "that doesn't mean solitude. I don't know why you think of such a thing as isolation. I have greater understanding and sympathy than your one hundred friends, don't I? You don't need friends. I think it fine for you to be by yourself."

Masako cried even more bitterly. What a lonesome life this would be—she cursed the man as she continued to cry.

Eventually, their love restored them to where they had been. Ashamed of his jealousy, Nitta apologized to Masako. His jealously, naturally, was what had insulted her. She was again able to return to her merry life. She was able to talk to Nitta freely and with emotion about her friends' impassioned words.

"Mutual understanding is really pleasant. It makes me happy. I should never disappoint Masako," he swore to himself.

But that was just for the moment. After Masako spent time with her friends, no matter how he tried Nitta was unable to wipe away his displeasure. Wearing a cheerless, cloudy expression on his face, he did not speak to her for some time.

"He's suffering after all," she thought. "He forgets what our marriage was like. He's after all an ordinary man. He cannot understand a woman in a new way." Masako sometimes reviled him to herself, but even as she did so she knew that deep down gentle sympathy for him flowed like water from the thawing snow.

She had to bend herself at the depths of despair in her dark daily life. There was nothing that made her fear her husband, but she could not bear seeing Nitta's displeased expression.

"You don't believe me. You don't understand me. You insult me," she pleaded many times; but stirred by sympathy for the man tormented by uncontrollable jealousy, she felt like forgiving everything. As a result, she unconsciously began to avoid her friends. Before she realized it, the young artists, who had no guilt whatsoever and were on friendliest terms with her, were gradually distanced from her.

"I'm sorry I have a lot of work to do right now. . . ."

"We have a visitor right now. . . ."

Making such excuses, she tried as much as possible to reduce the source of Nitta's torment. When Masako did not see her friends, he cast his face down before her like one penitent for a crime. On such occasions, they loved each other even more than usual.

Still, Masako felt lonesome. "What can I do?" Irritated, she constantly looked around with searching eyes. While wishing for her life to be broad, she sadly realized that it was on the contrary becoming more and more narrow. To have to be with Nitta alone was too confining. Although she loved no one else but Nitta, for the moment she could not refrain from having friends in art around her. Their ideas cast various reflections on hers, stirring something new in her desire for art that had been beginning to decline. They were stimulating to her. But she had to sacrifice those precious friends for his sake.

Nitta too had many friends. Naturally they were not of the different gender. He had meetings with them and also visited them at home. If Masako suggested that he cut off his relationship with those friends, what would his answer be?

"They are my precious friends," he would definitely say. Wasn't it the same with men and women? Why was Nitta himself able to seek friends, but not Masako?

"If my friends too were of the same gender as mine, there would be no problem."

When she thought this way, she was disappointed that there was none among her acquaintances of the same gender whom she wanted to have as a true friend.

Around that time Nitta had just begun translating a full-length foreign novel. He had to take up various jobs for the sake of earning a livelihood for two. Because Masako considered it humiliating to a woman to force her husband to support her, she assisted, partly for her own study, taking over easy parts. She did not neglect to comfort Nitta in the evening when he was exhausted from work. Half her daytime hours went to housework, but Nitta too comforted her. Seated face-to-face in his study, when the two of them busily wrote with pen and ink or discussed the meaning of a passage while being mutually taught and helped, winds of June blew through green leaves outside the windows, occasionally filling the room with a fragrance of the trees that was like fresh wine. They were indeed happy. Nitta was particularly happy. She was talented. She was bright. She was gentle without affectation. She was clever with her hands in everything. She was good at putting work in order. Her loving smiles were beautiful. Male visitors having gradually disappeared, by then she was totally by herself at home. She was able to distance from herself even her own mother. She stayed by his side to help with his work healthily and diligently—Nitta found in this their happy life.

"I will never love another woman," he said to Masako.

IV

Masako's health was gradually failing. She felt that something was wrong with her but could not locate the source. Her chest felt tight, or she had a headache; in particular her brain was constantly muddled in an unhealthy way. Although Nitta said that it was probably because she did not exercise much, she could not persuade herself to go out any more than before.

Masako was scared when she thought of how very stable her life had become. It was the kind of stability found in a patient when a disease has become chronic. She found it frightening that, while she had an illness, she was no longer troubled by it. She was not really happy. When his love and her love coincided, she thought she sensed infinite happiness, but it eventually changed into a fearful, unhappy feeling. And she could not avoid keenly sensing that Nitta's love leaned toward selfishness in all situations. While she felt sympathy for the circumstances that unconsciously made his demands upon the woman self-centered, his egoistic love constantly made her uncomfortable.

There were times when her creed of love was completely shaken off. The creed gradually faded from her heart. Trying to protect her creed meant that she also had to embrace his one-sided, egoistic love. She knew she was hardly capable of doing such a thing. It was all too ludicrous that she had attempted to place love at the center and infer the meaning of her daily life from there. She realized that she did not necessarily have to love. For her own sake, rather, she had to be prepared to fight against him. Such a thing as a creed of love meant debasing herself. She should not be so weak as to lose herself under such an ambiguous, doctrinal name as a creed of love. She had somewhat too large an ambition in her soul to live within this sort of inflexible love. Occasionally she felt impatient at heart, somehow wishing to break through her surroundings.

Having stopped assisting her husband with his work, she began to hide in her study. There, she was absorbed in her own creative writing. What was frightening, however, was that after nearly two years of housework, the habit never stopped neurotically urging her to attend to chores of all kinds. When she was at her desk, chores around her suddenly occurred to her and tormented her. Nor was she able to completely forget Nitta. While he was out she was peaceful, but when he was home, her attention was drawn toward him in ways that obstructed her thoughts.

Her creative writing did not at all proceed. For days in a row, she was absentminded whenever she was in her study. In the end, she even considered herself unable to create her own world. She gradually sank to a condition resembling that of a sufferer of hysteria. Now and then, she bitterly cried or lost her temper. Sensing the overflowing vigor of Nitta's entire body was enough to make her envious. And the man's invisible power that constantly ate its way into her life was simply hateful to her.

More frequently than before, she turned on him or resisted him. Learning to enjoy picking a violent quarrel with him on trivial matters, she felt proud as if she had subjugated the man if but for that moment. Nitta mistakenly ascribed her play with this sort of ignorant emotion to her natural disposition, hitherto hidden but now coming out in the open. He could not refrain from blaming her waywardness. There was no longer proper understanding or spiritual affinity between them. Even the effort to understand each other was, for them, humiliating. The two, who at the beginning understood each other on the basis of their pledge to walk along the supreme path of life, now hurled insults at each other as if toward a base, vulgar being.

"Marriage is to blame."

Both Nitta and Masako were made to think this. In their marriage was nothing of the metaphysical or spiritual that they had had in mind at the start. The only thing that remained was carnal union. Helped by its impressions alone, they barely managed to continue with their bestial love—Masako sometimes even went to the extreme of thinking thus.

"The wife's obedience, loyalty, modesty, and best behavior were part of life manners especially chosen as an important means for beautifying married life. These were expected patterns of married life rather than female virtues, and, unless studying them and hiding under their shadow, a woman can hardly bear the humiliation of the bare sight of married life." This was what Masako jotted down one day on the edge of a piece of paper.

After a while, however, the intelligent woman attempted to once again recover her own life. If she could not cast off her present life, she thought, there was no choice but to make that life adjust well to her. She decided to follow the feminine fate she had taken a step into and to look for herself afresh therein. It was a miserable decision, but she thought it would allow her to determine her spiritual direction for the time being.

Her efforts were not wasted. When a critical essay she finally finished writing was published, it instantly met high appraisal from some young men and won popularity. The essay, which poignantly introduced the lives of women imprisoned in marriage, revealed her thorough thinking, candid expressiveness, and ardent emotion. Referring to how this young woman, unlike others, at any rate demonstrated a flare of strong self-awareness, the men praised her as being full of promise. Following the publication of this piece, many people visited her again. The old artist friends who once distanced themselves also came over. She found joy in freshly associating with those people. Strangely, there were some around her who wished to direct special, intimate feelings toward her. She did not feel contemptuous of them at all.

The home situation improved at the same time. Nitta was pleased that Masako could undertake her own work for the first time since marriage. Seeing his response, she too naturally felt happy. Her life began to brighten. For her, everything was a source of pride. Even tending to housework brought her a pride she had never experienced before.

"For women to handle housekeeping on the one side and, on the other, keep step with men socially means that they work twice as hard as men. The difference in power aside, in terms of the amount of work women are superior to men."

This kind of pride increased her vitality even more.

V

The two of them were again able to love each other without disruption. Never at all being bothered by her daily life, Masako could fully focus on her creative world. Around that time she learned to halfheartedly leave undone the housework on which she had once placed so much emphasis.

It was precisely when Masako was feeling vaguely enticed by one of the men around her who tried to be particularly intimate with her, when she was making painful efforts to overcome the temptation. She found something physically unusual, and this weighed on her for a long time. When it was known to be pregnancy, she was shocked as if she had collided with an unforeseen situation. All day long that day she cried in her room.

"It's all over now," she thought. A sad despair—rather than thinking of the folly of having believed there would never be a child between them, she dwelled desperately on another new responsibility added to her life.

"I have to additionally think about becoming a good mother. I have to think about maternal responsibility."

Nitta had no compassion whatsoever for her despair. He was pleased by the expectation of the birth of a child between them.

"Are you pleased that I am going to be a slave? You are delighted about sacrificing my life for you and the child," she said through her tears. Nitta was silent. He asserted that he ought to think about parental responsibility just as she did. The only difference was that he wouldn't experience the pains of childbirth. But nothing could be done about it—Nitta kept so silent about her coming sacrifice that he began to appear in her eyes as a man of insidious wiles.

Masako was embarrassed by her appearance. She felt even greater embarrassment when face-to-face with the man by whom she felt tempted. Why was this? She disliked even thinking about it.

"When the child arrives, promise to send it away somewhere right away. We share something more precious than a child."

When Masako said this, Nitta agreed. If raising a child obstructed her work in her room, he said, it was fine to do as she suggested. Naturally he loved her more than the child not yet born.

"Why do women have to give birth?"

Masako thoroughly cursed women's fate. Hatred for Nitta began to roughen her feelings again. She walked outside in desperation day after day. Irritability, which nearly led her to destroy her body by throwing it against something, always kept her from staying still.

Physically, however, she was all the healthier. The child in her womb kept growing with no knowledge of its mother's agony. As if to demand the mother's love, it was trying to transmit the subtle warmth of love from the womb to the maternal sense of touch. Masako often received stimulation from that sense.

"Self-knowledge ultimately means that I become aware of being a woman."

It was difficult for Masako to be saved from this despair. She abandoned the work she had begun. Regardless of such circumstances, nine months quickly passed before her eyes.

In winter, the third year into their marriage, a lovely boy was born.

Nitta chose a good name for the child. Masako, who had insisted that the child be given away, did not mention this after the birth, as if she had forgotten all about it.

"Maternal responsibility."

Such a thing was no big deal for her. Aside from loving what she loved, no thoughts occurred to her at this point. Her nerves were tightly strained as she loved what she loved. She was unable to let others hold the child even for a moment. Covered entirely by beautiful, natural love, no other sentiments surfaced; she was simply gazing at the lovely thing.

Masako had to have a babysitter for the child. Her daily chores increased. She was not, however, bothered by them. It was not rare that, for the child's sake, she hardly slept at night. While perceiving the expression of pain on the little thing's face, her attention never lapsed for a moment. With all the attention, all the care, all the cautiousness for the little thing, she had no leisure to think about herself. While her eyes were bloodshot and her skin was rough and pale from lack of sleep, she never felt any fatigue. Unable to watch her miserable state morning and nights, Nitta started to talk about sending the child away.

"How can I entrust the boy in another's hands? I will raise him myself. He's really dear to me. I have already transcended things like maternal responsibility or sacrifice. I have nothing to think about any longer," she answered.

VI

Once again, her soul started waking to the world of ambition. Holding the lovely child in her hands alone was no longer sufficient to fulfill her desire for life. Especially, seeing her husband have to work twice as hard as before and seeing his efforts to do so, Masako could no longer sit still. She thought she must assist him if only in material ways.

She entered her study with her baby in her arms. But it constantly obstructed her work. When excited about her creative desire, she simply held him tight and shed tears unable to hate or revile the lovely obstruction. When tears of fretfulness fell from her eyes, she just sat limply afterward, idly embracing the little life.

The babysitter was totally useless for caring for the child. Rather, she caused more trouble. Nitta suggested having Masako's mother over so as to eliminate at least the trouble with the child. Masako's mother was a good person but was not the kind of person who could really understand Nitta's and Masako's life. She was convinced that everyone in the world lived with the same kind of sentiment as she did. Both Nitta and Masako could only keep company with her with wry smiles.

Although the mother came over right away to be with her daughter and grandson, she behaved assertively toward her daughter, who was unused to handling a baby; this did not please Masako. The child-raising approach Masako envisioned differed totally from what her mother had in mind. Over this, Masako daily complained, or, helped by the willfulness allowed between blood relatives, flew at her mother. The feelings of Nitta, who stood between them, were an added bother to Masako.

"If she were Nitta's mother, I would be more patient." This was Masako's thought when she decided that she would ask her mother to leave. Her mother was unable to help in the family long, either, for she had the children of Masako's siblings to care for.

Once again, Masako kept the child by her side. It was not rare that she read while carrying the child on her back, or wrote while breast-feeding him. The child grew in good health but occasionally surprised the young mother by running a fever, or simply crying and crying miserably, unable to convey what he wanted. Falling into a situation similar to that during the time following marriage when she could not work in her study, she was unable to handle half what she wished to do.

"How much time in the world do I have?"

Masako began to think about her time again. Unlike when she was troubled only by housekeeping, now that she was troubled by her child, she was unable to demarcate her own time from hour to hour. All she could do was steal some unplanned free time from the child. There was no choice but to do her real work during those intervals.

Soon, however, a second habit entered into her life. Just as she first came to be able to leave her housework half completed, this time she learned to keep her attention toward the child halfway. It was fine for everything to be halfway. She came to be able to search for a thought while handling the child, conceive an idea while cooking in the kitchen, and contemplate while laundering. She was now able to sit at her desk with complacency while hearing the baby cry.

What enabled her to do so was precisely the strange power latent in daily life. She was able to equally divide the double and triple portions of her life, harmonize them, distinguish them, separate them, and coordinate them. When looked at from outside, her life was rather tragic. Yet, while handling that much housework, she was publishing larger numbers of creative and critical pieces. She seemed to be struggling, with effort and willpower alone, amid prohibitive binds against inevitable female fate. A miserable life, a pitiful life—but she did not feel that way herself. She felt the mother's pride in the child, the wife's rights toward her husband, and her pride in her own art. Yet she tried to avoid interpreting that pride as pride. It was not pride, she thought, but something that should be named love. It was her love for the child, for her husband, and for herself. Everything was love. Her life was love. She thought the strength of her daily life was the strength of love.

She felt as if her perception of love were infinite. Different from a creed of love she once pursued, she was now reaching an interpretation by which she herself was an incarnation of love. While shining with joy, she did not neglect to create her own world either.

Was this problem of daily life a problem that never again had to be repeated? She would probably have a second child. A temptation, similar to what she experienced with that man when she was pregnant with her first child, would assault her again. For her artistic sentiment would not allow her to remain aloof to fascinations and temptations of all kinds. The world of her creativity would expand infinitely as she dashed toward it. Then she would have to fight again against her present life of love. Unlike those small fights that had flashed from time to time in her past life, greater strife would undoubtedly oppress her soul.

And when she realizes that she can hardly run away from the pitiable, inevitable fate of femininity, she would once again advocate a new "life of love."

3

The Song the Owl God Himself Sang: "Silver Droplets Fall Fall All Around"

Chiri Yukie

Long ago, this spacious Hokkaido was our ancestors' space of freedom. Like innocent children, as they led their happy, leisurely lives embraced by beautiful, great nature, truly they were the beloved of nature; how blissful it must have been.

On land in winter, kicking the deep snow that covers forests and fields, stepping over mountain after mountain, unafraid of the cold that freezes heaven and earth, they hunt bear; at sea in summer, on the green waves where a cool breeze swims, accompanied by the songs of white seagulls, they float small boats like tree leaves on the water to fish all day; in flowering spring, while basking in the soft sun, they spend long days singing with perpetually warbling birds, collecting butterbur and mugwort; in autumn of red leaves, through the stormy wind they divide the miscanthus with its budding ears, catch salmon till evening, and as fishing torches go out they dream beneath the full moon while deer call their companions in the valley. What a happy life this must have been. That realm of peace has passed; the dream shattered tens of years since, this land rapidly changing with mountains and fields transformed one by one into villages, villages into towns.

Nature unchanged from ancient times has faded before we realized it. And where are the many who used to live pleasurably in the fields and the mountains? The few of us Ainu who remain watch wide-eyed with surprise as the world advances. And from those eyes is lost the sparkle of the beautiful souls of the people of old, whose every move and motion were controlled by

---

"Fukurō-gami no mizukara utatta uta" (1923). From *Ainu shin'yō-shū* (Ainu Songs of Gods), republished in Iwanami Bunko (Tokyo: Iwanami Shoten, 2006). Translated by Kyoko Selden. This translation first appeared in *Japan Focus*, January 2009. Translation copyright 2009 by Kyoko Selden.

religious sentiment; our eyes are filled with anxiety, burning with complaints, too dulled and darkened to discern the way ahead so that we have to rely on others' mercy. A wretched sight. The vanishing—that is our name; what a sad name we bear.

Long ago, our blissful ancestors would not for a moment have imagined that their native land would in future become so miserable.

Time flows ceaselessly, the world progresses without limit. If at some point just two or three strong persons appeared from among us, who, in the harsh arena of competition, now expose what wreckage we have become, the day would eventually come when we would keep pace with the advancing world. That is our truly earnest wish, what we pray for day and night.

But—the many words that our beloved ancestors used to communicate in their daily lives as they rose and as they lay, the many beautiful words they used to use and transmitted to us: would they also all disappear in vain together with the weak and vanishing? Oh, that is too pitiful and regrettable.

Having been born an Ainu and grown surrounded by the Ainu language, I have written down, with my clumsy pen, one or two very small pieces from the various tales that our ancestors enjoyed reciting on rainy evenings or snowy nights as they gathered at their leisure.

If many of you who know us read this book, together with our ancestral people I would consider it an infinite joy, a supreme blessing.

March 1, the eleventh year of Taishō [1922]
Chiri Yukie

The Song the Owl God Himself Sang: "Silver Droplets Fall Fall All Around"

"Silver droplets fall fall all around,
golden droplets fall fall all around." So singing
I went down along the river's flow, above the human village.
As I look down below
paupers of old have now become rich, while rich men of old
have now become paupers, it seems.
By the shore, human children are at play
with little toy bows[1] with little toy arrows.
"Silver droplets fall fall all around,
golden droplets fall fall all around." So singing
as I passed above the children
running beneath me,
they said the following:

"A beautiful bird! a divine bird!
Now, shoot that bird,
the one who shoots it, who takes it first,
is a true valiant, a true hero."
So saying, children of paupers of old now rich
fixing to little golden bows little golden arrows
shot at me, but I let the little golden arrows
pass beneath me and pass above me.
Among them, among the children
one child carrying a plain little bow and plain little arrows
is mingling with the rest. As I look
a pauper's child he seems, from his clothing too
it is clear. Yet a careful look at his eyes[2]
reveals that he is the offspring of a worthy person,
a bird of a different feather he mingles with the rest.
To a plain little bow he fixes
a plain little arrow, he too aims at me.
Then the children of paupers of old now rich burst into laughter
and they say,
"Oh how ridiculous[3]
a pauper child,
that bird, the divine bird
doesn't even take[4] our golden arrows, one like yours,
a pauper child's plain arrow of rotten wood,
surely he'll take it all right
that bird, the divine bird."
So saying they kicked and beat
the pauper child. Not a whit minding,
the pauper child aimed at me.
Looking at how it was, I was touched with pity.
"Silver droplets fall fall all around,
golden droplets fall fall all around." So singing
slowly in the big sky
I was making a large circle. The pauper child,
one foot far out and the other foot close by,
biting his lower lip, aiming awhile,
let it go. The little arrow flew
sparkling toward me, so I extended
my hand and took that little arrow.
Circling around and around
I whirled down through the whistling wind.

Then, those children ran toward me
stirring up a blizzard of sand, they raced.
The moment I fell to the ground
the pauper child ran to me first and took me.
Then the children of paupers of old now rich
came running from behind him.
They said twenty bad things, thirty bad things
pushing and beating the pauper child:
"A hateful child, a pauper's child,
what we tried to do first you did ahead of us!"
When they said this the pauper child covered me
with his body, firmly holding me under his belly.
After trying and trying, finally from between them
he leaped out, and ran and ran.
Children of paupers of old now rich
threw stones and splinters of wood at him but
the pauper child, not a whit minding,
stirring up a blizzard of sand, ran and arrived
at the front of a little hut. The little child
put me into the house through the honored window,
adding words to tell the story that it was thus and so.
An old couple from within the house
came out each with a hand on their forehead
and I saw that they were extremely poor yet
there were signs of a master, signs of a mistress.
Seeing me they bent themselves at the waist with surprise.
The old man fixed his sash
and made a ceremonial bow.
"Owl god, great god,
to the meager household of us paupers
thank you for presenting yourself.
One who counted myself among the rich in bygone days
now I'm reduced to a humble pauper as you see,
I stand in awe of lodging you
the god of the land,[5] the great god,
but today the day has already dusked
so this evening we will lodge you the great god
and tomorrow, with *inau*[6] if with nothing else,
we will send you the great god on your way." So saying
he repeated his ceremonial bows over and over again.
The old woman, beneath the eastern window

laid a spread and seated me on it.
And then the moment they lay down
with snores they fell fast asleep.
Seated between ear and ear of my body[7]
I was, but not too long after that around midnight
I rose.
"Silver droplets fall fall all around,
golden droplets fall fall all around."
Thus singing quietly
to the left seat, to the right seat[8] within the house I flew
making beautiful sounds.
When I fluttered my wings, around me
beautiful treasures, divine treasures scattered down
making beautiful sounds.
Within a short while, I filled this tiny house
with wonderful treasures, divine treasures.
"Silver droplets fall fall all around,
golden droplets fall fall all around."
So singing I changed this tiny house
in a short while into a golden house, a large house.
In the house I made a fine treasure altar,
hastily made fine beautiful garments,
decorated the interior of the house.
Far more finely than for the residence of the rich
I decorated the interior of this large house.
That done, as before I sat
between ear and ear of my helmet.[9]
I made the people of the house have a dream:
Ainunishpa[10] unluckily became a pauper
and by paupers of old now rich
was ridiculed and bullied. Which I saw
and took pity on, so although I am not a plain god
of meager status, I lodged
at a human house, made him a rich person.
This I let them know.
That done, a little while later when it dawned
the people of the house rose all together,
rubbing their eyes they looked around the house
and all fell on the floor their legs going numb.
The old woman cried loudly,
the old man shed large teardrops.

But before long the old man rose,
came to me, ceremoniously bowed
twenty times, thirty times in repetition and said,
"A mere dream, a mere sleep I thought I had,
but what wonder to see your blessings in reality.
To our humble, humble,[11] meager house
you have come, and for that alone I am thankful,
the guardian god, the great god
pities our misfortune
and behold, the most precious of blessings[12]
you have given us." Thus through tears
he spoke.
Then, the old man cut an *inau* tree,
beautifully carved a fine *inau* and decorated me.
The old woman dressed up,
with the little child's help she gathered firewood,
scooped water, prepared to brew wine, and in a little while
arranged six casks at the seat of honor.
And then, with the old woman of fire,[13] the old female god,
I exchanged stories[14] of various gods.
In two days or so, wine being the gods' favorite,
inside the house the fragrance
already wafted.
Now, the child, deliberately clad in old clothes
to invite[15] from throughout the village
the paupers of old now rich,
was sent off on an errand.
As I saw him from behind, entering each house,
the child delivered the message he was sent with,
at which the paupers of old now rich
burst into laughter:
"This is strange, those paupers,
what wine they brew,
what feast they invite people for,
let's go and see what's there
and have a big laugh." So saying
to one another, many of them together came,
and from a long distance, at the mere sight of the house,
some went back startled and embarrassed
while the legs of others became numb upon reaching the front of the house.
Then, as the lady of the house went outside,

took all by the hand and ushered them inside,
all crawled and sidled,
none raising his head.
Upon this, the master of the house rose,
spoke in a sonorous voice like a cuckoo's.[16]
Thus and so, he said, was the situation:
"Like this, being paupers, without reservation
to keep company with you was beyond us,
but the great god took pity,
no evil thoughts did we ever entertain
and so in this manner we have been blessed,
from now on throughout the village we will be a family
so, let's be friends
and keep company—to you
I convey this wish." Thus
he spoke, whereupon the people
time and time again rubbed their palms together,
apologizing to the master of the house for their wrongs;
from now on they would be friends, they said to one another.
I too received ceremonial bows.
That done, their hearts mellowing,
they held a cheerful banquet.
With the god of fire, the god of the house,[17]
and the god of the altar[18] I spoke
while the humans danced and stepped,
watching which I was deeply amused.
Two days passed, three days passed, and the banquet ended.
The humans made good friends,
seeing which I felt relieved and
to the god of fire, the god of the house,
and the god of the altar I bade farewell.
That done, I returned to my house.
Before I arrived, my house had been
filled with beautiful *inau* and beautiful wine.
So, to nearby gods and distant gods
I sent a messenger to invite them to a cheerful banquet
I was holding. At the party, to those gods
I spoke minutely of how when I visited a human village
its appearances and circumstances were,
upon which the gods praised me highly.
When the gods were leaving, beautiful *inau*

were my gifts, two of them, three of them.
When I look toward that Ainu village
now it is peaceful, humans are
all good friends, that *nishipa*
being the village head.
His child, now having become
a man, has a wife, has a child,
is filial to his father, to his mother.
Always, always, when he brews wine,
at the start of a banquet, he sends me *inau* and wine.
I too sit behind the humans
at all times
as I guard the human land.
Thus the owl god told his tale.

Notes (by Chiri Yukie unless otherwise indicated)

1. In bygone days, adults made small bows and arrows for young boys. While enjoying shooting for enjoyment at trees and birds, before they knew it, the boys became skilled archers. In the Ainu word *akshinotponku*, *ak* means "archery," *shinot* "play," *ponku* "a little bow."

2. *Shiktumorke*: "a look." When trying to learn a person's identity, the best way is said to be to look at the eyes. When one looks about restlessly, one is scolded.

3. *Achikara* means "dirty."

4. When birds and beasts are shot down, it is said that they take the arrows because they want the human-made arrows.

5. *Kotankorkamui*: god of the land or the village. In the mountains, there are *nupurikorkamui*, the god who has the mountain (bear), *nupuripakorkamui*, the god who has the east side of the mountain (wolf), and so forth, and the owl is placed next to the bear and the wolf. *Kotankorkamui* is not a wild, hasty type like the god of the mountains or the god of the eastern mountains. Usually, he is calm with eyes closed and is said to open his eyes only when a serious event occurs.

6. Ceremonial whittled twig or pole, usually made of willow, with shavings left on—trans.

7. Chiri Mashiho explains in a footnote to his translation of this same poem that when the owl god was seated on the patterned mat beneath the honored window, its spirit was believed to sit between both ears of its earthly birdlike garb ("The Song that the Owl God Sang and Enacted," in Hanasaki Kōhei, ed., *Shimajima wa hanazuna*, 113)—trans.

8. *Eharkiso*, "the left seat." *Eshiso*, "the right seat." There is a fire pit at the center of the house. The side against the eastern window is the seat of honor. Looked at from the seat of honor, the right is *eshiso*, the left, *harkiso*. Only men can take the seat of honor. A visitor who is humbler than the master of the house refrains from taking the seat of honor. The master of the house and his wife always take the right seats. Next in importance are the left seats, while the western seats (near the entrance) are the most humble.

9. *Hayokpe*: "armor." Whether birds or beasts, when in the mountains, though invisible to humans, they each have a house that resembles a human house and lead their lives in the same shapes as humans. When visiting a human village, they are said to appear in armor. Their corpses humans see when they are shot dead are actually their gear, and their true forms, though invisible, are said to dwell between ear and ear of the corpses.

10. *Nishpa*, meaning a well-to-do man, a wealthy man of high status, or master, is the antonym of *wenkur*, "pauper"—trans.

11. *Otuipe*: one with a tail cut short. [Annotating the phrase *wenash shiri otuiash shiri*] A dog tail so short that it looks cut off is not much respected. An unworthy human is bad-mouthed as *wenpe*, "bad fellow," and *otuipe*, "one with a tail cut short."

12. When a god unexpectedly brings great happiness to his favorite human, the phrase that human utters with joy is *"ikashnukar an* (blessings are given)."

13. *Apehuchi*, the old woman of fire. The god of fire, the most important of the gods in the house, is always an old woman. When gods of the mountains, the sea, and so forth visit a house as does this owl god, *apehuchi* takes the lead in conversing with the guests. It is also acceptable to call her *kamuihuchi* (divine old woman).

14. *Neusar*, "chatting." While worldly rumor is also called *neusar*, usually it refers to such things as *kamuiyukar* (songs of gods) and *uwepeker* (old tales).

15. *Ashke a uk*. *Ashke* means "fingers or hand"; *a uk* means "to take." This refers to inviting people when there is a celebration and so forth.

16. *Kakkokhau*: "cuckoo voice." Because a cuckoo's voice is beautiful and clear, one who articulates so everyone understands is likened to the bird.

17. *Chisekorcakui*, the god who owns the house. The god of fire is like the housewife, the god of the house like the master. The god of the house is a male and is also called *chisekorekashi*, the old man who owns the house.

18. *Nusakorkamui*, the god who has the altar, an old woman. The god of the altar too is always female. When something bad happens she may appear before humans in the form of a snake. So, when a snake appears near the altar or near the eastern window, people say, "Perhaps the old woman of the altar went out on some business," and they never kill that snake. It is said that if one kills it, one will pay dearly for it.

4

Miss Cricket

Ozaki Midori

Even if we were to reveal her name, few readers, perhaps, would know the heroine of our tale. For she had few friends in this world and was something of an ephemeral creature. We could of course uncover any number of reasons for this, yet they would have little relevance to this story. Still, in the past we have heard one or two faint tidings borne by the wind. According to one story brought by the wind, the god of social relations and the god of friendship mismeasured their doses when our heroine was born into this world. Or, it is said that our heroine unfortunately came into the world as these gods took their brief afternoon naps. Yet again, our contentious wind told us earnestly that when the ephemeral heroine of our tale was born, a certain philosophy was circulating through the land of the gods. A fragment of this philosophy happened to lodge in a corner of our heroine's mind, or perhaps in a corner of her heart. This certain philosophy (or so the contentious wind continued) was said to be an extremely tranquil one, but there was also a theory that it was extremely riotous. The true state of heaven cannot be grasped by those like us, the wind said, so let us leave that to the gods. So perhaps our heroine took in a fragment of this tranquil philosophy and came to dislike loud places—those where many people gather, for example—or perhaps instead, she was deafened by the riotous philosophy of the gods. The deaf (and our contentious guest suddenly raised its voice slightly to make its final statement) are low on social proclivities to begin with! They fall easily into misanthropic ways! They are escapists!

"Kōrogi-jō" (1932). Translated by Seiji M. Lippit from *Chikuma Nihonbungaku zenshū* (The Chikuma Complete Works of Japanese Literature), vol. 20 (Tokyo: Chikuma Shobō, 1991), copyright 1991 by M. Hayakawa et al. English translation rights arranged with M. Hayakawa, et al. through Henshū Jōhō-shitsu, Chikuma Shobō. The translation first appeared in *Review of Japanese Culture and Society,* VIII, Josai University, December 1996. Translation copyright 1996 by Josai University.

We felt as if we only half understood the opinions of our contentious wind. Let us entrust those aspects we did not understand to the mists of heaven. And we thought vaguely: the heroine of this tale must be quite a misanthrope. If so, we must be especially careful in dealing with her. Let us follow her quietly, taking care not to lose sight of her shadow.

We have soiled the beginning of this tale with so many rumors, yet there still remains one rather significant story we have heard about a certain kind of medicine. Our heroine, it is said, is a regular user of a certain brown, powdered medicine. There are various theories about its color, and we don't know which to believe. Some say the medicine is not brown at all but yellowish, and others that it is made of small, white crystals. It must be a powerful drug, they imply, since it is only the color of the jar that makes the substance appear brown. Still others believe that it is the soft wafer wrapping that gives it the yellow hue. In any case, it is best to leave these questions to the gods who preside over troublesome matters. We children of the earth can only pray that dealing with such matters as the color of medicine will leave the gods' nerves all the more delicate and their senses refined.

Whatever its color may have been, our heroine was a regular user of a certain kind of powdered medicine. That is beyond doubt. Yet we have not had reliable reports of its effects. We said before that the heroine of our tale may have been deafened by the riotous philosophy that surrounded her. Some say she began using this powdered medicine to save herself from the melancholy of this deafness, while others claim it is only to make herself even more deaf that she continues to take it. Whatever the case may be, it is a kind of narcotic and there is no question of its evil nature. No one with a healthy conscience or good sense would place it in her mouth.

We have also heard a handful of rumors concerning the side effects of the drug. The powder works on the human cerebellum and capillary vessels, producing a sensitivity to sunlight and an aversion to crowds. In the end, users of the drug come to dislike leaving home during the daytime. Only when the blinding sun vanishes from the earth do they at last regain their humanity and leave their second-floor boarding rooms. (We hear that users of the drug tend to live in rented second-story rooms.) As for their destinations once they leave home, we have heard stories filled with evil vices. Addicts of the powdered medicine would rather grasp for air that is someplace far away than for what is close at hand. From their own peculiar interpretations, they grow to fear and disdain the world they live in and try to keep their distance from it. Finally, they come to think the world unfolding on a theater screen or the world spread out on library desks a more comfortable place to live. It may be the drug's fault, but what a terrible side effect it is. When we first heard this rumor, we sighed sorrowfully and murmured, "No matter how you think of it, this powdered medicine must have been invented by the devil. To keep one's distance disdainfully from the human world in which one was born: what a profane affair!" As long as users of this drug do not abandon this invention of the devil, a tremendous whip may at any time spring from the middle of the earth to snap at their hearts. We must at least save our tale's heroine, if no one else, from succumbing to this drug.

Yet despite such intentions, we didn't run into her again for a time. Then, as though possessed of some grand purpose, she began to go regularly to the library.

We have wasted too much time listing so many rumors one after another. Yet people should not decide from these stories that our heroine has turned her back on virtue. For they are all merely distant rumors. Let us go back now to the beginning of the tale and say that, for various reasons, it makes no difference whether or not we expose our heroine's name.

It was the month of May. A cluster of paulownia flowers bloomed in a corner of a field, and when it rained, their fragrance spread even to Miss Cricket's dwelling. Miss Cricket lived in a rented second-floor room 108 square feet in size. The open verandah beyond the paper screen was made of terribly old wood, and even when the mistress of the room walked upon it softly, it creaked and creaked.

Today it was raining just the right amount and the sun was not so bright. Miss Cricket decided to leave for the library during the day. As she made her various preparations to depart an hour early, and as she pondered the appearance of clouds in the sky, our Miss Cricket began to feel drowsy. Stretching her legs beneath the desk, she gathered a number of magazines for a pillow and napped for about an hour. When she awoke, the sound of rainfall had happily begun, and the scent of paulownia flowers, pale and faded, filled the air around her. Then, after simply putting on her overcoat, she was ready to depart. Miss Cricket's coat was an old one, and as spent as the smell of the paulownia flowers. In the left pocket lay a small handbag that had seen more years than the coat itself. The edge of a thick piece of clothing protruded from the right pocket. This was, in sum, her appearance, and it was not a very fresh or vivid look. And we must say that the young lady inside the coat, to our eyes, appeared about as fresh as the coat itself.

She entered the rain-soaked fields. The scent of paulownia flowers began to fill the inside of her umbrella. This was inevitable. In these fields this time of year, as long as there was air there was also the scent of paulownia. Yet Miss Cricket seemed not to enjoy this air. From the depths of her nostrils she expelled two or three breaths in succession back into the atmosphere. But so long as she remained in these fields, her every breath was tinged with the faded scent of paulownia flowers. So Miss Cricket grasped her handbag from her left-hand pocket and drew it up to her face, expelling her breath several times.

We should explain why Miss Cricket refused the scent of paulownia flowers as she walked through the rainy fields. To our knowledge, paulownia flowers have appeared in the poems of sentimental poets since ancient times, and to reject their aroma seems highly profane behavior. Still, it is true the fragrance enveloping Miss Cricket came from flowers about to fall, that were spent and tired, and that by now were afflicted with a nervous illness. Miss Cricket herself was by this time suffering from her own nervous illness brought on by overuse of the devil's medicine.

We once knew a doctor named Kōda Tōhachi, of a hospital called the Schizophrenia Clinic. Immersed in his study of schizophrenia, Kōda Tōhachi wandered the country armed with a collection of plays and a single notebook. At his destination, he would have a young girl read aloud a number of intense love plays, taking careful notes on her psychological state and pronunciation. He was a doctor who blasphemed against the mystical gods. We have a handful of favorite stories concerning Tōhachi's notebook, which we shall nonetheless save for another day. We would like, however, to foreground one dimension of Kōda Tōhachi's travel findings as we continue our narrative of Miss Cricket's psychological state as she headed in the rain for the library. All across the open May fields there fell a drizzling rain, leaving the air awash with the fragrance of spent paulownia flowers at the end of the season. Only two minutes after leaving her rented room, Miss Cricket's faded spring coat was covered with moisture. The sight of a retreating figure sometimes dampens the viewer's spirits, and faced with the scene of the open fields in May, we naturally let out a sigh. Miss Cricket's appearance was ill suited to the spring landscape. The young lady's retreating figure was wrapped in a single spring coat that had faded and had the feel of an autumn coat. We felt all the more like placing Miss Cricket's figure within the autumn wind. Now Kōda Tōhachi's theory is roughly as follows: once a person's cranial nerve has deteriorated from a drug's side effects or from psychological burdens, she will try to escape from intense phenomena such as the summer sun. She will also reject such delicate things as the scent of flowers about to fall. This reflects a psychological necessity arising from her physical condition and is not the distortion of us researchers of schizophrenia! If such a patient needs to go outside during a season when the sun's rays are strong, she will postpone going out until nighttime, or else remain hidden in her room with shades drawn to wait for a rainy day. And when forced to pass paulownia flowers at the end of spring, she will flare her nostrils, trying to prevent the neurotic fragrance of paulownia from entering her body. It is, in short, the neurotic rejecting another neurotic. It is an attempt to prevent the feeling of sympathy for one's own kind, for between her and the paulownia flowers, in spite of the difference between humankind and the plant kingdom, there is the kinship of those suffering from nervous illness.

Our unreliable memory may have altered Kōda Tōhachi's theory somewhat, yet it was just such a psychology that led Miss Cricket to avoid smelling the paulownia flowers. The young lady passed by the flowers, and from the bus stop was taken to the library.

Let us whisper now a secret. Following the dictates of the devil's medicine, the heroine of our tale has fallen in love. How can we explain the beginnings of her love? For it is a rather roundabout affair.

One day, Miss Cricket happened to discover the following story:

"A long time ago, a man and woman fell deeply in love, and had no thoughts for anyone else."

With this antiquated beginning, it recounted the love affair of a peculiar poet. The poet's name was William Sharp, and because of a chance impulse of his heart, he fell in love with the poetess Fiona Macleod. Their tenderhearted love was greater than any in all the world. They passed many heartfelt love letters and poems between them. To draw upon examples from our own tradition, the poems they sent back and forth most likely ran thus:

> From you I learned at last
> of what people in the world
> call love.

Response:

> Since I knew nothing
> of what the world calls love,
> it was I who asked you to teach me.

Yet here a mystery arises, for the people of the world never once set eyes upon Miss Macleod. She thus seemed to the world at the time to be a poetess like air. The young lady lived in a secluded corner of the world unknown to others, and wrote pale, mystical poetry. On occasion she stayed with our Mr. Sharp, where she would pass several days. Yet we can only wonder about where and how she spent those hours. The young lady was a poet of mystique who devoted herself to her muse away from the prying eyes of the world. From time to time, Mr. Sharp would receive complaints from his friends. They were the kind of people who could not allow for mystical poetry, and would press him, saying, "Miss Fiona Macleod is by all accounts an exceptionally beautiful and dazzling poet. You thus behave rudely to your friends. You have not once introduced Miss Macleod to us. Today, at least, we are determined to meet this young lady. We are prepared to wait for any length of time until our wish is granted."

Upon hearing this, Sharp's face clouded over, and he murmured to himself, without looking into their eyes. He himself seemed not to know what he said, and it was a fragmentary murmur, like Bashō in late autumn. "Ah, what an unhappy request! Macleod has already left on a journey. The young lady is no longer by my side. It was yesterday evening. I have lost all presence of mind and seem to have forgotten the passage of time, but it must have been last night. Side by side, Fiona and I gazed up into the starry sky. The planets, standing slightly apart . . ."

"Sharp!" At last the guests spoke cruelly to him. "What we want is an earthly thing. Not something of the heavens! The stars and planets! What are they? This is what it means to feign ignorance. They say people in love are careless yet shrewd. He tells us only half the story of his love affair, and for the rest escapes into astronomy. Mr. Sharp! You drew close together and then you . . ."

Sharp then answered. For this type of guest requires stories of embraces and of the bedchamber. With a sigh he said,

"Naturally, we then kissed. But what are kisses between Fiona and myself? As I watched the planets, my Fiona escaped from my heart, and now I no longer know where she is. . . ."

"What an unpleasant love story! Please bring us now a bunch of citrons and a round paper fan. A tan-colored fan of the Far East, the kind used to fan a charcoal stove. Make it as large as possible, for we have heard that this article is used to send a cool breeze to sullen ears that have endured such amorous talk."

In the end, Mr. Sharp fell silent. His guests continued to insist they be allowed to meet Miss Macleod, saying their noses were especially sensitive to beautiful women. The young lady is undoubtedly close at hand. Ah, this fragrance! Miss Macleod must be in the next room, applying powder! This is a fragrance known to the world since the age of Tutankhamen! When it blends with the scent of a beautiful woman's skin, how it captivates dandies like us! Mr. Sharp! Bring Miss Macleod from the powder room! So they yelled. Sharp was silent to the last.

In such fashion, many years passed in the lives of William Sharp and Fiona Macleod. For these many years, the world failed to catch even a glimpse of Miss Macleod. Finally, some months after Sharp passed away, people heard that she had been called to eternal heaven on the same day and at the same hour as William Sharp. It was even in the same bed and from the same illness as he. Yet, only one body was ever found. The one, male body of William Sharp.

We must now return to Miss Cricket, who had been reading this antiquated story. After finishing the old tale, she felt as if the autumn wind had pierced her very body. Whenever she was impressed deeply by something, she would feel it pass through her body. We don't know whether it was a psychological effect or a visceral, physical sensation. Yet always, after the autumn wind passed through her, Miss Cricket would fall in love, her passion directed to the someone or something that had sent the autumn wind through her body.

Our impulsive thoughts seem to have led us to expand greatly the definition of love. In any case, by this order of events, our heroine had fallen in love with a poet from another country.

We are now telling our story out of order, but the antiquated tale ended in the following way. Only one body was found, yet two souls had vanished. It was an unprecedented form of death. Yet who could know at the time the details of what had transpired? People mourned only for the corpse of William Sharp, born of this earth and returned to the great sky. (He too, like his lover, Fiona Macleod, was a mystical poet who had offered his poetic soul to the wanderings of the sun and to the play of the planets.) A number of mourners wondered to themselves, on what soil does Miss Macleod mourn William's death? Some gentlemen (the sort who always kept French ham stuffed in their pockets and ended in becoming even fatter during the funeral procession), felt their emotions overflow and spoke loudly in their own hearts: Sharp only ever talked of clouds and mist, and now he has at last risen to heaven. Pale soul, it is as if you have returned home! The moon, the stars, the pathway of the sun, limitless and infinite eternity. What do such things mean? You spoke only of what is immaterial, and now your soul has gone to ride the wind across the limitless sky. It is almost nonsensical! Now, when the funeral procession reaches its destination, we must offer, representing these fat gentlemen, a eulogy for the spirit of Mr. Sharp. What a contradiction! Our procession will soon arrive. There is nothing to be done. With dampened voices, let us call out:

Ladies and gentlemen!
William Sharp was a poet of the atmosphere.
In his glorious life, he wrote three, perhaps
seven volumes in the genre of poetry,
but they are, in fact, works of high philosophy
strung together with abstract nouns.

Next, of Fiona Macleod. Ah, Miss Macleod! Because of Sharp's lack of generosity, we failed in the end to gaze into your eyes. He would always maneuver his way out and refuse to introduce you to us. What jealousy! Miss Macleod! Now at last you are free of Sharp's jealousy and are likely yawning comfortably elsewhere. For women will not hesitate to eat at another table the day after losing their lovers. It is a timeless philosophy formed of our experiences with a thousand women. While their eyes are filled with tears, their mouths are already busy eating another meal. Our Miss Macleod, in what land do you now hold a new plate in your hands? Our noses sense Tutankhamen's fragrance once more. We will seek you out to the uttermost ends of the earth! Then our quandary shall be what fragrance to spread around our beds. Every woman's skin has a different scent according to her body type. Ah! Because of Sharp's unreasonable jealousy, we have yet to enjoy the scent of Miss Macleod's skin! Was there ever anyone as jealous as he? Nothing will stop us from pursuing her to the ends of the earth! In her poetry, she speaks like Sharp of clouds and mist, but when we seek her out we may find her possessed of a surprising body. Rumor has it her love letters to Sharp are quite intense, in contrast to the world of her poetry. This is as it should be! Miss Macleod would not be a slender-waisted creature like the clouds of mist. We have heard recently of a strange hospital somewhere in the Far East. According to a doctor there named Kōda Tōhachi, slender women tend to write lush poetry, while full-bodied women will write poetry like smoke. What a splendid theory! Now we must stop at nothing to uncover the body of Miss Macleod.

In this way, the quiet funeral procession containing all these various thoughts arrived at its destination. Yet these gentlemen were mistaken in their conjectures about Miss Macleod's whereabouts. At that very moment the young lady was lying unseen, in disembodied death within William Sharp's corpse, herself receiving a funeral service unknown to others. Fiona Macleod was a purely illusory poet. A poet without flesh, formed only as an alter ego of the poet Sharp. For this reason, the young lady disappeared from this earth together with him. Yet their exchange of love letters during their lifetimes had actually occurred. When his heart was male, the divided poet took up Sharp's pen and wrote letters to his lover, Macleod, and when the poet's heart was female, she took up Macleod's pen and wrote love letters to Sharp. Later, psychiatrists may take this exchange and unmask Sharp's soul according to the complex phenomenon of the "doppelgänger." Or perhaps an ephemeral poetess living in an attic in the Far East may chance someday, because of her own ephemeral poetry, to write of the crystalline poetess of a strange land. The psychiatrist and poet. What profane types! In every age, those dwelling in the land of Eros and the Muses have produced only harmful effects. With their every move, the world of mystery inhabited by William Sharp only disintegrates the more.

So ended Miss Cricket's antiquated tale.

The library stood atop a mountain close to the sky and afar from the street.

It was covered all in gray. The structure appeared to Miss Cricket like a capricious turkey. When the sun shone it became a brightly colored ivory tower, and when it rained it turned a dark, inviting color. The rain-darkened gray did not cause any further pain to her head, already weakened by the powder.

Still, the William Sharp who had captured Miss Cricket's heart was such a faint presence within the library. Even after several days of research, her notes were not abundant. And so she fell into a deep melancholy and in the blank spaces of her notepad drew fragments of the clouds that came and went in her heart. She decided to stop reading her massive literary histories. (For the larger the body of the history, the less the writer would deign even to touch upon the poet she searched for. This was Miss Cricket's sad discovery.) Our heroine began to question the value of literary history itself, and she fell into a vegetative silence, killing time to no end. This activity was of no benefit to the world.

Miss Cricket's notes on Sharp were thus quite meager. In the end she found, in one of her volumes of literary history, a preface perfectly worthy of her melancholy.

"Finally, there is something I must acknowledge. The publisher of this volume is the possessor of a certain lofty philosophy and has announced to me that he shall not publish a single line of any material having to do with unhealthy literature, any literature suffering from nervous illness. Therefore, I was led to excise from my manuscript several poets deserving of my master's hatred. I will merely list here the names of these beloved poets as consolation. In no particular order, then: three poets of *roseau pensant*, several members of 'the school of yellow nerves,' all followers of the 'neo–cocaine school.' Oscar Wilde, for his immoral activity. William Sharp, because he assumed the guise of a woman and so distressed society."

Of what use was such a preface for Miss Cricket? It only increased the ache in her head. When people are sad or disappointed their chronic illnesses grow all the more pronounced. For this reason, the young lady walked unsteadily from the reading room and into the dark air of the library basement.

After descending the narrow stairs, she turned into the corridor on the right. To her right was a row of two or three shops. She entered the women's cafeteria to her left. Apart from mealtimes it was always empty, and the dim air inside remained unmoving. There was always hot water available here, boiling in a large kettle, for Miss Cricket to take her powdered medicine. Seen through the dim light of the window, the boiling water seemed ashen. Miss Cricket swallowed some powdered medicine from her old bag. People may have seen her. The air in this room was truly stale, and beyond the glass window the drizzling May rain continued to fall in the basement garden. At times like these, people may feel like singing in a loud voice or conversing with someone or eating bread. From her daily experience of living in a rented room, our heroine fully understood this human feeling. And now Miss Cricket wanted at least to eat bread. Just at that moment, from a corner of the dining hall came the sound of someone sharpening a pencil. In the darkest corner of the hall was a customer who had entered before her. Miss Cricket had no doubt she was a student of midwifery. She would be a perfect conversation partner. Yet she showed no sign of returning Miss Cricket's greeting, and simply continued with her studying. Just as Miss Cricket had not noticed her for some time, she in turn did not notice Miss Cricket. What could it mean? There was nothing to be done, so she left the cafeteria for the bread shop.

"One roll, please."

Miss Cricket's throat, so unaccustomed to conversation, spat out unpleasant sounds. The girl behind the counter looked upon her with bemusement and handed her a bag containing the bread.

Perhaps we should explain something of Miss Cricket's state of mind as she ate the roll in the cafeteria. The young lady was immersed in her bread. She seemed by now to have forgotten her terrible distress upon reading the preface to her book of literary history only moments before. After she finished half her roll, her eating pace slowed, and as she idly licked the chocolate filling she began to speak in voiceless conversation with the other woman sitting in the corner of the hall.

"Midwifery is a difficult skill, isn't it?"

Yet the other woman remained bent over her material in the same unchanging pose. Miss Cricket sat two tables away looking at her dimly lit face and sent one more voiceless message. "Please study hard, Widow. (Miss Cricket did not know any other name for this dark, thin woman.) May you become a midwife by autumn. And as you step on a cricket at dawn, may your work flourish each morning. You may laugh at me for mentioning crickets. But let me make a quiet confession to you. I always worry about things like crickets. That is why I always think of things that are quite useless. Yet even for this type of thinking, I need bread. So I always need to surprise my mother with telegrams all year long. Letters and postcards are too embarrassing and too much trouble for me. My mother lives in the countryside. Widow, do you also have a mother? I hope she will live for a hundred years. But Widow, mothers have never, in any age, had a pleasant role to play. When her daughter succumbs to a sickness of the mind, a mother suffers many times more in her heart. Ah, Fiona Macleod!

"While you lived as a poet, did you ever think to make a request of the scientists? For a way to extend people's lives by breathing only mist? I am always hoping for such a thing. But I don't wish to keep clamoring for bread all the time."

Evening had fallen on the underground cafeteria.

5

Thorn

Mori Mari

One day, I suddenly became aware of a coolness that had come between Father and me. Deep in my heart, I was bothered by that chill. Prone to dreaming and not very clearheaded, I was bewildered by that chill air, the way a child not given to deep thought would feel. At all times, in all places, that air stood between Father and me. The loneliness simply would not go away. It was always there. Thin but obstinate, it seemed to refuse dispersing. The awareness of it left me feeling lonely. Why was it that I could no longer bask in Father's love as I had before? There really was no tangible change. He would smile when I laughed. He would say something kind when I spoke. All this remained the same. Yet there was a difference. The fact that everything appeared the same as before made the strangeness all the more unbearably isolating. It made me insecure and sad that somehow I could no longer lean on him with all my heart, that somehow there was a distance between us. Sometimes I tried to approach him. But somehow the air between us did not let me do so. It seemed that Father and I could not help but drift apart. I kept walking without trying to change my course. That air appeared to be like the pale, sweet twilight of the evening dusk, yet it was absolute. It possessed the strength to prevent me from going back the way I had come.

Little by little I became distanced from Father. One evening, we sat together upstairs in our small house, Father peering at the baby in my arms. I could feel the coldness. At the time I was living with my husband in a small

---

"Toge" (1957). Translated by Angela Yiu from *Mori Mari zenshū* (Complete Works of Mori Mari), vol. 1 (Tokyo: Chikuma-Shobō, 1993). Copyright 1993 Masako Yamada, Tomoko Yamada, and Reo Yamada. English translation rights arranged with Masako Yamada, Tomoko Yamada, and Reo Yamada. This translation first appeared in *Review of Japanese Culture and Society*, VII, Josai University, December 1997. Translation copyright 1997 by Josai University.

place. The room in which Father and I sat was quiet. Against the dimly lit paper screen, he somehow looked like a different person. I silently watched Father's smiling face bent toward the baby. His gentleness, like a rustling tree laden with spreading branches and fragrant flowers, had not changed at all. It was the same as before. Yet that gentleness no longer reached out to embrace me. It was congealed. Like something that immediately congeals upon exposure to air, it hardened around him. This congealed gentleness, a gentleness that no longer embraced me, made me unbearably lonely. Until recently, that gentleness had wrapped me completely. Although I no longer sat on Father's lap, it was the kind of gentleness that would have allowed me to had I wished. In those days Father used to go to the Ueno Museum and the library in Toranomon on alternate days. My house was in Shimizu-chō in Yanaka, so it was on his way to the museum. Every other day Father would drop by my place carrying something or other for my lunch, but he would always just stop at the entrance and rarely came into the house. I looked at him wishing to ask him to come inside, but that cold air had settled between us. Every time it happened, I felt unbearably lonely. Why was I no longer able to indulge in Father's love? Why was I no longer able to throw myself at his chest and cling to him? Such feelings of despair floated between us, and I felt powerless as though cast under a spell. I felt there was nothing I could do to struggle against that air. But once I did attempt to resist that binding force and said to Father, "Papa, won't you come in?"

He smiled, nodding two or three times, but he cast his face down just enough so that it was slightly shaded. That smile, so brimming with love, was somehow restrained. It looked as though it had turned inward and withdrawn into itself. The thick cloud deep between us painted even his smile, which had always been a sign of his love for me, in the color of smoke, and it seemed to weaken and vanish. Making up for the vanishing smile with a few meaningless words, he left, the gentleness that could have wrapped me still sealed in the space around his gray coat. "I'll come again." Those words of Father's echoed in me emptily. He looked sad at not being able to come close to me because of the mysterious smoke cloud between us. I watched his receding back for a long time—Father in his brown hat and gray overcoat. It was a narrow street with the Ueno woods on the left and, on the right, a continuous row of cluttered low residences with shops opening to the front.

Along this white street shining bright in the morning sun, Father walked in his usual deliberate, pensive manner, and slowly disappeared into the distance.

In this way I grew apart from Father and moved toward a new person who appeared in my life. Pushed by an irresistible and transparent force, I eventually became estranged from the gentleness and intimacy that almost could have been called romantic love between Father and me. Words that Father had said to Mother when I nearly died from a grave illness in childhood—"When I see the pond at city hall, I think of showing it to Mari when the irises are in bloom, but perhaps there won't be a chance anymore. When I ride the streetcar, it occurs to me that maybe Mari won't be able to ride with me anymore. I realized that up until now I've been living my life with the sole thought of taking Mari somewhere or showing Mari things. I've been living just for Mari." My mother told me that she felt her chest stiffen into a board as she watched Father standing at the entranceway saying those words.

I grew apart from Father that way and entered a different world. That world was, so to speak, the real world. After entering that world I changed very quickly. My speech and looks began to take on for the first time a kind of frivolousness, and things that were not found in the atmosphere of Father's home were now added to me. At that time I did not know I was extremely sensitive to the atmosphere around me and disposed to being easily influenced by it. I simply felt lost and anxious. I could not tell whether it was good or bad to become like this. But I was anxious that Father would no longer love me because of the way I was changing. As I lived awkwardly in a different kind of home, I was aware of sadness, a sense that I might no longer be loved by Father, beginning to form a fine web in a corner of my heart. Would he abandon me? Would the lonely feeling between Father and me increase and finally become unbridgeable? While living the days and months the best I could in my new environment, beneath it all I tasted the loneliness of being abandoned by Father. When I heard his remark to Mother, "When Annu talks to Mari, she begins to sound like Mari," my heart ached. The sadness of being the only one excluded, the sadness of earning Father's displeasure, hurt my heart. I wrote Father a long letter. Although the household I had joined was headed by a prominent businessman, the lives of the other people under the same roof were so cheerful and lively that when I spoke in my usual serious manner, it broke the harmony of the environment. I could no longer talk the way I wanted to. I wrote all that to Father. He did not reply.

After being married for some time, I said to my husband, "I keep the memories of Papa and me locked in a beautiful box inside me." Hidden in those words were a small regret and a source of pride. That was because I believed that the love between Father and me was beautiful. My young mind knew intuitively that Father was someone with poetry in him while my husband had none. And I really lived out what I said. I determined to keep that beautiful world, with its noble love washed in gray and the embers of that love, deep within me until I died. At the age of fifteen years and ten months, I began to live in a different house from Father's, and in March of the following year, plagued by uncertainty and sorrow, I left with my brother for Europe, where my husband was. Father was with everyone at the station, but when I saw him standing still behind the rows and rows of people under the window, I was seized with a sudden anxiety. I did not know what it was. That anxiety soon grew bigger, and spreading like a rain cloud, it suddenly threatened to block out the faces of children, the colors of kimonos, the slightly pale face of Mother, as well as other images in my heart. How shall I describe that anxiety? I felt as though I were abandoning Father, as though I were treating him cruelly. I felt as though Father were going to die. Perhaps I could describe that anxiety as something cold, thick, and wet that quietly smothered my heart. Yes, that was how I felt. Even if I could have gone to his side, clung to his chest and tried to ask what's wrong, the chilly air would still have been between us. I could not do that. I stood looking down. My eyes wandered restlessly between Mother's sad face and the hat of my sister, who was holding on to the window ledge as though she were hanging from it. I could not look at Father's face. And yet I was telling myself, "I must look at him! I must look at him!" and this seemed to threaten my heart that was filled with anxiety. I could not look at anyone's face with composure. Just as the departure signal sounded and pierced my anxiety, a strange sensation brought me back to reality, and I began to focus on the single idea of parting. Until that moment, my heart had been seized by a strange feeling, the feeling of being pinned down stealthily by the skirt of my kimono. Yes, I was seized by this feeling. As the car began to sway, my eyes moved toward Father's face. He smiled. And then he nodded twice, three times. It was the smile that I had seen so often since I was a child. It was filled with love. Father's face grew dim, and I wept like a child. In the depth of weeping, my chest was choked with the image of Father's face, choked hard for reasons that I could not explain. On that day we young travelers were leaving for Europe, a departure that was considered gay and splendid. Yet beneath that glorious surface flowed the cold air between Father and me, the strange anxiety, the fleeting premonition of Father's death, and a sorrow invisible to the eyes. I felt all this as though in a dream. Beneath this gay scene of departure, with its sporadic merry laughter, the strange shimmering air between Father and me congealed into a loneliness that resembled a dim piece of glass. During the voyage, and during our sojourn in Europe, I tried to forget Father's face at the time of departure. I buried it at the bottom of my consciousness and left it covered all the time. To touch it was, for some reason, painful and unpleasant. That day, when Father returned home, he said to Mother, "Today Mari was like a dove." The image of a dove in the West was symbolic of a pure maiden before marriage. I felt it was a small redemption that this was the last image of myself reflected in Father's eyes.

One morning more than forty days after our departure, my brother and I disembarked at the sooty platform of Gare du Nord. Cobblestone paths where empty wine vats lay, old folks vacantly watching the passersby, shaggy dogs whose dirty fur covered even their eyes. The white tin flags, lowered when hired, of the taxis that raced around town as though dancing . . . The Parisian mood that gently relaxes people's feelings lodged, already at that moment, a certain sweetness that nearly made me forget all about home.

It was spring in Paris. The sky was deep blue. Rows of horse chestnut trees, reaching up like seaweed, flared high up in the valley of the gray street. On café terraces, people filled the orange and white chairs. Boulevards were buried in slow-moving taxis, buses, and the carriages loaded with printing paper drawn by white horses. The smell of dust and flowers . . . Parisian nights were deep. They were deep, sweet nights. Lights from cafés flowed along the cobbled streets, gas lamps in the back streets of Saint-Michel. Footsteps from somewhere disappearing into a side alley. Lovers with arms around each other's waists forming a single shadow. As I stood looking at the cafés glittering like diamonds in the rain-wet darkness, or glimpsing by a midday road some ancient lamps and picture books of the reigns of the emperors coated with dust in show windows, I was immersed in Paris. I went to the forest, I went to the suburbs by boat, I saw plays, I walked along the Seine. I lived in the gentleness of Paris as though in a dream. I spent countless days in the warm sun and the mistlike rain. It seemed that the strange anxiety I had felt at my departure as well as the inexplicable pain of my wounded heart would be slowly soothed and healed by the gentleness of Paris. When we went to London in early summer, I heard the news of Father's critical illness. The day after I received the telegram about his critical condition, news of his death reached me. I cried for two nights without sleeping. Yet the memory of the cold air between Father and me occupied my sobbing heart and seemed to deprive me of pure mourning. Although his final image hurt my heart so, for some reason I could not mourn with purity. The fact that I could not become pure at heart despite Father's death made me terribly sad. Perhaps more than sadness, I felt pain. And in that pain there was a certain amount of discomfort. It might almost be called guilt. We were staying in a cold, white hotel room in London. The huge window next to the bed was open, and moonlight flowed on to the sheet. As I wept, I noticed the distinct creases on the sheet, and I sensed a pale loneliness.

From London we moved on to Germany, and after staying two months in Berlin, we went to Munich. It was moving to have come to the city where Father had lived for a long time, and the wound in my heart that Paris had soothed once again became raw. Whether walking along the bank of the Isar, or in the midst of the sounds of the German language, the froth of beer, and the whirls of tobacco smoke in the bar, I dreamed of Father's life and thought of his life's work, despite the fact that they cast only faint shadows in my young mind. I remembered Father's murmuring, "My memories of Europe have grown faint." One day I was waiting for my husband in a large bookstore as he was choosing books. Goethe, Schiller, Rilke—these names in gold glowed in the dimness. All of a sudden I experienced a strange sensation. I sensed that Father's spirit—a spirit that desired to master even more yet had to succumb to death—lingered among those bookshelves. I felt I could see Father's will, his spirit lingering there. At this point, I was overcome with an indescribable melancholy. How transient is a human life! I thought about the brevity of life. As I thought about Father's life and his death, something that seemed drawn toward death echoed in me. From some other place, perhaps from the realm of death, it echoed in me. The four walls of books surrounded me like the walls in Faust's monastery and stared down at me. I stood still, and became somewhat frightened. Somewhere a book seemed to be turning its own pages. From the pages came the clanging of swords, and I could hear the moans of Valentin and the laugh of Mephistopheles. I could almost see the breasts of the virgin Gretchen behind a veil of clothing. It seemed that along with the spirits of Goethe and Schiller, Father's will rose before me. Perhaps it was because of those several moments during which I remained in that state of illusion. Young as I was, I thought of death and was frightened by its coldness. My husband, who was standing on the ladder against the bookshelves and peering at the books as though he were removing insects from a tree, came down, brushed off the dust from his large hands, turned around to me, and said, "Shall we go?" I put my hand on his arm and we walked outside to the cobbled street warmed by the golden rays of the evening sun. I felt as if I had finally returned to the realm of the living. Yet in my sad longing for Father, I was aware of a transparent barrier of air that existed between Father and me, and there remained in my heart an element of malaise akin to bitter regret, as well as an uncertain sorrow.

Once again we returned to Paris. And then, after some time, we returned to Japan. After that, whenever I was overtaken by an unexpected mood, I would be sunk in thoughts of Father. But whenever I thought of Father, a strange sense of doubt always occupied my memories and made me uneasy. Not wanting to touch the lonely and sore spot, I always tried to bury the pain deep inside me, to put it out of my mind. But one day, while talking to Mother, I discovered what that strange air between Father and me was about. When I had been feeling lonely, Mother suspected Father's aloofness and asked him the reason for it. Father said, "I want Mari to become close to her husband, Tamaki. That's what I am trying to make happen." Father deliberately created a distance between us, all the while bearing his own loneliness. Perhaps Father was also thinking of his imminent death. In order not to make me sad, he tried his best to hide it from me. Perhaps Father thought it was best for everyone to send me to Europe. Seeing my desire to be with my husband, and reading the letters that my husband sent him, Father, despite his poor health, visited everyone concerned and persuaded those who were against the idea. Then he came to the station, said good-bye to his daughter, whom he knew he would not see again before he died, and endured his own loneliness. The anxiety that overcame me when I saw Father at the station was the death that Father sensed in himself. It was the final parting that Father sensed between us. What pierced my young heart was Father's silent wail.

When I heard this story from Mother, my last memory of Father became a deep sorrow to me. The golden box is still hidden in my heart. But a small, sharp thorn pierced my heart the day I heard what Mother said. When a lover dies, he or she leaves a deep wound in the other's heart. In the same way, Father left a piercing thorn in my heart. Every time I think of my parting from Father, I feel the pain of that thorn. It is a gentle thorn, like the soft, supple thorn of a young rose. And that only makes it all the more painful.

6

Masks of Whatchamacallit

Hayashi Kyōko

By the little stream is a trapezoid-shaped stone. Sitting down on it, Takako looks around. There are no trees. No houses. No people on the streets at midday.

Fires burn along the rubble-strewn horizon. When will they be extinguished? The sun is too hot. Takako wishes for the shade of a tree. She wishes to see life, alive and moving; even a small ant will do.

Takako died. In October 1974, when she was forty-five years old. The cause of death was cancer of the liver, or of the pancreas according to some, from A-bomb aftereffects. Some said that the autopsy revealed the pancreas to be rotten, resembling a broad bean.

Takako was consecrated this year at the A-bomb ceremony in the memorial tower of Peace Park. Her name is bound into a single-volume death register along with those of over one thousand others who died of illness caused by A-bomb radiation in the past year.

Our classmates who died in the atomic explosion thirty years ago are also consecrated in the park. Those girls, still fifteen or sixteen, must have frolicked around inside the dark monument as they welcomed Takako at this thirty-year reunion, saying, "We've been waiting for you!" I can see her troubled expression as she tilts her head, surrounded by those innocent girls, not knowing what to do. She had become the age of their mothers.

Takako and I went to different girls' schools. Hers was a missionary school, located halfway up the hill overlooking Nagasaki Harbor. My alma mater was near Suwa Shrine. This locates her school in the southern part of Nagasaki,

---

"Nanjamonja no men," published in *Gunzō*, February 1976. Translated by Kyoko Selden with the permission of Hayashi Kyōko and Nihon Bungeisha Kyōkai. This translation first appeared in *Review of Japanese Culture and Society*, XVI, Josai University, December 2004. Translation copyright 2004 by Josai University.

mine on the western outskirts of the city. Takako was also one grade ahead of me.

We came to know each other at an arms factory just beyond Urakami, where students were mobilized to work. Both of us were bombed there, but, strangely, sustained no external wounds. The factory was not even a mile away from Peace Park, where Takako is now consecrated, just fifteen hundred feet from the epicenter. Nearly everyone in town met an instant death.

On August 9, the day of the atomic bombing, both Takako and I ran desperately from that area. I worry that she may not be able to attain Buddhahood if brought back to the place from which she managed, at great pains, to flee; but perhaps she is simply resting in peace, not thinking of anything now.

I last met Takako ten or so years ago. It was early October, just before the autumn festival of Suwa Shrine. The sound of festival drums could be heard from the woods surrounding the shrine. The festival ranks among Japan's three biggest, and the entire city was excitedly making preparations.

When I returned to the city for the combined purpose of seeing the festival and visiting my mother, I chanced to meet Takako.

Walking as far as Kajiyamachi through the arcaded streets of Hamamachi, the bustling quarters of Nagasaki, one comes to a quiet shopping street with less traffic. One of the stores there is a "gift shop" carrying unusual dolls sold nowhere else. I found them by chance when I happened to drop in fifteen or sixteen years ago. The artist, I heard, was a physically handicapped young man who had suffered polio when small.

Because they were the work of a single person, the number of dolls was limited. Twenty at most were placed casually on a shelf in the furthest corner of the shop. In the gloom where neither outdoor light nor store lighting reached the shelf, each doll stood in a queer posture. They were made of red clay, baked unglazed so as to make the most of their color.

Measuring two or three inches in height, each had a different expression and design. What they had in common was that the neck of every doll was forcefully twisted heavenward. And they were wailing, each with a different expression.

When I took some in my hand, I noticed the artist's fingerprints on the sticklike torso, which measured about a quarter of an inch in diameter. One doll had a flowing fingerprint from its forehead to the pointed nose of its inverted triangular face, which was upturned to heaven, creating a warped expression as if it were about to break into tears.

Like a snail's, two eyes of another doll protruded from its head, with two additional red eyes placed just below. The torso of another doll stretched from the legs to the neck, then, at the tip, a face opened up like a plate. On the plate were two eyeballs, lips, and two ears, taken from the face and arranged like fruit.

The one that most resembled a human shape was a minister dressed in black paint. Hands raised like those of an orchestra conductor, face turned up to the sky, he peered heavenward, wailing. All that was there for eyes were two *X*s inscribed with a bamboo carver, but they made him look as if he were crying.

Inside the gift shop where showy local toys were displayed, the shelf holding clay dolls looked like a dark hollow, alone by itself. As I stood gazing at them, the dolls almost seemed to crowd together and press toward me, making me avert my eyes.

They seemed to have been created from the shadows within the heart of the physically disabled artist.

Uncanny as they were, each time I returned to my hometown I bought a different one.

On that day too twenty or so clay dolls were arranged on the shelf. Among them was one whose style struck me as novel. Its mouth, gaping from ear to ear, opened across its face. White spots covered its body, and the inside of its wide-open lips was colored with vermilion paint.

Picking it up and placing it on a palm, I looked at it.

"A scream, yes?"

I heard a woman's voice behind me. When I turned around surprised, my eyes met those of a long-haired woman. Taller than me, her lean body was dressed in a navy blue sweater and jeans. Perhaps because both top and bottom were in cold colors, she looked all the more slender, her facial complexion unhealthy and subdued.

This was how I reencountered Takako. She had long been slender but seemed one size thinner. I asked her, "Why does he scream, I wonder?"

"He's in pain," she answered confidently in Nagasaki dialect.

"What from?" I asked again.

"*Remaining* this way. It's painful to be forever exposed to the world."

Takako picked up a doll with red stripes. It looked like a prisoner, but also like a priest.

"Are you buying that?"

Nodding, I bought the screaming doll. She bought the one with red stripes. We left the store, each with a doll wrapped in a small fancy rice-paper bag.

"I saw K. yesterday," I mentioned our common friend who had visited me at my mother's place. Takako responded with an ironic smile on her lips, "You heard some unsavory rumor about me, I suppose? Fine to spread it as you like."

Then, looking me in the eyes, she said, "Would you keep company with me too for a half day?"

A few houses down, there was a shop that sold freshly baked French bread with two red pay phones side by side at the front. I called my mother, asking her to eat lunch by herself because I would be late.

I bought a fresh baguette for my mother.

"It's warm," I said, pressing the bag against Takako's cheek.

"It's nice to see a woman buying warm bread look happy, for the moment at least," she smiled. Then she asked, "Have you been well all this while?"

Apart from a series of A-bomb symptoms that followed my exposure to radiation, I had had no serious illness that would keep me in bed. But I experienced dizziness every day.

"Not necessarily all well," I answered.

"We're both flawed merchandise. We must always handle ourselves carefully," she said thoughtfully and added that when she felt well enough, she worked as a volunteer at a mentally and physically disabled children's facility in the suburbs of Nagasaki, work she intended to continue as long as she lived.

As if the autumn sun were dazzling to behold, she blinked incessantly. Taking a good look at her eyes in the bright outdoor light, I saw a bloody bubble in her left eye. It was round, the size of a drop from an eyedropper. The center of the bubble rose slightly and, alongside the black pupil, produced an odd semblance of two pupils in one eyeball.

"Weird, isn't it?" Takako pointed at her eye.

"A-bomb illness?"

"Maybe, maybe not. It looks like spot bleeding. It looks like the pupil will absorb it if I leave it alone. My illness, whatever it is, always looks like a matter of *looks like*."

Viewed through her red eyeball, she told me, the faces of healthy, beautiful women appeared to be those of red demons. The prim looks of those women who assumed they were beautiful were so absurd, she added laughing merrily. They may have really looked red, but it was Takako herself, who so perceived them, that appeared weirder to me.

"That can't be true," I said, looking her in the eyes. "It's true, it is," she laughed aloud.

The café was at the far corner of a narrow alley in Kajiyamachi, a small shop with a wooden door that needed to be opened by hand.

It was dim inside. A bartender stood behind the counter. Takako lifted her right hand casually to him. The young man behind the counter said "hey" in return.

Takako seemed to be a regular. She also seemed to have a fixed seat, and the bartender placed a glass of cold water and a whiskey bottle on a table near the wall.

She sat with her back against the ecru wall, I on a chair facing her.

The bartender turned on the light that hung on the wall. In the illumination, the left half of Takako's face was brought into relief, and somehow I felt that the bubble of blood was glistening at me. Before thinking, I looked down. She might have been telling the truth when she said people looked like red demons. The bubble of blood might possess vision, adding color to objects that did not please her. She might not be merely applying that vision to distinguish between beauty and ugliness, but was perhaps observing me and other things in the world with three pupils.

As I took a fresh look at her with this thought, sure enough I felt that her gaze perceived something.

"Any children?" Takako asked, pouring whiskey in her glass. I raised one finger.

"A boy," I added.

"Are his limbs and brain all functioning?" Takako asked unceremoniously. I made no reply.

"Sorry," she apologized, quickly reading into my feelings.

"I meant no harm," she added as she lowered her head, "I've experienced so many things that I've lost all sense of shame."

Nobody knows where the story began, or whether or not its source was that of a single person. But that story, which spread right after the explosion in a twinkling with speed and accuracy to be marveled at even when looked back on today, was of a reliable nature.

On the twelfth, three days after the bombing, a girl attendant at city hall came by, collecting old newspapers to be used as medicine for treating the burns of *hibakusha* [A-bomb victims]. Newspapers, she explained, were burned to ashes, mixed with sesame oil, then applied to the burnt skin. "I heard that everyone exposed to that light will die. No matter what medicines are taken, nobody will be cured. It's scary," said the girl, twelve or thirteen years of age, to my mother from the shade of a tree in our yard. She was even frightened of the sun's rays.

Just as she said, those who had bathed in the flash of the A-bomb explosion died one after another. Those who fled without wounds began to die, blood oozing from their eyes and mouths. Within ten days after the bombing, most of those people were dead.

Takako and I were among those who managed to survive, but the A-bomb demonstrated its real, relentless power over our group. Having projected a fatal amount of radiation at that instant on August 9, it now waited for the deaths of those of us who had survived.

The general outline of the symptoms was nearly the same from person to person.

Green diarrhea and vomiting, a sense of lethargy all over the body, then eventually purple spots. Some lost their hair, others spit blood, and in the end they died in a derangement caused by high fever. In the intervals of this outline, other symptoms appeared, suiting individual physical constitutions. For example, skin eruptions all over the body. Inflammation of the oral mucosae, which spread like liverwort from tongue to gums. Not just a sense of lethargy, but a true loss of energy from the entire body with a prolonged period when one could not even chew.

If there was one person who took on all these symptoms, it was Takako. Though slender, she was not necessarily delicate, yet she succumbed to each symptom.

"I'm a superior guinea pig," she would say, as she spoke of a new symptom each time I saw her.

Around two weeks after the bombing, Takako began to lose her hair. She would grasp some hair, cross her heart with a prayer, "Please stay," then pull it to see.

The strands that she held in her hand would come off just like that.

She became bald almost instantly.

With no distinction between face and head, she looked unfocused. The area from the corners of her eyes to the back of her head looked like an extension of her face, and when she talked, only her lips looked oddly soft.

Takako covered her head tightly in a scarf so that no more hair would fall out. This was during an era in which there was a shortage of goods. No such luxury items like Western-style scarves were around after the war. As a substitute she used a *furoshiki* cloth wrapper, the last article her mother had refused to part with and kept in a corner of a chest of drawers.

It was made of high-quality silk, a bright vermilion color that burst in the light. No matter how high in quality, it was still a *furoshiki*, making Takako feel that she was wrapping her head in it rather than wearing it on her head.

When walking through Hamamachi, it was easy to spot her approaching. The contour of her head showed clearly, suggestive of a small watermelon wrapped in cloth and indicating that her hair had fallen out.

"I can tell you have no hair left," I whispered to her frankly.

"Oh yes, I still have some. See, take a close look," she said, taking off the *furoshiki*.

Heedless of being out in the streets, she extended her head before my eyes. "See? There's some, isn't there?" She waited for my answer with great seriousness.

In the sunlight, I noticed gray ciliation that resembled mildew on rice cakes. It wasn't something that could be called hair, but I answered, "Yes, there seems to be a little."

The same ciliation stuck to the reverse side of the *furoshiki* too, but I pretended not to notice.

Takako too looked indifferent.

"You'll lose yours soon too. It can't be that you're the only special case," she said as she pulled my braided hair.

It didn't come off. Looking at her fingertips pulling at my hair, she said, "It'll fall suddenly," repeating that it was impossible for only one person to be special.

Next, Takako began to bleed.

A heavy dose of radiation causes problems like kidney disorder and the delayed development of bones, but it strongly affects reproductive organs as well. The majority of male inmates who were bombed at the Hiroshima jail were found to be impotent.

With women, many cases of sterility were reported resulting from the death of reproductive cells. The percentage of miscarriage was also high.

The greatest disturbance, I heard, was seen among growing children. It was not rare that menstruation began suddenly after the bombing, or that bleeding did not stop.

The majority of people, however, stopped bleeding within a month. Takako was an exception. Right after the bombing, while fleeing near Peace Park, she passed water. Her urine was fresh blood.

It was not bloody urine, but bright-red blood.

Not one hour had passed since the bombing.

Looking at the blood soaking into the rubble, she first mistook it for menstruation. She was not shocked because she had menstruated previously, but this was not that; it was clearly discharged as urine.

One week later, menstruation began. One week passed, two weeks passed, and there was no sign of its stopping. The amount was also more than usual. The condition lasted for three months, never skipping one day.

She took to bed in diapers. Purple spots the size of red beans broke out all over her body. Her fever ran above 104 degrees. "She's going to die," the rumor gradually spread.

Around that time, a cure using the patient's own blood began to be talked about as the most effective method for blood troubles caused by A-bomb illness. This meant a hip injection of the patient's blood mixed with a certain medical liquid to avoid coagulation. Takako seemed to have received this treatment.

Among my friends was one whose menstruation lasted as long as six months. She had the same symptoms as Takako, and the bleeding never skipped a day in those months. An amateur, I cannot tell if one can call six months of bleeding menstruation. I simply call it by that name because it took the same form.

That friend, the only daughter of a doctor, also received blood transfusions.

According to her story, less than an ounce of blood that was of a completely *different* type than her own was injected during one session. This was repeated three times.

Even an amateur knows that the transfusion of a different blood type leads to the rejection of heterogeneous protein and death.

"You don't say," I said, incredulous.

"Well, listen then. My relatives are all doctors. But they thought this the only way, and used treatment that even amateurs laugh at."

After the transfusion, she ran a fever over 104 degrees and a violent quiver assaulted her entire body.

It seems to have been a form of shock therapy, a kill-or-cure venture, grabbing death as a weapon against death.

My hair did not fall out. But, as Takako said, the A-bomb provided no special exemptions.

One morning, I found a red spot on my wrist. It was just an ordinary spot. It held liquid at the tip, which, when I scratched it with a fingernail, burst open with a faint yet powerful sound. That powerful burst on my mind, I put my arm out from the blanket to check on it the following morning. Around the spot, new spots clustered like deutzia flowers.

I carefully crushed them with a fingernail.

Constitutionally, I was not prone to suppuration. Even if I scratched my skin with a fingernail, a reddish black scab would form by the following day and the wound quickly healed. I crushed those spots assuming the usual outcome, but they gradually suppurated, losing their shape.

This was a kind of rash from radiation, limited to areas of skin that were directly exposed to the air or covered under black clothing. In my case, it occurred only on my arms and legs. When one spot began to rot, the heat of the wound seemed to speed up the suppuration of other spots, which too turned rotting, viscous.

When I walked, bloody pus fell on the tatami. My mother wiped it clean with a rag if she found any, but my sisters kept pointing out more, saying, "Here too, look, some over there."

My mother boiled a well-worn indigo kimono bathrobe in a large pot, split it into two- or three-inch-wide strips, and, in place of bandages, dressed my shins in them. Kimono patterns showing here and there, I was a straggler no matter how I looked at myself. "White Tiger!" schoolgirls my age jeered in unison when I walked through town to commute en route to the hospital, referring to the boys' troop of Aizu province that was routed in the Boshin War.[1]

"Tell me which grade, which class you're in and who your homeroom teacher is," said my mother, who accompanied me, angry enough to report them to the teacher.

It felt better to expose the wounds than to protect them under bandages. The wounds pulled in the wind and hurt, but it was refreshing because the wind lifted the heat from my skin.

On days when the wounds held more heat than usual, I would spend the entire day without bandages under a room-size mosquito net in the well-ventilated living room. If I was inattentive, flies laid eggs on the wounds. Many green bottle flies flew around the mosquito net.

In that condition, I experienced my first menstruation.

I wondered if mine too, like Takako's, might refuse to stop. I had no idea whether its coming meant normal development or was an unexpected result of the A-bomb illness. Each time a clot of blood was discharged, I felt it in my as yet narrow pelvis, and each throbbing flow of blood took something away from my body. I felt insecure.

I crouched in a corner of the room, holding my lower torso in both arms. Unfortunately, both my older sisters, who might have shown me what to do, were out. My mother had gone to nurse *hibakusha* housed in a nearby elementary school.

I traced my memory of a lecture we received soon after entering the girls' school during a child-care class.

The female teacher, dressed in a traditional blue serge divided skirt, explained menstruation to us while pointing at an anatomical chart with a bamboo stick. I had learned the lesson by heart because the topic was to be covered in the trimester-end test, but nothing was of help in an emergency. Listen, she said, menstruation is there to tell you that you are physically ready to have a baby. This portion of the lecture had made me feel cheerful.

If things were as she said, the beginning of my menstruation was a healthy sign. I had no reason to feel insecure. From that moment, my A-bomb disease may have taken a course for recovery.

I waited for my mother's return. She would be pleased to hear the news.

She had a simpleminded side and always knew how to interpret things to her advantage.

Would my daughter die today, or tomorrow? This was the question on her mind as my mother spent her days measuring my life span. She would take her daughter's menstruation as proof of her health. Even happier than at the time of the first menstruation of my sisters, who had grown up uneventfully, she would certainly steam rice with red beans, a celebratory dish that had become customary at home. Because we're celebrating, she would say, taking out the precious store of black-market rice from the closet.

We must get some Queen Rose, she would say in the affected standard dialect she had used when we lived in Shanghai, and rush to the drugstore herself.

Queen Rose was the brand name for sanitary napkins. When I was in elementary school, I often ran through the streets of Shanghai to a drugstore to buy Queen Rose for my sisters and mother.

Come here for a second, my mother would beckon me to a corner of the room and whisper in my ear: go get some Queen Rose. Unlike usual, her voice then carried a womanlike tenderness.

Sensing from the private tone of her words a woman's secret, I ran with short breath at those times, if never on other errands, along the streets of Shanghai.

Queen Rose came in a crimson cardboard box decorated with the image of a white rose on the chest of a princess. I never saw the content.

Let me see it, I would say with a conscious gesture of sweetness as I handed over the box. "Mother, how indecent can she be," said my sisters, glaring at me, their glares full of delight.

"It's too soon yet," my mother would say in a high-pitched voice as she joined their merriment. "I'll buy you some to celebrate when the time comes," she added.

Before that time came, I scented out what the content might be from how my sisters appeared.

When I could no longer contain myself I would open the talcum-powder-scented crimson box alone in a room—I felt as if that would be enough to make me a beautiful adult.

The day of celebration that my mother had promised came when my skin had begun to rot with A-bomb illness.

Made of rubber gently touching rubber, like *yuba*,[2] Queen Rose held two meanings for me: a sign of passage to beautiful adulthood and, more than anything else, a healthy body capable of giving birth.

I'm not Takako, I told myself.

I pulled out a cottony blanket from the closet.

In those days, rationed blankets were woven mostly of cotton with waste yarn mixed in here and there. When pulled with a little force, the coarse texture was uneven. When it rained, it sucked moisture and became difficult to handle.

I sat in the corner of the room, firmly wrapping my lower torso in the heavily moist blanket so that blood would not flow down from my thin summer clothes.

When she returned in the late afternoon from nursing, my mother found me wrapped, in midsummer, in the blanket.

"Do you have the shivers?" she asked in Nagasaki dialect as she brought her lips to my forehead.

She always felt my temperature with her lips. No, I said, confused, pushing her chest away from me. Menstrual blood develops a strong smell when it sits. Each time I smelled it, I felt as if I were becoming stained. I felt awful, this being my first experience. A sudden shyness assaulted me. I didn't want anyone to know.

But my mother was too sensitive to miss what was happening.

"It can't be," she said as she looked at my body, and asked directly, "Your period, isn't it?"

"No!"

I lied on reflex. The expression my teacher used in class, though equally a physiognomic term, had a wise ring that celebrated women's health that my mother's lacked. It washed away in a twinkle the scent of talcum power that I had cherished carefully until that day.

"Buy me Queen Rose, please?" I asked my mother. She bluntly replied that there was no such thing nowadays. "At such a time, of all times," she added, knitting her eyebrows.

She couldn't determine whether her daughter's menstruation meant normal growth or was owing to bleeding caused by the A-bomb disease. And because she couldn't, she was in a bad mood. On the brink of life or death, her daughter may have begun preparing for womanhood. It seemed that, as a woman, my mother had an aversion to the body moving ahead with the instinct to birth in the absence of all else.

I missed my "genderless" girlhood. I remained seated on the tatami floor of the room, now dark, thinking I would much rather that all the blood flowed out of my body as with Takako.

"Hey," the bartender called.

When Takako looked over, he said, "There's a guy who's interested in making some money."

"Is he young? How's his build?"

"Perfectly okay," he said, rounding his fingers behind the counter.

"I'll think about it before I leave, so hold on for a bit," Takako stopped him as he put his finger on the phone dial.

"What's okay?" I asked Takako.

"What?" Takako asked back, then answered without hesitation, "Oh, just a male."

"A male? A human male?" I asked stupidly, recalling the rumor I had heard from K. the day before.

K. had eagerly told me, eyebrows knit, that Takako regularly bought young, healthy men for their bodies. Impossible, I laughed at the rumor, which seemed much too wild. Was K.'s story true?

As I remained unable to discern Takako's intentions, she looked at me and grinned broadly.

"She's liberal with her money," the bartender jested, shrugging his shoulders.

Takako married in 1957, at the age of twenty-eight. I hear it was an arranged marriage. Arranged marriages were rare among *hibakusha*. No one would choose to marry a woman with a bad background. At the same time, we ourselves did not much feel like waging our lives on marriage. Rather than considering marriage as something that would last throughout our lives, we rather tended to view each day as the beginning and end of married life. This was the way to live without disappointment for those of us who never knew when our illness might relapse.

Takako did not seem to have any particular hopes for marriage either.

Her partner, from Kansai, was a part-time college instructor. He was five years older and of course was not a *hibakusha*.

At their meeting held with marriage in mind, Takako took the initiative to announce that she was a *hibakusha* and related all the symptoms she had then.

At each previous such meeting, her parents had tried to suppress the history of her exposure to radiation so as to smoothly bring about the marriage. Because the arrangement had fallen through a number of times because of an agency's investigation that revealed her past, her parents had tried even harder on this occasion.

The man who later became her husband heard her story through and said, "It doesn't matter at all, to me at least. The war damaged more or less all of us who lived through it. You and I are fifty-fifty in this sense."

Her husband-to-be seemed to interpret her story as a reflection of her victim mentality, covetous of sympathy.

Her parents thought him broad-minded and concluded the proposal, perhaps too rashly, with an offer of a small, sunny mountain wooded with Japanese silverleaf and of one of the old houses they owned.

The man who became her husband was engaged in painstaking academic research that involved digging ancient earthenware up from the ground. He put lost time back into shape, which was like fitting puzzle pieces into empty space. Perhaps because of the nature of his work, he was not too particular about daily life.

Takako continued to run a slight fever of ninety-nine to one hundred degrees. With a husband well suited for a woman of delicate health, who left her alone as he thought fit, her marital relationship was ideal. She neither loved nor was loved.

In their second year of marriage, Takako's A-bomb illness recurred in the form of breast cancer.

It was a sultry, warm day during the rainy season, when the sun broke out. She suddenly felt like washing her hair and took a bath.

Partly because of having lost her hair after the bombing, Takako was obsessed with it. Her hair was long because all she did was trim it, hardly ever using scissors for a real haircut.

Combing her freshly washed hair with a boxwood comb required a fair amount of strength from her fully extended arm.

As she combed with her left arm, she felt some tension in the muscles in her chest. She changed the movements of her arm, but the tension was still there. On probing the breast with her fingertip, she came upon a stiff mass the size of a rice grain.

Each time she took a bath, she examined herself with her finger. There was no pain, but the stiff spot was always there in the same place. She suspected cancer.

She was only thirty. Pouring warm water over herself in the bath, she saw drops of water trickle down her skin. Her skin was lustrous, even ruddier with life than when she had been a girl.

Takako trusted her youth just as any other woman would. Afflicted by the A-bomb aftereffects as she was, she still believed in her physical youth.

The stiff spot fattened. By now she could feel an unevenness under her fingertips when pressing it. A pale pink hue developed on the surface of the skin. It was just a growth after all, Takako thought with relief.

The absence of pain worried her, but she knew cancer would play no such tricks as drawing attention to itself by adding color on a swelling. Suppose it were cancer. Given the fact that a fair number of days had passed since the rainy season, Takako would already have been dead.

Still, the absence of pain was ominous. When she thought about it, she realized the color was much paler than that of other growths. It didn't come to a head with pus, as would an ordinary growth. Somehow, just the left nipple looked dark and felt strained. Feeling uneasy, after a bath Takako showed her skin to her husband: "Take a look, it can't be cancer, can it?"

Her husband took a quick look at her skin, fresh from bathing, as if stealing a glance at that of a stranger's.

"The possibility could exist," he said simply in his usual polite, standard dialect.

"When breast cancer is found too late, it's because of the husband's negligence, I hear. I suppose we can't help it if our relationship is suspect," she said half in jest, trying to arouse his interest.

"Please don't joke about it," her husband said, seated upright without a smile. "One should manage one's own health. Even between husband and wife, it's each person's responsibility. Not only that, in the first place I never wish to see a wound on another living person," he said.

The cancer continued to grow unhindered inside Takako's tender chest.

Cancer that has nested in a young body grows surprisingly fast.

Takako had been wrong to have trusted her young body.

Partly because of the warm weather, which reached a temperature of ninety degrees that day, she felt sluggish and stayed in bed all day, then rose to prepare dinner.

Putting her hands on the kitchen counter, she looked up to turn on the electric switch, when she felt the back of her head grow weightless and her knees buckle. About to fall backward, she unconsciously bent forward to support herself on the counter.

At that moment, she banged her chest. It was a nasty knock, right against the corner of the counter, on the growth of her left breast.

She heard the sound of bursting flesh, then came the raw, warm smell of ripe fruit.

Takako pressed her breast with both hands. Under the swaying light, bloody pus slipped through her fingers. It had been this rotten, she thought as she measured the amount of blood in both hands, and momentarily regretted having left it alone for so many days.

Be that as it may, she also told herself that it wasn't much compared to the amount of her earlier bleeding, which had continued for three months.

She heard the voices of her husband and neighborhood women, the siren of an ambulance went off, and Takako was taken to the hospital. She was carried directly to the operating room, right on the stretcher, and the affected breast removed.

When she was still half asleep after the operation, her husband informed her, "They say it is cancer. I thought you would want to know."

Takako was not so frightened. It can't be helped, she thought. Besides, she knew how the A-bomb behaved. It attacked unyieldingly in waves over months and years. Without exception it took what it intended to take.

Where next? she wondered, looking at the white bandages tied around her entire chest.

She could no longer raise her left arm. Nor could she reach her back. Her freedom of movement was restricted, as if her arms and torso were sewn together.

I'm going to lose my freedom step-by-step over the years, Takako realized.

As he read, her husband spied on her awkward movements. He did not say to her, "You must feel inconvenienced." He merely peered at her steadily.

"I can't move, please help me"—she wished to say this, honestly disclosing her difficulty, for that would have helped heal her feelings when she was easily depressed. But when she tried to talk to him, he quickly shifted his eyes back to his book.

"When things are hard, I make it a rule to recall the day of the bombing," she told me. "If I think of that, I can put up with anything."

"Yes," I agreed. "But how lonesome that is."

Takako just nodded, then said, "Look, it's gone."

Abruptly stretching her right hand across the table, she grabbed my wrist.

"See? You can tell it's gone," she said as she pressed my fingertips to her left breast.

"It's there, of co-o-ourse," I jested, not knowing what to do, in a tone of girlhood exchanges. Takako laughed aloud.

"You often lie to me," she said. "When I lost my hair too, you lied and said, 'It's there.' Look, feel it carefully. It's just sponge."

Pressing my fingers now to her right breast, she made me recognize the difference.

I pulled my hand back unsympathetically. "It's okay if it isn't there," I said almost angrily.

She shook her head and said, "It's not okay."

How can men take breastless women seriously? This was what K. had said to me yesterday, jiggling with pride her breasts, which she said fit only an American B-cup brassiere.

The reason that Takako bought men with money, K. explained, was because she had to compensate for the breast that had been surgically removed. Here was a woman paying a man to hold her, K. said humorously.

"But why does she buy men?" I insisted on knowing.

"How do I know? She was fond of men," K. replied nonchalantly as she left, "from long ago." It was hard for me to think that this was the only reason Takako bought men.

"May I have some ice?" Takako asked the bartender and pushed her bottle toward me, saying, "You can drink too, can't you?"

I poured a few drops into my coffee.

Recalling the fresh-baked French bread I had bought at Hamamachi, I asked the bartender if he could fix ham and eggs. An item not on the menu came with an extra charge, he pointed out and asked if it was okay.

"Put it on the house," Takako said in a loud voice. There were no other customers in the store. Straining my ears, I heard the festival drums of Suwa Shrine mixed in with the noise of the town.

"Are you going to display that doll?" I asked, pointing at the paper bag at the edge of the table.

"I have more than twenty, but I don't mean to display them. I store all of them wrapped in paper in a wooden box."

"Why do you buy them if you don't display them?"

"I want them to be cremated with me when I die. They are my burial figurines," she said, picking up the paper bag between her fingers.

The bartender brought over ham and eggs, skillfully fried to half done, along with thick-sliced cheese.

Takako picked up a slice and bit into it with her front teeth and, leaving an arch-shaped impression, put it back on the glass plate.

Breaking off a piece of the French bread, I handed it to Takako. She gazed at the piece, still warm, for a while.

"Thanks," she said in a small voice. "I wonder how many years it's been since I felt this relaxed. It seems I have struggled and struggled, squaring my shoulders. I feel like sleeping restfully in the arms of someone who knows every bit of me, doesn't ask for any compensation, and holds me without saying anything."

Takako knew that spot bleeding of unknown causes was associated with breast cancer. Sooner or later, something would find its vent in that little wound and burst out. That something, she knew, was already in progress.

"I haven't even told my mother. There's stiffness in my right chest too. Look, it's here," she said without expression, placing my finger on the stiffness and rotating it around the spot.

"This is definitely cancer," she said. "But I'm not going to die so readily."

In August, one year after her operation, Takako became pregnant.

"What?" I asked back when I heard of it. The effects of the postoperative X-ray treatment on the fetus was a matter of concern, but perhaps it was all right because we *hibakusha* have more than enough immunity against radiation.

What was more unexpected was that her husband, who had coldly announced that he did not wish to see wounded bodies, was willing to hold his wife. I had automatically assumed that they were physically distant.

Takako was ecstatic about her pregnancy. Because of her girlhood bleeding lasting three months, she had thought herself infertile. She rejoiced at her lean body now growing rich with fragrance.

She told her husband the doctor's diagnosis in detail.

As usual, he listened while reading, then asked, his eyes rounded, "Can you be with child?" He added, "More important, I am surprised that you intend to give birth. In the first place, you are a *hibakusha*. Second, you are the one who explained to me how radiation would affect the genes."

She didn't have to be told. She knew that. Knowingly, she rejoiced in her pregnancy. Amid all those grim symptoms, the smallest sign of health was a delight she could not resist.

"There is a possibility," she spoke formally, switching to standard dialect, "that the baby may be deformed. Therefore you say it is not right that I give birth, is that so?"

"It's not a sentimental matter of good or bad. You showed me a photo of a microcephalic child exposed to radiation. I simply saw it as one example of what can happen, but I cannot accept the same for my child. Not just my own child's, but any deformity that can be prevented should be rationally checked ahead of time. Wouldn't you say it's our responsibility to leave superior people for future generations?"

"A married couple," Takako noted, "is a strange thing. Even if you don't love the man that much, if you start a life together, you feel like building something together. Give birth to his male child, foster, and build. Build, or reach a certain point of building and let it fall apart again. I don't know exactly what, but anyway, you feel like having something in common to foster. Marriage and home are something like that, aren't they?"

Takako sipped a little whiskey.

"Is there a single microcephalic or otherwise deformed child among your classmates or mine? I haven't heard of any," she said.

I hadn't heard of any such examples either. Rumor would spread right away if a child was born microcephalic or had any trouble with the functioning of limbs and body.

It may be that a child with physical deficiencies, even if born, dies soon afterward because of its natural fragility. The rate of death within the womb must also be high. Disgraceful stories such as these would be buried from darkness to darkness. However, rumors of concealment tend to spread.

Judging from the fact that not one story existed, it would seem that none among us had given birth to a disabled child that would breed rumor.

Takako's husband one-sidedly enumerated her shortcomings, but there must have been some risk on his side too of causing deformity. Statistically speaking, such a risk exists at the rate of one in fifty healthy couples. One could not say it was Takako's responsibility alone if by one in a thousand chances a disabled child was born.

She restrained her desire to protest. The disadvantage, after all, was larger on her side.

"I would like to have the child," she told him.

"Can't you please think about the arrival of a healthy child rather than worrying about a deformed birth?" Takako asked her husband.

"I don't think I'd like that," he declined plainly. "You can't give birth by way of experiment. You are talking about a life."

Takako acquiesced to his words. The fetus was in its fifth month.

This is almost like a premature birth, said the doctor, who feared for the mother's health and encouraged her to carry the baby to full term.

"Because I'm a *hibakusha*, I worry about deformity. I was under treatment for A-bomb disease till recently," she explained and added that this was her husband's wish as well.

After the operation, the doctor said to Takako, "Let me tell you this for future reference. It was a healthy baby boy, a little larger than average, with perfect fingers and toes." He added encouragingly, "Next time, give birth with peace of mind instead of worrying about unnecessary things."

"I killed a healthy baby," she told her husband after reporting every word the doctor had said.

"So you want to judge me," he said. "Then why didn't you disregard my opposition and have the baby? You were worried too. You feared the misfortune of one in ten thousand cases, just as I did. Neither of us had the courage to accept a mentally or physically disabled baby as our child."

"It's not the life of the baby that was an issue for you," he continued. "You wished simply to live freely without problems. All you wanted was a 'perfect' child as a component of the family, a component necessary to a healthy family life like a television set, an air conditioner, or a car. *You* have no right to criticize me; we are equally to blame."

"Before I realized it," he added, "I was as involved as you in your A-bomb 'disease' and found myself looking at our unborn child with the mentality of a victim. I was made to see clearly the fragility of reason. I feel miserable. I have had enough of former soldiers begging on the train, and I have had enough of your A-bomb 'disease.' " With this he left the room.

Takako recalled his words from their first meeting: all Japanese were scarred by the war. Whenever he wished, she felt, he could promptly distance himself from the scars of war. Her parents too had found her a husband and gotten away. Takako was always left just as she was. She was left in the midst of raw wounds that had lasted since August 9.

Takako and her husband divorced. Their marriage had lasted four years.

After the abortion her right breast swelled up, blue veins rising to the surface. When she squeezed the breast, it released yellow milk.

She felt a pain even on the left side of her chest that had no breast. As her husband said, it was not a matter one could gloss over. For their aborted child, there was a tingling even in the taut-skinned part of her chest. Wishing to make what little atonement was possible, she began volunteer work with handicapped children.

"Your husband's great," Takako commented. "I'm impressed that he let you have your baby. Didn't he say anything?" she asked, pouring her third glass of whiskey amply to four fifths full.

"Is it okay to take that much?" I asked, concerned.

"Though it's a banal thing to say, this disinfects the rotten body," she joked, drinking half the glass in a single gulp.

Her words make me think that my husband may indeed be great. He approves of most of what I say and do.

His assent may come from disinterest, however. In a way, he seems to calculate the inconvenience of placing restrictions on his own neck by putting fetters around his wife's.

He showed no interest in his unborn child. He had no unnecessary worries about his wife being a *hibakusha*. Nor did he ask me to go through with the pregnancy.

I seem to be with child, I informed him. "Are you," he groaned, eyes on my flat abdomen.

I told him of my insecurities. "I wonder if the baby will be strange."

"No telling," he said. He took another look at my abdomen and said, "I feel strongly that the fellow inside you belongs to you. No, it's my child, and I'm not arguing about that. Frankly speaking, I feel like you should discuss it with the fellow inside you."

In other words, he was telling me to ask if the fellow inside me wished to be born. Oh, I see, I thought, comprehending my husband's mind.

In short, he left it entirely up to me to keep the baby or have an abortion. Because I thought it our child, I had wanted to know his intentions as its father.

I decided to keep the baby. I cared for the little life that was doing its utmost to be born, regardless of its parents' speculations. In order to give birth to as healthy a child as I could, I began putting things around me in order. Fearing prenatal influence, I put together the A-bomb-related photos on my desk and placed them in a large envelope.

I closed it with adhesive tape and wrote "sealed" with a red magic marker I had bought for this act of sealing, which I viewed as a matter of celebration.

I would not unseal this envelope until the baby's birth. If there were such a thing as prenatal influence, I would seal my past along with these photos and raise my child in an unstained womb.

I placed the sealed envelope on my desk and said to myself: this does it. I remained gazing at the yellow envelope for a while.

Among the photos I put in the envelope was one of a little girl in a padded air raid hood, eyes and nose indistinguishable because of burns. Whatever might have happened to her mother, the girl sat all alone amid the rubble. Her face was expressionless.

I put the photo of a mother's charred body into the envelope too. A baby was by her side, charred uniformly black just like its mother, round eyes open and hands firmly together—I found myself going over in my mind every one of the photos I had put in the envelope.

The photos came back to me all the more vividly now that they were sealed in. Not only that, the tragic scenes in them were the very scenes I had directly witnessed a number of years ago. Memory and photos mingling, I had an illusion that the children sealed inside were scratching the envelope, making dry sounds.

I pushed the envelope into the space under a chest of drawers. I trapped it firmly under the chest so that a charred baby could not break free and crawl into my womb.

Labor began at midnight on a cold March day. I woke my husband at midnight. "Perhaps you can wait till morning," he said.

Wait? Wait for what? Did he mean put up with the pain till morning, or hold the birth till morning? Was delivery that easy to maneuver? Was he by some chance confusing delivery and excretion?

He seemed to forget that the fetus came to life with a will of its own.

The labor pains grew intense and occurred at shorter intervals.

Please take me to the hospital, I asked.

He rose and sat on the bed. He lit a cigarette and took a savory puff, but immediately crushed it out, looking displeased.

"I have to go to work tomorrow." Then he added, "On the whole, you lack planning. Didn't you even make sure which day and time to expect delivery? If this is pain that meets the expectations, I will of course take you to the hospital. But if you are simply complaining about pain, all I'll do is catch cold to no gain. It's bad for your health too." That said, he pulled the comforter over his head and went to sleep.

The clock showed it was past midnight.

I began to make preparations myself. I wrapped bleached cotton diapers that I had sewn and two soft gauze undershirts in a *furoshiki*. I also put in a pair of booties I had knit with the finest yarn, right and left different in size by one-quarter inch.

Would these uneven booties fit its little feet? Wouldn't the baby dislike these unshapely things that looked like small rice-bran bags used for rubbing the body? I felt somewhat cheered, imagining the sight of the baby not wanting them and wrinkling its red face.

I walked along the midnight road by myself. When the pain came, I crouched by the side of the road and waited till it eased off. Though it was the season when the cherries would soon bloom, frost was on the road.

At 6:20 in the morning, I gave birth to a boy.

"Congratulations! He's on the small side, but plump. He's nourished enough to have creases in his thighs," the doctor said, raising the baby, which was still covered with lardlike mucus, high in the morning sun.

I asked to see the baby's face. It was red faced with black, lustrous hair. Eyes firmly closed, it seemed to be resisting the first sunlight with its entire body.

I was relieved. My child was not expressionless like the children I had sealed away in the envelope.

Past seven o'clock in the morning, my husband came to visit me at the hospital after breakfast. He forced open the fingers of the child's tight fists and counted them one, two with his own thick fingers. He even pulled its feet, drawn into the baby robe, and counted the toes. When he finished checking to see if all the fingers were there, he looked at me with a smile.

"I wonder if he looks like me," he said, bringing his face to the child's cheek. Then he lay stretched out. "I think I'll skip work today!" he said happily. Soon he was asleep, snoring loudly.

I resented his counting the child's fingers. Every parent would naturally check them, yet it bothered me.

If the baby had had defects caused by the bomb, my husband would never have asked if it looked like him. As the fellow within you belonged to you, so it still belongs to you after birth—this might have been his thought.

I knew of a boy who was microcephalic because of the A-bomb disease. His IQ was low and he was mentally retarded. The mother, who was pregnant at the time of the bombing, lived near Peace Park, where Takako is now consecrated. It was an area where nearly everyone met instant death. At the moment of the bombing, the mother was in a shelter, rearranging clothes and emergency food.

All the other members of her family who were inside the house died instantly.

The boy had an extreme language disability and managed just barely to utter sounds. His arms and legs were round like wooden pestles. Fingerlike joints were attached here and there but had no function as fingers. From early childhood he had ill-defined convulsions of the entire body. They were ill defined simply because they could not be explained medically; in fact, they were caused by exposure to radiation while inside his mother's womb.

When he grew to twelve or thirteen, he developed sexual desires. Not knowing how to control himself, he threw himself on his mother as led by his instincts. The mother tied his waist with a rope and leashed him to a pillar in the living room. He howled like a dog, trying to break the rope with his teeth. Upon consultation with the doctor, the mother had the boy's testicles removed.

He became a "good" boy with dulled responses, a quiet boy who would do no harm to healthy people.

In the spring of his fifteenth year, he was overcome by intense convulsions and died after quivering all day long. The only humanlike response the boy had ever demonstrated was his unrestrained sexual desire before the operation.

"Would you have had him operated on if he had been yours?"

"No," Takako replied instantly. After gazing awhile at the amber-colored liquid in her whiskey glass, she continued:

"I wouldn't have had him operated on. We would try leading a life, however bloody, parent and child together. Now I think that way. I think often about the day of the bombing. I was really happy I survived. I wished to survive even if I lost an arm."

After the abortion, when she heard that the child was without any physical defect, she regretted the little life she had given up. For the first time then, she realized clearly what she had wanted. She had wanted a human baby whole of limb and meeting ordinary standards, and she didn't need her husband to tell her that.

"Just suppose the aborted baby had had defects. I would probably have felt relieved thinking I had done the right thing. I wouldn't have regretted its life," Takako said.

She told me about mentally and physically disabled children. Twenty-two or twenty-three children are housed at the place where she works. They include second-generation *hibakusha* and those who aren't. There was one who was Mongoloid. Five or six years old, the child could not even eat properly. Nor did the child have the desire to eat. Takako was drawn to the child sitting in the sun in the hallway.

Each time she visited the place, she found the child sitting in the same spot, vacant.

Takako bought a little bouncing ball decorated with red thread. Seated face-to-face with him, she threw it at him to see if he would respond. His eyes remained directed toward her face as vacantly as before.

She went to fetch the ball, which had rolled away, and threw it at the child. Repeatedly, she threw and fetched the ball.

She threw it at different places on his body, at his hands or directly at his chest, trying to make him catch it somehow. One day, after a few days of having made this effort, the child smiled when she threw the ball.

The child had been taking note in a corner of his heart. While observing Takako over the days, he had been taking in something.

"Fine for healthy children and handicapped children to be as they are," she said. "The mixture is what humans are." If the value of life were forgotten, August 9 would be meaningless to her.

Suddenly, she burst out laughing, looking really happy. "I'll tell you about my only rebellion," she said as she brought her face closer to me.

She kept a stray cat. She fed it only nutritious dairy products. The cat grew robust and fat. To bring it up as an agile wild cat, she hit its tail if it sprawled in the sun. The cat learned to be as sensitive as a dog to footsteps. It ran before Takako approached.

As Takako wished, the cat grew like a puma. It had nasty eyes. If human, it would have been the type to be tailed right away by the police.

Whether cheese or ham, Takako threw the food at it. It jumped agilely to catch it in its mouth. It had black, shiny hair. Moreover, it was a male. It roamed freely, impregnating female cats in the neighborhood.

A woman from the Society for the Prevention of Cruelty to Animals came to ask that the cat be sterilized. Takako paid no attention.

"Cats live as cats should," she laughed delightfully.

"What do you say? Shall I make the phone call?" The bartender asked.

"Yeah, try calling."

She winked at me as she poured another whiskey, already having consumed several glasses.

"Call—a man?" Aware of the bartender's presence, I whispered my question into Takako's ear.

"A man to buy with money. He's strongly built, that's all," she said without self-consciousness.

"What do you buy him for? Do you want a man?"

"Want . . . maybe it's a little different. I wish to hold young men, imbibe some of their energy, and make sure of my own life. I want a solid sense of being alive. There's nothing else in my hands."

"You'll get pregnant. Are you going to have another abortion?"

"I'll have the child. No, it's not sacrilegious; I'll have the child of my own free will. Fine if it's deformed. I'll let it live in my stead."

There are plenty of men, I commented with common sense. It's not recommended to buy a man with money. Takako laughed.

"You only stand on your feet and look upward, so you talk like that. Crawl like me and set a red eye on the ground. You can very well see human essence or whatever it's called," she said, slapping her left breast. "Who would take me seriously? As you know, rumor flew after the bombing that I was dying. But I was thinking there would still be something in store for my future, it would be a waste if I died just like that. Now, though, there's nothing left. Unless I test myself against another person's strength, I don't even have a real sense of being alive; still, I want to remain alive."

It's one year since Takako died. After our last meeting, her right breast was removed. The wound left after the operation rotted, even the area sewn with thread.

Her whole body, I heard, was nested by cancer. Infused with the body fluids of young men, the cancer cells might have affected Takako all the more energetically.

In the letter she sent me right before her death she wrote, "I'm already exhausted." Cancer made the gesture of slowing down for a year or two following an operation. Each time that happened, Takako saw some hope. And she was betrayed.

It's too painful, she wrote.

Her symptoms indicate the course I must trace. She has carefully guided me along the way *hibakusha* must follow. Takako has already lived enough. Her vitality still surprises me.

What I dread most is not being able to die easily.

I feel relieved that Takako died. Even in the worst of situations, I can trace that passage.

I burned Takako's final letter in the yard. Going out to the yard after the rain, I collected moistened fallen leaves and placed the letter on the heap.

I took from the glass case the clay doll I had bought with Takako at Hamamachi, and put it on the letter. I emptied the entire contents of an economy-size matchbox around the body of the doll.

I set fire to them. The red heads of the matchsticks flared all at once.

The clay doll burned, mouth wide open.

I picked up a small rock from the ground and crushed to pieces the corpse of the clay doll, charred black. "Takako's burial figurine," I muttered as I scattered the pieces on the dirt.

Nearly twenty clay dolls remain in my glass case. These are my burial figurines. The wailing clay dolls are called "masks of whatchamacallit."

Notes

1. The Boshin War refers to a series of battles leading to the overthrow of the Tokugawa shogunate and the restoration of direct rule by the emperor. It began in the first month of 1868, or the year of *boshin* in the sexagenary cycle, and ended in the sixth month of 1869. Byakkotai, or the White Tiger Brigade, was a corps of a few hundred youths, organized in the third month of 1868 by the pro-Tokugawa Aizu province (now part of Fukushima prefecture) to resist the forces of restoration. It was decimated by an imperial army. Twenty survivors made their way back to Wakamatsu Castle, the Aizu stronghold, but committed suicide on a nearby mountain. The group became a popular symbol of loyalty, determination, and courage.

2. The thin film that forms on bean curd in the tofu-making process.

7

Water's Edge

Tsushima Yūko

Water was trickling on the other side of my bedroom wall in our fourth-floor apartment. In my sleep it sounded soft and distant. I dreamed that our building, wet from rain, shone with all the colors of the streetlamps and neon signs. When in the night had the rain begun? I had a feeling that it had started before I went to bed, but then, on waking up, I wondered if I had just imagined it: in the morning when I threw open the windows, I was greeted by brilliant sunshine and the noise of the traffic below. The sky was bright blue and the streets, even the parts still in shadow, were completely dry.

Pleased that it was another fine day, I went to wake my daughter, who was still sound asleep. I didn't wonder what had happened to the rain that had fallen in the night, nor did I find it strange that there weren't any puddles. But the sensation of falling water stayed with me. I felt as if it were still raining somewhere out of my reach, like an itchy spot between the shoulder blades. I was sure it wasn't just a dream.

Had the people downstairs not complained, no doubt I would have heard the same soft pattering again the next night, and not given it a second thought.

Just as I took a bite of my toast, I heard a knock at the door. I opened it cautiously, wondering who it could be so early in the morning. The vaguely familiar face of a fat middle-aged man appeared before me, but I couldn't remember where I'd seen him before. I was disappointed that it wasn't Fujino; I hadn't seen him for over a month.

"Mizube," from Tsushima Yūko, *Hikari no ryōbun* (The Territory of Light) (Tokyo: Kōdansha, 1979). Copyright 1979 by Tsushima Yūko. Translated by Gillian Kinjo and Susan Bouterey. English translation rights arranged with the author through Sakai Chosakuken Jimusho. This translation first appeared in *Review of Japanese Culture and Society*, VI, Josai University, December 1994. Translation copyright 1994 by Josai University.

"Where's all the water coming from?" the man asked, looking around my apartment crossly. My daughter stood in front of him and stared curiously, with upturned face, first at me and then at the man.

"The water! You must have spilled something or left a tap running. Do something about it, will you. We're in a terrible mess downstairs."

It finally dawned on me that he was the man from the office on the third floor. Hurriedly greeting him, I said, "What do you mean? I don't know what you're talking about."

"Listen, water's pouring into my office. It must be coming from your apartment. If you aren't aware of it, you'd better hurry up and find out what's wrong."

He owned the company that made gold crests. They probably weren't actually made in the small office downstairs, but cardboard boxes were always piled up at the open door, packed and ready for dispatch. I often saw him carrying out cartons and checking their contents against a list. Either it was a very demanding job or he simply enjoyed working, for he arrived at the office around eight every morning and frequently stayed there until closing on midnight. I found this rather annoying, since it was my job to open and close the shutter at the main entrance to the building. He must have found it inconvenient too, for on mornings when I slept in he was kept waiting outside, and on nights when he worked late he had to call out to tell me he was leaving. Two months after he moved in, the owner of the building agreed to give him a key, which made things a lot easier for us both.

His wife, who was the only other worker in the office, was usually there with him until late at night, though I hardly ever saw her. While he was fussing over the cardboard boxes outside, she would be bent over the desk inside, hard at work. She always wore an apron, which made her look as if she had just stepped out of the kitchen.

The man insisted that the leak came from somewhere on the fourth floor, so although it was time for me to go to work, I checked the kitchen sink, the washing machine, the toilet, the bathroom upstairs, and anywhere else where water might possibly be leaking. I even checked the small living room. Just as I thought, there was no sign of a leak.

"The water doesn't seem to be coming from here, does it?" I said to the man, then promptly scolded my daughter, who, in all the excitement, had forgotten about her breakfast and was running around the apartment.

"We'll be leaving in a minute, so hurry up and drink your milk. The teacher will tell you off again."

"Don't give me that! Look, what's this puddle? Come out and see for yourself."

Scowling, he took two steps down the stairs, leaving me with no choice but to follow him, still in my slippers. No sooner had I stepped out than he slammed the door and pointed to the floor. Sure enough, a small puddle had formed there. I looked up at the ceiling. There appeared to be a stain in the corner, but there was a similar stain on the ceiling in my apartment; the real estate agent had told me that before it had been repaired, the roof used to leak quite badly.

"That's funny. I wonder where all this water came from?"

The minute I began to speak, my daughter started to cry on the other side of the door. I immediately went to open it but the man grabbed my arm. "The water is definitely leaking from this floor," he said. "We opened the door to the office this morning only to find our papers and everything soaking wet. Right at this very minute my wife is trying to clean up the mess. Come down and you'll see what I mean."

My daughter's crying had grown louder. Ignoring the man, I took a step down the stairs to wrench open the door. Left with no room to stand on the narrow landing, he hastily followed me.

"There's obviously no water leaking in my apartment," I said as I picked up my daughter, who was hot and flushed from crying. "It must be coming from elsewhere. I have to go to work now. If you still haven't sorted things out by this evening, come back at six. I'll be home by then."

Without waiting for his reply, I banged the door shut. The man went back downstairs. By now it was time for me to leave. With a damp face cloth I wiped the red, tear-stained face of my daughter, who was clinging to me, and rushed out forgetting about breakfast. Afraid that the man might try to stop me, I crept down the stairs. Through the open door to his office I could hear him rudely abusing his wife, no doubt to appease his own anger.

I paid no attention to the water trickling down to the third floor; I was angry, not so much because of the water but because my morning had been disrupted. My daughter hadn't had her breakfast, and when we arrived at the nursery school, although most days she would cheerfully wave good-bye to me, that morning she let out a wail and clung to me, shaking, as if she would be eaten alive if she went anywhere near the teachers. In the end, she had to be forcibly taken inside by the two teachers. Then, after all that, I was late for work. I was annoyed with the man; it was selfish of him to come to my home and make such a fuss, whatever the reason. I had forgotten all about the gentle sound of water I had heard in the night.

I usually had lunch at work with my boss, Mr. Kobayashi. That day, we were just starting on our bread rolls and milk when my husband, Fujino, rang. Mr. Kobayashi answered the phone.

"It's your husband," he said and casually handed over the receiver.

"Thanks," I mumbled and put the phone to my ear. At the sound of Fujino's familiar voice, I felt a tug of nostalgia that immediately turned to intense anger. I had decided that if Fujino rang, I would try to remain calm and composed while we discussed our situation so as not to worsen our relationship—we had our daughter to consider, after all. I had even thought that I would like to try to find the words to explain why I too had come to want a separation, although I didn't really understand my own change of heart. But I couldn't even speak in my normal voice, so conscious was I of Mr. Kobayashi's presence.

There was another time, four years ago, when Fujino rang me at work and Mr. Kobayashi answered. It was after I had moved in with Fujino but before we were married. I didn't recall our exact conversation, but we probably discussed going out for a meal together that evening. We could afford to eat out a lot in those days. We were better off then than at any other time in the four years we spent together, as Fujino was receiving a university scholarship as well as an allowance from his parents. I liked my new lifestyle, relatively free as it was from domestic chores. That day, I chatted away on the phone as usual when Fujino rang, oblivious to Mr. Kobayashi. However, when I hung up, Mr. Kobayashi glanced up and said, "I hope you'll settle down soon."

Disconcerted, I blushed. I had been convinced that he was just an old man too engrossed in his books and papers to be concerned about the private life of his assistant. I wondered if he had overheard other conversations too. I didn't tell him that I had started living with Fujino, but he must have known what was going on. On reflection, it was only natural that he should be concerned, although it had never before occurred to me.

"You're trying to do too much for a woman. You'll run yourself into the ground if you're not careful."

I nodded, embarrassed.

Mr. Kobayashi used to work as a radio announcer. I found it hard to imagine, with his hoarse voice. In any case, it seems that after nearly twenty years on the job, personal problems had led to his being shuffled from post to post. Eventually, he was placed in charge of the recently relocated library division. He was a brusque, pasty-faced man in his sixties, but the young employees at the station referred to him rather fondly as the "old fellow." Nearly everybody enjoyed spending time with Mr. Kobayashi. They all seemed to like deliberately saying things that might offend him, just to see the change in his dour expression. I gathered from the way he spoke that he was a bachelor.

After Mr. Kobayashi voiced his concern for me, I felt confused; I was flattered by his interest in me, but, at the same time, I didn't want his sympathy. Unsure of how I should respond, I began to smile at him more often. He started taking me out for coffee during working hours, and on the way home he would take me to a bar where they kept a bottle of whiskey for him.

"Come here anytime you like," he would say, "even women should be able to have a drink now and then." But I never went there except in his company; I could hardly take Fujino with me. Having nothing in common, his kindness was almost an embarrassment. Wherever we went, however much he drank, Mr. Kobayashi never lost his dour expression. He would chat about work or books, but never again mentioned my private life. And when he saw me off at the station, he would always set off for yet another bar in another part of the city; everyone knew how he enjoyed drinking.

Nevertheless, Mr. Kobayashi's attentions must have left me with the impression that he was concerned about me. When Fujino and I got married, the first person I wanted to tell was not my mother, but Mr. Kobayashi. Whenever I arrived home late after a night out with Mr. Kobayashi, Fujino would reproach me for making a mockery of our relationship. This would make me resent Mr. Kobayashi; at times I even wondered whether he might be deliberately trying to make trouble for me. Even so, I sincerely believed that no one would be more pleased to hear of my marriage to Fujino than he.

When I announced my marriage, thanking him for all he had done for me, he gave a forced smile and muttered, "Nothing to do with me." That was all he said, but I felt as if I had received his blessings, and once again I thanked him with a smile and a bow.

Shortly after that I became pregnant and stopped going out drinking with Mr. Kobayashi. We got into the habit of having lunch together, although it was not really to make up for not going to the bar. I would buy bread rolls and milk for the two of us, and we would listen to music on the transistor radio I had brought to work, or to some of Mr. Kobayashi's favorite old programs on the library tape deck. Sometimes customers brought their lunch and joined us. After my daughter was born, I often monopolized the conversation over lunch, showing photos of her and telling Mr. Kobayashi what a sweet, funny baby she was. Once I spent the entire lunchtime boasting about how Fujino planned to stay on at the university and make a career out of "new film." Having the last word as usual, Mr. Kobayashi had simply said, "Shame he doesn't film his own child though, isn't it?"

Observant as he was, Mr. Kobayashi must have noticed how quiet and withdrawn I had grown over the last year. And the changes in my life must have become only too apparent once I started visiting real estate agents during the short lunch breaks. When I let him know that I had moved house, I couldn't bring myself to tell him what had really happened. I felt ashamed, remembering how I used to talk about my life with such self-satisfaction.

As I took the receiver, I wondered angrily why Fujino had phoned me at work. I didn't know what to say with Mr. Kobayashi there listening. I had kept telling myself to discuss things amicably with him, that there could be no better resolution than if we then managed to get back together again. But in spite of myself, I couldn't say a word, not here, not now. "He's gone and ruined everything by ringing me at work. Why did he do that?" I fumed.

"How are you? Been a while, hasn't it? How's our daughter? What is the new apartment like? It's about time we met for a chat, don't you think? Hey, say something will you? Is someone listening? Never mind. But surely you can say something. I'm your husband, after all, there's no need to be embarrassed. Are you listening? At least say yes, can't you even say that?"

"What do you want?" I asked him coldly, having paid no attention to what he was saying.

"What's got into you? Can't I phone you without a reason?"

"No. Good-bye."

I put down the receiver. Unable to look Mr. Kobayashi in the face, I kept my eyes lowered and concentrated on eating my bread roll. When I finally glanced up at him as I took a sip of my milk, I saw he was busy reading the newspaper, a hamburger in one hand.

Out of respect for my job perhaps, Fujino never again bothered me at work. When I hung up, my legs were trembling and my throat stung. I couldn't believe what I had done. Knowing how angry he must be, I felt sick with regret. It was not Fujino but I who had destroyed any chance of saving our marriage. It was too late now.

Crushing the empty milk carton and the paper bag that had contained my bread roll between my hands, I stood up. Mr. Kobayashi spoke.

"Would you mind making me a cup of tea? I'm rather dry today."

At the sound of his voice, I at last raised my head. "Certainly," I said, trying to sound cheerful. Disappearing into the kitchen, which was separated from the work area by a screen, I carefully prepared tea for us. My legs wouldn't stop shaking. Then, only a step away from his desk, I tripped and the two cups on the tray crashed to the floor. His cup was broken; mine remained intact.

"Oh no! I'm sorry. I'm so sorry. . . ." I mumbled, crouching down to pick up the broken pieces—his cup had split almost completely in two. I heard his voice above me.

"You'll cut your hand if you're not careful. Use a cloth."

"Yes, of course. I'm sorry. I'll go and get one."

Without bothering to straighten up, I rushed out to the kitchen. Back at his desk, I knelt down and pressed the cloth to the steaming floor. Immediately my palm was filled with a damp warmth.

"Your cup is stronger than it looks."

I glanced up to see him holding my cup in his hands, comparing it with the pieces of his own, which I must have tossed on to his desk.

"I'm dreadfully sorry."

"Don't worry, it was only an old one I got from a sushi restaurant."

"Oh..."

As the cloth rapidly began to lose its warmth, the events of the morning came flooding back to me. "Do you suppose," I asked, "that even a small amount of water such as this could leak through the ceiling to the floor below?"

"I shouldn't think so. If that were the case, no one would be able to work here, would they?" he replied, flashing me a rare smile.

"That's true, I suppose," I said, returning his smile. Staring fixedly at the wet linoleum floor, I slid the cloth over it. Tears sprang to my eyes. Avoiding his gaze, I continued to wipe the floor for some time, brushing away the tears with my left hand.

After a while, he stood up and went to the toilet. While he was gone, I finished cleaning up, throwing away the broken pieces of the cup, and then set to work making new library cards. Lunch break was over.

That day, Mr. Kobayashi said slightly earlier than usual, "That'll do for today. You can go now." I left without a moment's hesitation. My daughter squealed with delight when I arrived early to pick her up. On the way home we stopped at a local store to do some shopping.

As soon as we began to climb the stairs to our apartment, the man I had spoken to that morning appeared on the third floor landing; he must have heard my daughter's high-pitched voice. Directly behind him, I could see the face of the real estate agent, who acted as caretaker. Judging by the looks on their faces, they had been waiting impatiently for my return. It took everything I had to keep myself from running back down the stairs and outside. Instead, I pushed my daughter ahead of me and, taking one step at a time, slowly made my way up. My daughter climbed the steep stairs on all fours like a dog.

When I reached the third floor landing, the agent stepped in front of me as if to protect me with his slender frame from the angry-looking man behind him.

"I hope you'll excuse us. Actually, we've been waiting over an hour for your return. This gentleman said that we should let ourselves into your apartment, but I suggested we wait as you were sure to be back soon. I took the liberty of waiting with him...."

"Yes, even though we've no time to lose," the other man grumbled.

The agent smiled apologetically as if to say, "Don't worry."

"The leak seems to be quite serious. The water is now leaking through to the second floor, and since it's not raining, I think it must be coming from the top floor. I'm terribly sorry to bother you, but would you mind letting us check your apartment?"

The agent was a polite, unassuming old man, of slight build and with gray hair. Whenever I went to pay the rent, the owner, a woman in her sixties, would be there with him, seated on the sofa; together they reminded me of a mistress and her elderly butler.

I led the way upstairs to my apartment. What had only been a small puddle on the landing that morning now covered the entire area outside my door. The stain on the ceiling had also spread; drops of water were forming there and gradually growing larger and larger until they eventually splashed to the landing below.

I made the men wait at the door while I looked around the apartment first myself. It was exactly as I had left it that morning. The strong afternoon sun streamed through the windows so that the whole apartment shimmered with light. Staying close by my side, my daughter sang a song she had just learned at school, in a shrill voice.

After checking all the other rooms, I went to have a look at the bedroom, just to satisfy the man from the third floor. Not for a moment did I think there would be any water leaking there. Now, however, I noticed a large stain on the wall that I had never seen before. On the other side of the wall were the stairs to the rooftop.

I told the men. The man from the third floor immediately tried to push his way inside.

"Please don't go inside. Let's try the roof instead. I didn't check up there this morning."

I hastily showed them the way to the stairs, cringing at the thought of their seeing my bedroom with its unmade bed.

There was no water leaking in the bathroom. I opened the door to the rooftop and stepped out ahead of the others. A cry escaped from my lips at the sight that met my eyes: there, on what should have been a dry roof, rippled clear, sparkling water.

"The sea, Mummy! It's the sea! Look, isn't it big!" my daughter cried and jumped into it with her bare feet. Her laughter rang through the air as she began to slosh around in the ankle-deep water, scooping it up with her hands and splashing it on her face.

We traced the leak to the water tank. Water was gushing from the tank at an astounding rate.

"It's coming out here, flowing along there and down into the drain, and then overflowing from the drain and leaking downstairs. There must be a small crack in the tank. It's certainly quite a sight!"

Even the man from downstairs seemed overawed; his expression was much calmer than before.

"I suppose we should be thankful there's no real damage downstairs, considering the huge amount of water that's leaking. Look, your daughter's having a wonderful time."

"My grandchild loves playing in water too."

The two men gazed fondly at my daughter splashing about in the water.

"But you must have heard something, surely. It's directly above you."

Only when the agent said this did I recall the sound of trickling water that I had heard in the night. That soft, distant sound. To think that I would hear that sound again, only this time not in a dream. A shiver ran through me.

"Now that you mention it, I did hear something . . . but when I got up in the morning the sky was clear . . . so somehow I thought . . ."

"What! If you'd only checked, we could have had it repaired straightaway!" the man from downstairs exclaimed angrily.

"I . . . I'm awfully sorry," I stammered.

The men decided to have the tank fixed early the next morning and left.

That night, my daughter and I played barefoot in the "sea" on the rooftop. Although I wasn't in any danger, I felt strangely nervous and excited with my feet in the water. Splashing each other and playing tag, we both ended up soaking wet and inevitably grew cold; though warm during the day it was still, after all, only the beginning of May.

The phone stopped ringing just as we got back inside. I wondered how long it had been ringing. Fujino's face flashed before my eyes. I remembered how happy I had been when we first started living together; my even greater happiness when we went to the ward office to register our marriage; how I hadn't hesitated to have our child. I could hear myself asking Mr. Kobayashi if I must live forever with the consequences and pictured him nodding in reply. All of a sudden I was surrounded by a multitude of shadowy figures, all vigorously nodding their heads.

It was now over a month since my daughter and I began a new life together, a life about which Fujino, my husband and the father of my daughter, knew nothing and of which I told him nothing, not that there was anything much to tell. But the sheer uneventfulness of my life only made me more afraid of the days that lay ahead. In my mind, I pictured a fragile, misshapen, transparent mass that should have collapsed but for some reason didn't. Instead, it was beginning to spread its roots and send forth new buds. I was growing too attached to this fragile new gift, visible to me alone, to go back to being Fujino's wife. Fujino still spoke to me as a husband would his wife, but it only made me feel uncomfortable. I wondered if I would have to go on listening to that now distant, empty voice of his until he completely cut me out of his life.

Can't I forget Fujino, even though it was he who had wanted the separation? I looked questioningly at the shadowy figures around me. The shadows, who all seemed to resemble people I knew, solemnly shook their heads.

The sound of trickling water echoed in my ears once again that night, and in my sleep I felt as if I were wrapped in something soft and moist.

Next morning, the tank was repaired in no time at all. The clear water disappeared from the rooftop before our very eyes. My daughter scolded the plumber for me.

"Leave the water alone, meanie! I hate you!"

On the Sunday, two days later, the roof was painted. It took all day. In the evening, once the work was completed, I went up to have a look. I'd been warned not to touch the paint until it had dried, and I repeated the warning to my daughter several times as we climbed the stairs to the roof.

My daughter opened the door first, and at once let out a cry even more piercing than when she had found the sea. Wondering what on earth had happened, I looked out after her. To my astonishment, the whole surface of the roof shone a bright silver, burning my eyes with the glare. I had assumed that they would only repair and paint the crack, but the entire roof was covered from corner to corner with thick waterproof paint. If it was this bright in spring, we'd never be able to look at it in the summer. Here, in the midst of the city, we would burn our eyes, just like people walking in the snow or floating in the sea.

A silver sea. What a wonderful sight! And this time no one could take it away from us. I smiled.

"Isn't it pretty!" exclaimed my daughter as she gazed in wonder at the silver roof. "Like the stars."

The following evening, Fujino rang. Everything I said only seemed to irritate him further. For some reason, whenever I heard Fujino's voice, my legs would start to tremble.

That night, I dreamed I was sitting in a star-shaped vessel. The vessel began to spin faster and faster until my body was flattened against the wall. "Stop, please!" I cried, whereupon a woman looked up and said, "Why are you so hopeless?" She had been in my junior-high class, although I had never had much to do with her. An outstanding student, she was invariably chosen as form prefect. Not only that, but being very pretty, the boys always flocked around her. I knew it was silly to be dreaming about her now, but I pleaded, tears streaming down my face, that I couldn't help being what I was, no matter what she said.

"There must be someone, somewhere, who will care for me. There must be, there just has to be."

The woman shook her head sadly and walked away. She was just as beautiful as ever.

8

Cherry Blossom Train

Saegusa Kazuko

I flash my pass at the ticket gate and, as usual, climb up and then down the steps that lead to the train platform, but I feel slightly dizzy. The platform is bulging with young children. It looks five times wider than normal, a bit like a playground. 10:00 AM. At this hour, the station is always quiet. With just a few scattered silhouettes, a peace of mind descends after the rush hour. Although they are just ordinary commuters, the ones who come now appear somewhat out of place. The looks on their faces seem to express a sense of abandonment and loss. Latecomers. Part-time employees not bound by time. And among the mix, there might be a stray laid-off worker, who, feigning innocence, has left home as if to go to work. They all look timid as they wait for the train.

But today is different.

Is this a kindergarten field trip? No, it can't be.

The children's ages are too different for that. They range from toddlers just starting to walk to ten-year-olds. There are a dozen or so women who look like mothers. Given their number, there appear to be too many children. Yet this doesn't seem like a neighborhood group either.

"But the roller coaster . . ."

"No. It's mine."

"No. I said no."

"At her place, her dad's the . . ."

"Let me have it for a minute."

"Sakura densha," from Saegusa Kazuko, *Nomori no kagami* (Field Guards' Mirror) (Tokyo: Shūeisha, 1980). Copyright 1980 by K. Saegusa. Translated by Alisa Freedman and Kyoko Selden with the permission of Shū Yasuhiro. This translation first appeared in *Review of Japanese Culture and Society*, XVI, Josai University, December 2004. Translation copyright 2004 by Josai University.

"You know the magic mirror room?"
"Next to the haunted house, right?"
"Oh, hurry up. Hurry u-up!"
"Wow. That's cool."
"Show me. Show me, please!"
 Shrill laughter. Shouts. Out-of-tune songs clash. Already whiny voices mingle. Chiding voices. Yelling voices. A green baseball cap and a yellow Alpine hat run around. A large pink ribbon shakes. Faint nausea wells up within me. The smell of spoiled milk mixes with the children's body odor.
"Oh yes. Mine has been so excited since early this morning."
"There are sushi and sandwiches. Since I also made lunch for his big brother, who's staying home, I was so busy my head swam."
"Absolutely not. You look really nice in it."
"Oh, how lucky you are."
"I wonder if I am."
"And that's why my husband didn't go to the playground then. He said he already had plans to play golf. But I'm not so sure. I know he wanted to get out of going to the park. He took his lunch, but instead of meeting people at the course, he went to the driving range by himself. I'm sure of that. It's like this every Sunday."
"Mine doesn't leave the house. He just lies around, dozing. And that is even more annoying."
"I agree. It's exhausting. I wish school would start soon."
"Did you go see the cherry blossoms?"
"Watch out! You're a big girl, so you should know not to walk backwards."
"Be careful! The train's coming."
"Get back. Get back!"
"Don't run. Don't run!"
 There are no available seats on the train. Some children have to stand. They run around the train. There's a boy who's probably in the – – grade. He's a little overweight. The hem of his shorts digs into his thighs. A girl slaps him on the back with all her might. He gives a toothy smile. Two white hats peek into a white basket. Candies spill out. A child scatters gum wrappers. His mother scolds him.
 The mothers' faces all look the same. The foreheads beaded with sweat. The caked-up layers of foundation. The lipstick off-center. Now and then, they scold their children, yells coming from the tops of their heads. But between those times they incessantly chat with one another.
 At first, the mothers' outfits and those of the children all seem different, various colors, but I realize that they are really identical. As I idly gaze at them, they start to blur together. A wild dance, a whirl of soiled colors.

I shut my eyes, and beneath the clamor of the children, I hear the clatter of the train passing over the joints of the rails in regular intervals. The jolting roar. The creaking roar. The train stops. The sound of doors opening. The whistle. The sound of doors closing. The train moves again. I open my eyes and look around. A young man, perhaps a student, and a late-middle-aged man, briefcase in hand, both here when I got on, are now gone without my even having noticed. Since all the passengers who have taken their places seem accompanied by children, the train has become packed with children, just as if it had been chartered for a school trip.

In a group, children's voices seem different from usual. This is especially the case on a train. Shouts an octave higher fly back and forth, intensifying the feverish atmosphere of the train and making it painful to breathe. It's as if the air needed to breathe is rapidly thinning.

Where in the world are all these children going?

Recalling that I forgot to check the name of the last stop suddenly makes me anxious. It might just be my imagination, but the scenery outside the windows seems different from usual. Could I have taken a train going in the opposite direction?

I peer out the window. No matter how hard I look, I can't find any indication that we are heading toward the center of the city. Simply because the train came, I got on, as if pushed by the crowd of children engulfing me, but I wonder if that could have been track no. 1. Track no. 2 is for trains bound for the city. The station is built so that the stairs are connected to the passage through the ticket gate, which forms a sort of footbridge leading passengers to the platform. There's only one platform, one side used for trains going toward the city and the other for those going away from the city. I can't say that I have never gotten suddenly confused and almost boarded the wrong train. Those times, I caught my mistake before it was too late. But now not realizing my mistake until I have already boarded? Was I that absentminded?

Since I don't have to be anywhere at a certain time, it doesn't really matter if I am late. I will teach at a junior college starting this semester. So now I just need to get the class lists and straighten up the office. It's just that those bookcases have gotten so disorganized since students have been allowed to use the room.

It seems like it might be a while until we reach the next station. But as soon as I can make sure this is the wrong train, I hope to catch the right one. It's 10:20. If I get on the right train now, I should be at my desk before lunch.

Outside the window passes an embankment lined with cherry trees. Perhaps either because it is a bit overcast or because I am looking through a glass pane, the blossoms seem to fade into the sky, making it hard to tell where one ends and the other begins.

A feeling of bitterness suddenly burns inside me. I'm thirty-two. If I were married like most people, I might have two or three children around this age. Just the thought of it scares me. No, it depresses me. The depressing thought of having children and that of not being able to completely resolve this question overlap, driving me into a terribly damp corner.

Ultimately, maybe the problem is not being able to marry. Or it might be more accurate to say that I have not been able to decide how I feel about having a child out of wedlock. Looking at the faces of the women enshrined here on the train, smiling with the same carefree expressions as their children, more than anything, makes me unhappy, for, when I ask myself if my life is much better than theirs, I can't answer right away.

What am I doing with my life? I smile wryly to myself. I don't have a particularly special job. My salary as a lecturer at a women's college is only enough to support myself. Occasionally I go out with old boyfriends to the movies or the theater, or I might be invited to a concert. I have a good enough time then, but afterward when I get back to my apartment, the flow of time suddenly slows down, and I experience an odd pain. While I busy myself preparing for class or writing articles for the college bulletin, somewhere in my heart a space forms that is difficult to fathom.

It's about time to break up with the man I am now dating. He is a lecturer like me and is one year younger. He's single, so that's not a problem, but I have a very hard time figuring him out. I am okay with dating someone I don't plan to marry. With a tacit understanding between us, we cope with each other's feelings as we see fit. However, I sense that the longer I keep dating him, the harder it will be for me to get married. I neither love nor hate the man. Yet without my even realizing it, the feeling that marriage is nothing but trouble has spread like mold to every corner of my heart.

"I think I'm pregnant."

He replied at once, "So you'll have an abortion."

"Of course."

"Got money to cover the costs?"

"Yes, I have at least enough for that."

" . . . "

"It's my mistake, so I'll take care of it."

"I see."

We never again brought up the topic of the operation or its costs. I took care of it myself, and we continued our relationship as if nothing had happened.

Is it that women are able to just grin and bear it and persevere like this? I have no close female friends, so there is no one I can confide in or ask advice.

" . . . "

I get the sensation someone is talking to me, saying the words right in my ear. Looking around, however, I see this is not so. Yet it makes me very uneasy. I sense that someone might be trying to warn me of something, but I am not sure of what. The two boys seated next to me have begun to play "Hey! Look over there!" I watch the boys aimlessly, recalling that this game was part of an old TV program. They are absorbed in play. When the winner slaps the back of the loser's hand, both let out a whoop. Because of apparently slower motor skills, the boy in the navy blue Tokyo Giants cap keeps losing to the boy with the pageboy haircut and the face as gentle as a girl's. Pageboy is quick. He never falls for Giants' finger pointing when he says, "Hey! Look over there!" If Giants' finger points up, he looks down; if it points down, he looks up. If it points right, he looks left; if it points left, he looks right. Pageboy has his escape plan down to a pattern. Giants does not seem to understand his opponent's strategy. It may be that he enjoys losing. Each time Giants is slapped, he breaks into a big smile, looking genuinely happy.

"My little – –, I guess this is an express train." A woman, apparently Pageboy's mother, addresses him from two seats away, but the boy does not even turn around. He has obviously heard, but he merely quickens his pace and moves his finger and head even faster.

"Well, it seems the train is just speeding by the stations without stopping."

" . . . "

I hurriedly peer out the window. The train seems to be moving faster. It cuts straight through the wooded suburban landscape. There is no doubt that I am being whisked off in the opposite direction from the city.

A bulldozer moves slowly in the distance where an apartment complex is apparently under construction. A plastic greenhouse. The white roof of a cake factory. A station platform that seems to be blown backward right before my eyes like a sheet of waste paper. It takes a split second. I feel even more anxious because I can't make out the name of the station.

Could this be a chartered train?

Normally, express trains run nonstop from the city to a station near a mammoth housing development and make frequent stops after that. They stop at every station as they approach their terminus. But the youth who looked like a student and the middle-aged man with a briefcase had ridden only part of the way. So this can't be completely chartered. But they may have gotten off, warned that this train was reserved. That's probably it. I was mistaken for a chaperoning mother.

Realizing this, I suddenly feel very uncomfortable. I look timidly around. A nearby girl is staring at me. Wide-eyed, she scrutinizes me, a passenger who has wandered in by mistake. "She can't be a mother," the girl seems to think. "Mothers don't dress like that." She critically gazes at my short, unpermed hair and my Burberry coat with its showy checked lining.

Pageboy's mother quickly turns around and calls to her son. "Please, – –, be a dear and get the conductor for me. Or just go ask him what's the next stop."

" . . . "

At this, Pageboy, who has been absorbed in "Hey! Look over there!" abruptly stands up. Without answering, he begins to walk quickly away.

"Oh, – –, you're going to ask the conductor for me." Pageboy's mother slides the baby on her lap a little to the side as if she is about to get up. Without turning around, Pageboy nods once and disappears into the next car.

Suddenly left alone, Giants looks around, not quite understanding what has happened, but he does not seem to be looking for Pageboy in particular. He stands up and calls to anyone at random, "Wanna play 'Hey! Look over there!'?"

After her son has gone on his errand, Pageboy's mother perks up, seeming an almost different person. Exaggeratedly shaking her head, she chats with the woman seated beside her, also a mother past age thirty.

". . . It's really like that. Just as I have always said. You agree? It was also like that when he was in the second grade."

"Of course, nobody wants to bad-mouth the homeroom teacher. Nobody. But still."

"What about the other teacher, Ms. – –"

"I am not sure, but rumor has it that . . ."

Their voices drop a level. The mothers, heads leaning close together, look suddenly old. While continuing to talk in whispers, the one holding the now fussing baby in the crook of her arm gives the child a shake to calm it down.

A row of girls is seated across from them. They are eating something, moving their mouths in unison. Perhaps this is why they don't talk much. With serious expressions on their faces, they look out the windows and around the train car. The boys might be bored, for some have now started to do chin-ups from the hand straps.

By now, the small children have stopped wandering away from their mothers. Now clinging to their mothers' knees, they are whining about something. Seeming annoyed, the mothers hurriedly open their baskets. They quickly take out chocolates, tangerines, and such.

It is now about to pass 11:00. The train has not stopped since 10:20. And on top of this, Pageboy has not yet returned.

" . . . "

For some reason, I start to shudder. Although I am not sure why, it seems as if an underlying, formless anxiety has suddenly reared its head and let out a silent scream. The back view of Pageboy casually nodding without a care in the world and disappearing out of the train car is strangely imprinted in my mind's eye, an image that floats before me again and again. The sudden change in his behavior from ignoring his mother's request and continuing his game of "Hey! Look over there!" to walking off strikes me as very odd. I get nervous thinking that the boy might have been pulled in by some special force rather than moving on his own volition. I try to catch his mother's attention, but she is so absorbed in conversation that she seems oblivious to the passing of time. I look around to see if I can find another boy to help me. Since an innocent four- or five-year-old won't do, I spot a boy that seems a few years older, perhaps now in the fourth grade, and walk toward him.

He is engrossed in a comic book.

"Hey, little boy—" I call out, but he does not even turn around.

"Hey, little boy, what grade are you in?" I tap him on the shoulder, and he jumps in surprise. It confuses me that he is startled.

"Hey, you're a good boy, so could you do me a favor?" As I speak to that vacant look on his face, I carefully enunciate each word to make absolutely sure he understands my request.

"You know, this train hasn't stopped for a while. I would like you to go ask the conductor what is going on."

". . ."

The boy cocks his head. Then, finally seeming to understand my question, he says in a crystal clear voice, "Oh, so you don't know. There is no one driving this train. And no conductor. The train just keeps on going and doesn't stop anywhere. Right, everyone?"

And the ten or so boys and girls, who have gathered around without my even having noticed, all nod and shout in a chorus, "That's right. You know nothing."

". . ."

I gasped. That instant, all crumbles before my eyes, and the place where I stand tilts violently

"Yeah!" scream the children as they all stand up and start running around, paying no attention to me. Shrieking like animals, they run in circles around the train car. At the same time, the train seems to be moving faster.

"What are you doing? Stop it. I'm telling you, stop!" I yell. But the children ignore my order. Indeed, the more I try to restrain them, the more they happily run around, merely brushing away my hand.

What is going on? I just stand, amazed, in the center of the circle of moving children.

Some insane force must have infiltrated this train, driving the children to run around in this way.

Overpowered by the children's force, without even realizing I had done so,

I find myself sitting smack in the aisle. The children's faces, now seeming a dismembered, misshapen blur, rush before me. Eyes, all whites, their pupils dilated with excitement. Lips stretched up to the ears. Black mouths devoid of teeth. Bobbing bright red Adam's apples. A yellow Alpine hat flies by. A pink ribbon, wrenched off, coils around a neck. Frills swinging. A jumble of jeans. Red appliqué flowers scatter. A lion leaps. A cat is crushed. A giraffe twists and turns. Boys and girls now indistinguishable. Shouts like shrieks of laughter or sobs swoop down on me. When I try to escape, the commotion grows, and the children all become little demons. A horde of tiny devils. Red faces. Blue faces. White faces. But their eyes gleam with an identical glaring bloodshot glow. And they all bare their sharp fangs. I shut my eyes despite myself.

It is at this moment. Tinkling metallic women's voices fall on me from above.

"Where did she come from? How did she become one of us?"

" . . . "

I try to see whose voice this is, but I can't make out the face.

"My boy went to get the conductor, and it's her fault that he hasn't returned."

"No!" I try to shout, but no voice comes out. That boy's mother is still unaware. This train is not calmly making its way to some amusement park. But I do not have the words to tell her this.

"She probably came to kidnap the children. Mothers, you better watch out! I hear that after bathhouses, kidnapping happens most on trains."

"Bathhouses?"

"They say there is a woman who steals babies."

"How scary. Son, stop running around and come over here!"

"I doubt that's true. Where would she hide them?"

"Her plan is to take them somewhere far away. It happens a lot, you know. The kidnapper claims something like the child was so cute that she couldn't resist. But they end up throwing the child away when it cries."

"Maybe she is just one of those women who are too old to find a husband."

"Looks like it."

"Probably lonely."

"Because men aren't attracted to her?"

"My, you're harsh."

"It's because your boy is so cute. This is terrible."

"Let's call the conductor."

"No. You don't know what she might do then."

"If she wants a child, she should have her own."

"But she can't if men don't fancy her."

Then oddly suppressed laughter. The whispering makes the space between the women's lips and ears somewhat tepid and obscene.

"..."

I stand up. I have to hurry and stop this train. At this rate, it may race until it disintegrates in midair.

"Stop it. Don't butt in where you don't belong." It's that man. Why has he come all the way here? I shake my head. I try to escape him.

"You're immoral. And I thought you were a more rational woman."

"Immoral? Irrational?"

Here I go, falling for it again. And I told myself that I would just ignore him. But somehow I never feel quite free around him.

"So you're attacking me for having made you get an abortion."

"..." I can't come up with a response to this insinuation. What are you saying? I am not attacking you; I don't see it that way or bear a grudge against you for making me have an abortion because, first of all, you didn't make me have it, and it is none of your business. But it would be a lot of trouble for me to have a child, and, at any rate, this child might not even have been yours, so you have no right to act all self-righteous and try to manipulate me."

"..."

Then he says something. Hearing his voice, I wake with a start. Without realizing it, I had fallen asleep with my head resting against the back of the seat. Confused, I look around. It's quiet on the train. Beside me, the woman holding the child in the crook of her arm is deep in conversation. Pageboy, player of "Hey! Look over there!" is not here. Neither is Giants. What on earth is going on?

The train is moving at the same speed. But my watch says 11:05. Time seems to be virtually standing still. I shut my eyes. The quiet train is somehow eerie. Behind my eyelids, I sense that outside the cherry trees are gently spreading their pale branches. The train keeps moving, cutting right through the white flowers that look opaque on this cloudy day. A piercing cry cuts right through the mass of blossoms. I listen intently to that cry, not knowing whether it is coming from the train or the cherry trees or if the whole world around me is howling. As I listen intently, dragging a wisp of a tail like a comet, the cry fades into the direction the train is heading.

"Ahh!"

I open my eyes, startled. I wasn't the one who shouted. It was Pageboy's mother, sitting next to me.

"My baby is gone! What should I do?"

"What do you mean?" And the woman who has been talking to her all the while rushes toward her.

"Why did you leave the baby alone?"

"But everyone was here, so . . ."
"What happened?"
"She says her baby is gone."
"Maybe it crawled off somewhere. You should go check the aisles."
"I just left for a moment to go find my boy. Just a moment . . ."
"Stop crying and have a look over here."
"Everyone, please stand up."
"Conductor, stop the train, stop the – –"
"What are you saying? Please calm down. Maybe someone is holding your baby for you."
"He fell through the space between the train cars, where the coupler connects them. My child. He fell in there. Conductor! Conductor!"
"It's no use, madam." A cheerful voice resounds from around the middle of the train car. It's the boy who has been engrossed in the comic book. "There's no driver or conductor on this train. Making a fuss will get you nowhere."

The boy's voice is so dignified that there is no room for objection. That instant, the mothers look stupefied, as if they had dropped something.

I believe this boy who reported the situation twice in the same tone of voice. I have come to believe that the train will just keep rushing further into the cherry trees. And if so, that's fine with me.

"We all knew it from the start. Right, everyone?" Then the children all scream like animals and together break into a run, even faster than the speed of the train, in the direction we are heading.

9

The Strange Story of a Pumpkin

Kurahashi Yumiko

Mr. Bōbura, the former prime minister, had been called "Pumpkin" behind his back ever since he had held the post.[1]

In general, it's never a good sign when the name "pumpkin" crowns an appellation. First there's "pumpkin head," then "pumpkin fellow." Whatever the name, once "pumpkin" has been attached to it, it sounds foolish, ugly, and graceless. There's also the expression "eyes and nose put on a pumpkin." This too is no compliment, used to describe a woman who is plump and round faced, with no particularly felicitous countenance. Somehow, the awkwardly large fruit of this plant, hailing from the American continent, is despised, slighted, and often applied to refer to an ugly person.

As for how the nickname of former prime minister Bōbura was chosen, there are various theories, and the truth is uncertain. Many say that his appearance, especially the general impression produced by his face and head, was pumpkin itself. But there are pumpkins, and there are pumpkins. Some are dark green with abnormal indentations and protrusions; others are orange colored and smooth, aimlessly huge as if a winter melon had blushed with embarrassment; still others are funny shaped like gourds. When asked which one of these various types Bōbura resembles, no accurate answer surfaces. According to one theory, Bōbura is large headed and out of proportion given his short height. His head not only resembles an orange pumpkin but is also problematic in terms of its content, meaning that he's an idiot; that's why he

---

"Kabocha kitan," from *Kurahashi Yumiko no kaiki shōhen* (Kurahashi Yumiko's Short Tales of the Grotesque) (Tokyo: Ushio Shuppansha, 1985). Copyright 1985 by Sayaka Kumagai. English translation rights granted by arrangement through the Japan Foreign Rights Centre. Translated by Kyoko Selden. This translation first appeared in *Review of Japanese Culture and Society*, XVI, Josai University, December 2004. Translation copyright 2004 by Josai University.

is called "Pumpkin." But this theory itself is problematic. If the person serving as prime minister of a state were really an idiot, then it would follow that the citizens upholding him as their leader would likewise be idiots. Hence, the entire nation would be constituted by pumpkins.[2]

Even so, it would be a lie to say that Mr. Bōbura never conveyed such an impression. The large head, oiled and smoothly combed hair, unfocused face, eyes so thin that they once stirred criticism because he seemed to be taking a nap during a conference with the premier of a certain small state—not to mention his language, which lacked lucidity, stupid slips of the tongue, and errors in reading his own speeches—no matter which of these features one considered, it unavoidably evoked a pumpkinlike image. Ordinarily, one who at first sight appears to be an idiot gains popularity by making the masses feel at ease. As far as Prime Minister Bōbura went, he did not seem to be blessed by such a virtue of fools. Even as he remained unpopular, he stayed in his post for an incomprehensibly long time. When people got too used to the taste of this pumpkin to feel any particular way about it, he quit abruptly. The ridiculous reason that he gave was, to put it simply, that he could no longer stand being called a pumpkin.

This Bōbura, having retired from the post of prime minister and having been forgotten along with his nickname, "Pumpkin," died as suddenly as he had retired. He was still in his sixties, and health was his only strength. So the cause of his death was ascribed, at least for the sake of immediate purposes, to heart failure. But the real cause remained uncertain. It was a fact that he died, however. So, a few days later a grand funeral becoming to a former prime minister was to be held. His body was cremated in preparation for the event.

About that time, Bōbura found himself (what follows is indeed inscrutable, but judging from the facts as clarified later, there is no other choice but to proceed with the story for now) in the world of the dead and was going through an evaluation that would determine his future position in that world.

To sum up what Bōbura understood about the world of the dead: The newly dead must first be judged unconditionally. The deliberations partly resembled a court trial of this world, but there was neither public prosecutor nor attorney; no distinction between defendant and plaintiff, and no observers were present. Several referees evaluated the dead on the basis of documents recording their lifetime conduct and merits and demerits thereof, and also face-to-face cross-examination. They accordingly determined the rank and position of the dead, and established the nature of the punishment, in case comparison revealed criminal deeds outweighing meritorious achievements. The atmosphere of this office of deliberation was more like a refugee camp reception desk or an employment agency than a courtroom in this world. Separated by a humble desk and with the documents between them, the dead exchanged words with plain-looking referees. The referees neither behaved high-handedly nor uttered anything like criticism or reprimands, but processed matters in a business-like manner. The position or occupation the dead hoped for in the afterworld was one of the things the referees asked, though only just in case—"Not that we can necessarily suit your wishes"; they would add something like this. The world of the dead also seemed to be equipped with whatever or everything that is in the world of the living, such as governmental offices, schools, factories, business offices, theaters, and libraries. The only difference was that all these took the form of publicly founded and publicly run organizations.

Now, regarding Bōbura's case. It took an unexpectedly long time, because his evaluation was not easy to complete. The reason was that examining a politician's achievements and clarifying his merits and demerits require an exceptionally sharp analytical ability and high quality of judgment, and it does not follow that these desirable attributes, which cannot be found even among judges in the human world, are possessed by every referee in the other world. In fact, those in charge of Bōbura's case seemed to belong to a particularly mediocre class of people, even in the eyes of this owner of a pumpkin head. Thus, the judgment was deadlocked many times, and, as there was apparently such a system there too, specialists were called in as expert witnesses, along with ordinary people who could testify. Many of the specialists were political scientists and critics who were familiar with Bōbura's work as prime minister. General witnesses were senior politicians, who had also died just a short while before Bōbura did, and ordinary citizens. These people nearly unanimously agreed that Bōbura had been relatively unassociated with the "vices" that are normally inseparable from politicians, such as corruption, unscrupulous fund-raising, and Machiavellian schemes. On the other hand, they also commented that he had been devoid of any policies worthy of note, and that those he had ever initiated were almost all vapid.

Free of worries as he was, Bōbura felt depressed by all this in the end. Because the deliberations were prolonged, he sometimes went to take a look at other courtrooms. In the world of the dead, the defendants were relatively free until sentencing. Thus, this sort of thing was allowed. It was impossible, in any case, for them to run away back to the old world; there was no need to keep them detained, for there was no place to which they could flee. One of the deliberations Bōbura observed concerned a certain judge. The man who had been a judge in this world was now to be judged after death. What impressed Bōbura here was that in the world of the dead, everything—what each person did in his lifetime, including whether, for example, he had committed murder—was crystal clear, as though reflected in a mirror. Thus, a judge's misjudgment too was revealed with perfect clarity. This particular judge had never delivered a verdict of the death penalty. But according to what was clarified at the deliberations, he had declared as many as eight murderers innocent on account of insufficient evidence. This "crime of failure to punish those who should have been punished" was regarded as extremely grave, so it was determined that the judge be handed over to relatives of the victims to work as their slave. Witnessing such postmortem deliberations, Bōbura was greatly impressed by how retributive justice was carried through.

Now, Bōbura's own lengthy deliberations continued, but finally the referees reached a conclusion and the verdict was to be delivered. Bōbura was made to stand before three referees as he heard the following:

"Sentence. In light of the follies during your lifetime, we will pumpkinize you. The end."

"Wait a second, please," Bōbura said, flustered. "What does that mean? Is it permitted to turn humans into pumpkins or dogs? I am dissatisfied. I will appeal right away."

"Calm down," the referee in the middle said, restraining Bōbura. "In the world of the dead, there is no such thing as an appeal system that would allow the same case to be judged three times as in the world of the living. This is the final verdict. Moreover, one can become a dog or a snake depending upon one's conduct during life. You seem to be dissatisfied with becoming a pumpkin, but we believe this to be the appropriate verdict. We reached it after racking our brains in all kinds of ways. In the first place, you were already called "Pumpkin" during your lifetime. You should not feel too uncomfortable about turning into a pumpkin. Again, on searching for precedents, we find Emperor Claudius of Rome among those who were pumpkinized.[3] You must agree this is a fine precedent."

Thus reasoned with, Bōbura began to feel that it would not be so bad to turn into a pumpkin. The referees stood, bowed, and left the chamber.

From here on, Bōbura's memory suddenly became uncertain. Anyway, when he came to, he found himself at a gathering that seemed to be someone's funeral. He was standing in a line of many attendees waiting to offer flowers to the soul of the dead. Although he had no idea whose funeral it was, since it was common sense not to ask such a question, he thought he would at least finish offering the flowers. When he approached the altar, however, he was surprised to find it to be his own funeral. A fine, framed photo of him in his life was displayed there. Gazing on the face, Bōbura felt he understood why he was called "Pumpkin" during his life.

After offering the flowers, Bōbura greeted this and that acquaintance at the gathering, then addressed the former secretary of the cabinet.

"Thanks for your good job today. It looks like a pretty good turnout. By the way, now that I'm back here for some reason, let me make a final speech."

The addressee went quite blank, not understanding the situation. In the meantime people started to gather around them. The bereaved family, or so they were expected to be, lost color. They thought the ghost of the dead had appeared. The deceased, already cremated with his ashes supposedly contained in the urn, was there, identical in face and body as before, speaking. Of course this was hard to explain.

It was determined that a press conference be called immediately. The funeral hall was redecorated without much ado, Bōbura and his family sat at the front, and, in addition, all kinds of people, including the main doctor and the crematory attendants, were called in.

First, Bōbura rose from his chair, beaming, and explained all that had happened so far. He described the deliberations in the other world in fair detail, omitting the sentence he had received and skipping various other portions unfavorable to himself. He did not understand the situation of the other world too well, he said, and added that he had been thus sent back to the world of the living, possibly because the trial clarified that he had been sent to the world of the dead by some kind of mistake. A question-and-answer period followed. While listening to the testimony of persons concerned, even some press reporters who had first suspected this to be a deliberate farce grew excited, realizing that this was unmistakably a "resurrection," "a recovery from death." The hall was filled with feverish excitement.

Bōbura rose again and again to speak eloquently as "a miraculous returnee." In the midst of this, he demonstrated a hard-line stance totally new to him while quoting the trial of a certain judge that he had witnessed in the other world. He emphasized how much the type of trial in which "the suspect must be given the benefit of the doubt" hurt justice if justice were to be served. The situation even progressed to a stage where he was ready to announce his desire to return to the political world and once again take charge of the administration.

When the excitement of the gathering reached a pitch in this manner, a change occurred to Bōbura onstage. This is not to say that he collapsed with heart failure or stroke. His speech, unclear to begin with, grew even less clear, and came to a halt in the end. He resigned himself to a certain transformation, while still standing on the platform. His face was beginning to expand abnormally. Eventually, only his face sat on the table, continuing to expand. Eyes and nose moved around like a failed attempt at drawing a face blindfolded.[4] The result was precisely "eyes and nose drawn on a pumpkin." By then, his torso and limbs were invisible, absorbed into this object upon the table. Several minutes later, clear for all to see, the thing had turned into a huge pumpkin. A commotion occurred in the hall, and it was hard to distinguish whether it was a sigh of regret or of admiration. Bōbura's pumpkinization had run its course. People felt indescribable ease and satisfaction with how the series of miracles had culminated with such results. They discussed what to do with this pumpkin, with members of the family leading the core of the discussion. It was decided that they would display this fine pumpkin at the altar, change the gathering back to a funeral, and then have all concerned partake of it in memory of the virtue of the deceased.

Notes

1. The name Bōbura comes from *bōbura*, or *kabocha bōbura* (Cambodian pumpkin) in full, from the Portuguese word *abóbora* (pumpkin).
2. The expression recalls "idiotization of the entire nation," a celebrated phrase with which the critic Ōya Sōichi (1900–1970) described the introduction of television in the 1950s.
3. When Emperor Claudius (Tiberius Claudius Caesar Augustus Germanicus, 10 BCE to 54 CE) died at the hands of his niece and fourth wife, Agrippina, or was perhaps simply poisoned by mushrooms, Lucius Annaeus Seneca, the politician and satirist, wrote *Apocolocyntosis divi Claudii* (The Pumpkinification of the Divine Claudius).
4. A reference to *fukuwarai*, a New Year's game for children. A blindfolded player tries to place pieces of paper in the shape of eyebrows, eyes, nose, and mouth within the outline of a puffy-cheeked female face.

10

Mama Drinks Her Tea

Ogino Anna

1. Those Were the Good Days

In the living room, dim in the first light of day, Mama is drinking her tea. No rose-colored dawn is shining through the cross weave of the window blinds. Nor are the bulbuls chirping in the tangerine tree. The dregs of night still clinging to the corners of the chilly room, yet another sullen day is about to begin.

It is an uncertain moment—too early to do the calisthenics broadcast over the radio, and too late to catch another few minutes of sleep. Mama slouches and drinks her strongly brewed green tea, letting her thoughts drift in many directions: could she save the tangerine tree from the persistent attack of the bulbuls, and who decreed that morning follow the sleep of night? When she was younger, she could digest the night in dreamless sleep; but age brought with it problems of indigestion because the unabsorbed remainder of one day was carried forward to the next. These thoughts made her sad. As the caffeine coursed through her limbs, and the gray haze lifted from her brain cells, there spread before her a view of her hometown in the Banshū Plain, where the season was spring.

The wheat-stamping season is over. You see, wheat stamping is winter. Later, when the sprouts of wheat lengthen, and the ground is golden all around you, then it is summer. No, wait, it is spring, not summer, that I was talking about just a second ago. (She lights a cigarette and sends out smoke in a big puff.) *Violets are blossoming on the worn brown riverbank, and some wild thistle is pushing through the spaces between the dried eulalia. The sound of the water is beautiful, really. A slender creek cuts through the wide riverbank, and its*

"Uchi no okan ga ocha o nomu" (1989). From *Josei sakka shirīzu* (Women Writers Series), Kadokawa Shoten, vol. 22, 1998. Copyright 1998 by Anna Ogino. Translated by Vyjayanthi Ratnam Selinger with the permission of the author. Translation copyright 2011 by Vyjayanthi Ratnam Selinger.

surface has a sparkle here, a sparkle there. Fū-chan would chew "koppon" by the riverbed. I found it sour myself and didn't eat it so often. Eh? You don't know what koppon *is? It has a thick stalk, but the inside is hollow. More or less just a thick stalk. We cracked them in our hands, threw them into our mouths, chewed on them, and spat them out. At least, I think that's what we did. Me, I didn't eat them. But Fū-chan, why, she'd eat anything, even silverberries. Really tart, very tart, those berries were.* (She puckers her mouth.)

Fū-chan's older sister, Yae-chan, was so nearsighted she was practically blind. When she tried something new, she smelled it very carefully. Her eyes would pull into slits—just like this—and she would draw the food to her eyes until they almost touched. She would pore over it, putting it in her mouth only after looking it over really carefully. This is what I heard anyway. Fū-chan's house was always very clean. Most people clean by scrubbing only the dirty spots, right? Well, Yae-chan's eyes could not see the dirt, so she got into the habit of always doing a thorough cleaning. This is what I heard, like I said. That's why, no matter when I went to Fū-chan's house, it was always clean.

Yae-chan got run over by an oxcart when she was a kid. This, you know, is our village "mystery." It was a pretty wide road and there weren't any people on it either. An oxcart was trundling down the road, and for some strange reason, Yae-chan got run over by it. What's that? The speed of the oxcart? Come on, with an ox drawing it? It was just lollygagging along, just like a man sauntering. Why, even the feet of children move faster! When the oxcart passed by, five or six children walking home from school just plopped into the back, the empty carriage of the oxcart, that is. Once in a while, when we were walking home from school, we would pass an empty oxcart, and that's what we would do, hippity-hop, just get on. No question, walking would have been faster, but the swaying oxcart was more fun. And besides, it was no big deal for the ox to have five or six small kids piling on. You know, that's how it must have happened. Yae-chan, she must have been riding along, and must have been run over when she was getting off. This, right here (she points to the right calf), *became a swollen lump. Anyway, that's another story.*

Yae-chan's older brother, Take-chan, now his eyes were even worse.
"Take-chan, here comes a puddle!"
"All right, watch me go over it!"
Splash, he lands in the puddle.

In the end Yae-chan never married. You see, if she had ended up coming back to her parents, she would have been called a "back again" divorcee. She gave it some serious thought, especially since she had vision problems. So I heard that she turned down marriage offers that came her way, and that she and her half-blind brother stayed on in the house as sister- and brother-in-law, living with the family that their other sister made with her husband.

I wonder what she ended up doing later in life. . . .

There's a neatly clipped hedge of bitter orange plant around Fū-chan's house. The top is neat and rectangular, trimmed to be around eye level. It has big thorns. What's that, you ask? The bitter orange is what they call a citrus family fruit, one of those things. It has these big thorns, right? No, it's not like the rose or something. No, not on the trunk. On the branches, right on the branches, there are these big thorns. Even when you prune it carefully, there are thorns. So the neighbors would drop their washed laundry on these hedges to dry. See here, this is what it was like: it was great—the clothes wouldn't fly off with the wind because they would cling to the thorns. What, you don't understand? Listen carefully, you silly goose. There was a river close to Fū-chan's house. The neighbors would wash their clothes in the river and drop them off to dry on Fū-chan's citrus hedge, and then pick them up when they were dry. Omatsu-san, who lived with Toku-chan and Kitchan's grandmother, would drop off practically anything to dry, even underskirts. You think it's a bit like drying your panties on someone else's front porch? Well you're not far off, though a waistcloth is square, kind of like a big handkerchief, so maybe it is slightly better.

Kitchan's grandmother, she used to live really close to the river. Later on, she moved a little further away. She would carry her chopsticks and porcelain and wood bowls in a basket, and come down to the river to wash them. After she was done washing the dishes, she would reach under her kimono and tug at the end of the underskirt. It would slide to the ground, and she would wash it, just like that, after she was done with the dishes. And this is what she would mutter, "If it flows three inches, it is a great river." That's it. I heard this story from others too.

Fū-chan would bring two tangerines from her garden to the field trips. No, not a bitter orange. It is too small and too hard—it can't be eaten. Your mouth would get bent out of shape. By the bitter orange hedge, there was a tangerine tree. That's right, tangerines. She would share one of those tangerines with me, and I in turn would give her one of my boiled eggs. Eggs in those days were rare treats. Fū-chan would look so pleased. Fū-chan's tangerines were green, a really bright green. And oh were they tart!

It was always clean in Fū-chan's house. Fū-chan was one of those kids who would cackle happily at anything that was said. We played together every day *till the third grade. When we were young, we never stayed home. We would get up in the mornings and "do rounds" of the neighborhood. We were "gathering information" on the village, so to speak. We would go to the riverbank afterward, or go play at our houses—you know, every day, summer and winter. Those were the good days. Wild violets are the prettiest things. Growing plain pansies in parks, now that just isn't right. Yes, violets in the wild, grape-red violets. That's right, they used to have these things called grape-red violets. We would eat them by the riverbed, they were pretty sweet. You know, those things.* (She uses her thumb and index finger to draw a circle in the air. For a second, I mistake it for a coin.) *What's that they called the thing with the small berries? Ah, now I remember, the flowering almond. They weren't tasty or anything, mind you, but they were better than the silverberries. We would hunt for these like crazy and then munch on them. The flowering almonds grew in people's yards, not by the riverside. Some people also grew raspberries in their yards. Yeah, we got yelled at when we got caught. I joined in the stealing because the lotus seeds from the lotus pond and the raspberries were the only two tasty things around.*

Now Fū-chan's place had a large yard that stretched all the way from the citrus hedge to the house. Everyone called it "the corner". On summer evenings, all the children in the village would gather there. There were benches in the yard; two benches, I think. We would sit on those benches, just fanning ourselves to cool off. Only in the evenings, you understand. During the day, everyone had to do housework, even the kids—you know, babysitting and so on. I would spend the evenings either at Fū-chan's or at the "ten'ya" next door. What's a "ten'ya"? Ten'ya was the store next door; our next door neighbors ran a shop. A general store, I suppose you would call it. We used to gaze at the Milky Way as we lolled on the stools. That's how we spent our days all the way to the third grade. In fourth grade, though, we were put in different classes, and we lost touch. We haven't seen each other since then. I have no idea what happened to her after that.

But you know, just around the time when Fū-chan reached adulthood, her mother died. All the members of her family belonged to the Tenrikyō sect. They would chant, "Exorcise evil and save us!" Not just that. When her mother fell ill, they would not call a doctor. Instead, I heard, they fed her paper, small bits of paper, from the Tenrikyō sect. I bet they would be mad if they heard me call it bits of paper. I don't exactly know what it was, but I heard that she would swallow talismans. According to the story, that's how she died.

Fū-chan spoke to my grandmother in her sadness.

"You are alive, right, Auntie? Why did my mother have to die?"

They were eating very simply, to pinch pennies, and so they didn't call a doctor. Thinking back, that's probably why she died.

Whenever I went to Fū-chan's place, the only snacks they served were sweet-potato ends, hard, stonelike pickles, and coin crackers. Coin crackers are sugarless and hard, really hard. We'd cook them quickly in the baking pan, and oh were they tough to chew. You couldn't get them down your throat even after chomping and gnawing on them. You see, at Fū-chan's place, they farmed and, as a side business, they also sold fresh and fried tofu. They probably made twenty tofu cakes and a handful of fried tofu pieces every day. Sometimes, I hear, they would take just one sheet of fried tofu and divvy it up among the family members. Besides, they grew their own vegetables at home. That's how they built their family savings, and that's how they died.

That's pretty much all I know about Fū-chan.

No, no, you got it wrong! The story about the Western plates is not about Fū-chan—it's the one about the sewing store. We call it the sewing store, but they don't really sell sewing machines. It's really a clothing store. They sell men's suits made with the sewing machine. So one night, around dinnertime, one of the neighbors went to the sewing store. And right there, in the middle of the dining table, he saw coin-shaped slices of something bright heaped onto a Western plate. And some rice. That's it, just a bunch of people holding rice bowls in their hands sitting in a circle around a Western plate.

"*That's a beautiful thing you have there. What is it?*"

"*Oh, it's just eggplant.*"

Basically, they had cut some raw eggplant into round slices. Their grandma liked to chew on raw eggplant in the fields, and her son had taken after her. Raw eggplants must be really sour!

Mama poured some tea for herself while I got myself some coffee. During those hours "spent in idleness,"[1] I had experimented with different kinds of coffee. In the end, I had settled on a City Roast of Colombian beans finely ground into a light espresso. I would fill up my "aluminum Marilyn Monroe," my tight-waisted hexagonal coffeemaker, with water. Then, I would heap two teaspoons of ground beans and wait for it to steam. And soon it would deliver an Americano made from a French blend—a blended, stateless, piping-hot beverage. You too may want to try an aluminum Marilyn after reading my intricate recipe. And the nut-brown hot beverage that it delivers will perhaps also taste of loneliness and tedium.

These things are really immaterial. At the same time, if we were to cut away all the immaterial things in our lives, in the end we would all be like the snake that swallowed its tail—stuck.

Even when I am lazing around in the living room with my feet up, watching TV, and thinking these thoughts, I feel like there is a steep precipice behind me. I feel queasy, as if a slug were stuck to my back. If I close my eyelids, I see a naked baby floating around the pitch-black universe. That baby turns out to be me, and I feel the urge to start wailing. At such moments, I like to make my coffee as deliberately as possible, and repeat to myself that famous line "I am happiest when there is nothing to distract me and I am in stasis, alone and just being." What am I saying? Is it really a good thing to have nothing to distract me, I sigh to myself.

I have decided for myself that man is at all times, even in company, "without distraction and all alone." And yet why, I wonder, am I hopelessly diverted by random memories of the past? Thinking back, I always conclude that those days were the best. No matter who I am with, "those days" always seem better than "now." The self-indulgence of man is higher than the mountains and deeper than the seas. This self-indulgence, deeper than the seas, is what relieves you from your lonely idleness.

2. Verdant Barley and Bourbon

Toku-san's house was halfway through town. When Toku-san was young, he liked to go night crawling. No, no, night crawling isn't just men going after women. The Buddhist priest who lived in town—now he was a looker—people used to say that the village widow went night crawling to see him. I am not really sure whether night crawling is something men do or women do.

The young people would share their night-crawling exploits with one another. That is when Toku-san said of Omatsu-san, That woman is hairless."

Now he went around saying this, so all the young people knew. And of course, since they talked about it at home, the whole town knew as well. Toku-san had never once considered taking her as his wife. But, Omatsu-san, now she was a frightening woman. I don't know what happened, but in the end he had to marry her.

That Omatsu-san would get jealous. Was she jealous! Whenever Toku-san opened his mouth, he would say something like, "You know what I think? I wish that both men and women had their things on their foreheads. Then when we bowed to one another, our foreheads would touch. Wouldn't that be great!"

Toku-san was always talking dirty. Though Omatsu-san would rage with jealousy, Toku-san was never one to do anything—he just liked to talk.

One day, Toku-san was on his way home from the fields. Far off in the distance, Mitchan, with her hair down, was also walking home with a hoe. It was around the time of year when the barley plants begin to send out little green shoots. Green barley fields stretched between them in rows of neat parcels.

Since I was pretty close to Toku-san at that moment, I saw and heard everything with my own eyes and ears. Suddenly, Toku-can yelled out to Mitchan. I thought he had some business with Mitchan, but then—

"Hey there, Mitchan. (Pointing to the barley) Do yours come out this much?"

Mitchan stopped walking and yelled back.

"What's that again?"

"Your stuff over there, does it come out this much?"

"Whaaat?"

So they went back and forth about three or four times. Suddenly Mitchan realized. She scowled, brought up her chin, turned her body away from him, raised the hoe onto her shoulders, and stomped away. At first, I had no idea what had happened. Minutes after she had walked away in anger like that, it struck me. Of course, Mitchan would get angry at something like that!

What's that? How old was Mitchan? She was at that budding stage, you know, just like the barley shoots. She was about a year younger than I was. At that moment, there was nobody around but Mitchan, Toku-san, and me. It may have been lunchtime and everyone was at home. No, wait. Back then, there were very few people around anyway. In fact, it occurs to me now that Toku-san was shouting to make sure that I heard as well. It has taken this many years for it to occur to me. Ha-ha, that's funny.

So you see, those days were better.

You know, you probably shouldn't tell these stories to others. I might end up in deep-red shame. Hmm, I wonder if shame is always red.

Mama retreated to her bedroom muttering silently to herself about the color of shame. Mama sometimes drinks things other than tea and it makes her more talkative than usual. I, on the other hand, drink after I am alone. I break the seal on my favorite Bourbon in Toku-san's memory. It's called Four Roses and has vibrant roses flowering on its yellow label. Just four roses with four leaves arranged together in a circular pattern. It's an insipid design, but it is also strangely bright and lurid. It warms the heart if one keeps looking at it.

Bourbon is the drink that helps me remember "those days."

Helped by the drink, memories rise like bubbles from the sluggish, bottomless marsh of memory. Filtered through both drink and memory, the past is always available in a rosy hue. We like to color the past in a rosy shade because we know there is no rose-colored life.

Who am I? What kind of person am I at this moment in my life? I cannot find the answers to these questions even though they are so important to me. That is why I cling so tightly to the self that I see in my memories.

My rosy self in a rosy frame. Clasped by one specimen of the humanoid

species of the mammalian group inhabiting the opaque irregular present continuative tense. A scene that makes me sick to my stomach.
"Nothing prevents happiness like the memory of happiness." (André Gide)
It can be said more concisely, surely.
"Memories of happiness are the seeds of unhappiness." (Me)
Or, for that matter,
"Memory is the opiate of the human species." (Me)
Or,
"Happiness comes to the door of those who forget." (Me)
Or,
"Forgetting is like dieting for the heart." (Me)
And so, I would like to keep as many things forgotten as possible.

What I would like to forget first is the fact that I have loved so many cities—no, that I may yet love them. For some reason, the vessel of my heart seems to have been made to love stone-paved streets. I get intoxicated and lose myself when I smell the damp mildew rising from stone-hewn walls—who knows how many frosts and suns they have seen—of a Romanesque cathedral on the verge of collapse, forgotten in the flow of time. On fresh summer mornings, I listen from my bed to the sound of stiletto heels as they sound loudly against the cobbled pavement. Then I curl up and doze off in my cool sheets. Emerald skies filling the windows. The spire of a distant church. Crows. Rooftops linked to one another like wavelets rising and falling, and instead of the toss of ocean spray, the gleaming television antennas, adding color to the monotony of the sea of the city. It would be even better if a river cut through a city like this. And a tower placed in the center of the city—just perfect!

I used to live in a city called P. that was close to "perfect." Not that I wasn't in love with someone then, but now that face looks blurred and covered by mist. Behind it, I see right through the streetscape of P. I had been living, certain that I was in love with this person. But the moment I left P., everything disappeared, like an appendage falling off. This happened two or three times before I realized that it was really P. that had roused my affection, and that I had used my human lover as the release. Jupiter would capture the hearts of his mortal female lovers by transforming himself into golden rain, into a steer, and, at times, into a male swan. In my case, I wonder, can I win the city's heart only by becoming a city myself? Are cities sexed—male and female? How is it that cities "multiply"?

I traveled to other kinds of cities when I lived in P. In a manner of speaking, P. was the legal wife, and I was straying in search of another kind of "perfection." My drink today evokes nostalgic memories of B., a town I encountered during one such "cheating" trip.

City B. did not have a small tower. But it did sit on the estuary of the River G. before it poured into the Atlantic Ocean. The spirits of the sea and the river doted on B., for the ground was fecund and the skies sparkled; it was a country town where the hearts of its inhabitants were at peace.

What links B. to Bourbon? In the beginning, I will pretend as if I were moving away from Bourbon. Occasionally stealing glances, I will approach it again.

Speaking of B., there is a world-famous wine that honors the town with its name. In its appearance, B. is classical yet quietly showy; it is bright and reminds one of a perfectly clear yet strangely sad breeze. Come nightfall, this is a town whose back silhouette can look like a woman—doesn't matter, she could be a slip of fifteen or a hag of ninety—and this town gave birth to a liquor. I came to love both the town and the drink through a woman called C. who hailed from B. Like the prototype of women from this town, the structure of her face had many problems from a purely objective standpoint. But taken in its entirety, it was an utterly beautiful face. It was her eloquent love for her hometown that sent me into the arms of B.

I walk through the main street that runs through B. Not much of a main street, just a well-maintained long stretch of road. There should have been a thoroughfare of people, but the street that appears before my eyes now is empty and serene. Every corner of the street is bathed in the afternoon glow of early spring, and this gives the bleached-looking walls of the neatly aligned rows of buildings a creamy coloring.

Who knows where I walked? I traveled to the edge of town, where, suddenly, I came upon a scene that shook me out of my time frame. The proper little street with the tidy row of modern houses came to an end. Beyond it lay a Roman stone archway basking in the light of the setting sun, just as it might have eons ago. The arch was simple and elegant, quite suited to being the portal to the town. As I passed through this gate, the time that had enveloped me took flight—the silhouette of the town of today blurred over its visage of the past, creating a third and different time frame.

There was a shop near the gate that lured one into buying coffee. The shop mistress was a typical B. town beauty. She good-naturedly lent an ear to the chitchat of the travelers, and the travelers, for their part, took second helpings of the coffee while she plied them with tidbits of the chocolate that was for sale. The twiglike chocolate treats, a novelty of the B. region, had a whiff of orange. The coffee itself deserved to be called "the devil's sympathy," for it was guaranteed to set your stomach on fire after the third strongly brewed cup.

With a little coaxing from the coffee, the little demon who lived in my entrails took a trip to a seaside town far from B. in search of oysters.

He paused at the headland to watch the watery desertlike expanse of the

February ocean dissolve into the misty sky. A bedraggled dog jumped into the sea and seemed to swim forever and ever. Some citizens of B. disinterestedly looked on. An old man with a thick local accent muttered in a deep voice.

"They seem to swim great distances, don't they?"

Still the dog went on swimming. I wonder what happened to that old dog.

Bleak. Cheap eateries in desolate tourist towns during the off-season neatly fit this adjective. The chipped paint, the dust collecting listlessly with nowhere to go, the cold chairs. On the way back from the sea, he stopped at a joint like that and drank watery beer with some oysters.

The main purpose of the trip, now forgotten.

The little gut-dwelling demon has a bad habit—he gets overexcited whenever he travels. He said in coaxing tone, "Why don't you quit drinking coffee and drink something better?" I had not yet recovered from the strain of the previous day's travels, and my brain had morphed into a squelchy sponge, heavy with sleep. I drew my pillow in closer, and crushed the bait of the demon with a long yawn. But he was no ordinary foe. He gave a wicked kick to my abdomen while it was relaxing at the end of a breath, and screamed. "Come on, hurry up! If you don't drink while you can, you won't be able to drink later. That's how life works." The bitter words of the demon seeped from my abdomen through my esophagus to my tongue, and I found myself violently thirsty. *Sitio!* (Upon the cross, even the Lord Jesus says, "I am thirsty.")

I learned, to my surprise, that the municipality of B. was hosting a tasting of local spirits at its official House of Wine. A good-looking government official, a typical B. town beauty, was pouring glass after glass of different wines.

At 11:00 AM a foreigner left the House of Wine with tottering feet. A steely blue sky stretched over his head. In the taut light, the town was a blazing yet coolly white soul. The town square, the theater, the water fountain. To the tipsy eye, mere stone will look like marble. I wonder if stones dream too? I wonder if stone thirsts as well? *Sitio!* (Even he is saying, "I am thirsty. . . .)

Demons are persevering, and man never learns from his mistakes.

I undertook another journey the day after my visit to the House of Wine to sample the local spirits in the highlands to the north. We made our ascent up gentle slopes, rocked by a bus that plied only a few times to these uplands. The slopes of the hill were lined with vineyards, sure to be dripping in green by the summer. Even after the bus dropped us off, we continued our trudge upward, passing by rustic villages curled up in the cold.

Every house clung to the ground like a crushed toad, and the virtually slopeless roofs were covered with pebbles the size of large rice cakes. The giant gray rabbit who lived in the skies seemed to have relieved himself, from time to time, of ash-colored feces. The accumulated dung had formed the roofs, but under them there wasn't anybody to be found. It hit me—there was no sign of life whatsoever in this town. No rustling leaves. That is to say, the town had no body temperature. Even at midday, the town, empty of both man and sound, reeked of a nightmare.

The only soul I met that day was the town Bacchus on a bike. The old man's nose was a vivid burgundy. I stopped this man to ask him where the town's House of Wine was located.

"Much further away."

His scratchy nasal twang still clings to my eardrums.

That day, after journeying "much further" to get that one glass of wine with a kick, I learned a valuable lesson. Thou shalt not journey to vineyards in February. Naked grape trunks are eerily gnarled. Black rheumatic hands, warped in anger, reach out from the ground. Thousands of hands frozen to the spot as they writhe, in futile agony, to recall their fallen leaves, their snatched fruits, the memory of a summer now past.

Even trees dream.

Even trees do get thirsty.

The thirst for something lost to eternity renders the next season's fruits that much sweeter. A well-mellowed wine is born from an irrecoverable loss.

The night before I left B., I sat for a lot longer than I expected at an alley restaurant. They had a TV set. One gets sentimental sitting around a TV set in a foreign town. I left the place only after watching a singing show to the very end, nursing my nameless drink the whole while. Leave the side street, and it puts you in the main thoroughfare. Night it was, but barely 9:00 or 10:00 PM, and yet there was not a soul to be seen on the street. It was a serene night. Something, I couldn't tell gas or liquid, stole coolly across my cheeks into the night.

Not a human soul. But *something* was around. I was inside *something*. I was walking inside that *something*, all the while sensing the presence of something more furtive than a human or an animal. A second look at my surroundings—all the buildings and the sidewalks were made of stone. Mineral ores probably have their own breathing rhythms.

I called it city, the goblin I created in my mind with the stone entrails made by man. This goblin appears to have a figure, but in fact its outline is invisible. It has eyes all over the body, but lacks a head. It stretches its limbs, and the road ahead grows longer. A hundred arms twisting and locking with a hundred legs. Close it as frequently as you might, it remains open. And bottomless. The sky is the bottom of the city. If I were to stand on my head right here, I would feel as if I were being sucked into the bottomless trap of the night sky. I was probably a little drunk, for such thoughts were running through my mind.

Suddenly, from somewhere ahead of me, the sound of festive voices ricocheted off the streets toward me. A few B. towners in their twenties were reeling and lurching, making their way toward me with uncertain feet. As they approached me, a phrase popped into my head: good men and women. Radiant in their youth and drunkenness, their faces resembled those in Fra Angelico's paintings. Their blank faces, wiped clean of impure thoughts by the virtuous powers of alcohol, sometimes took on a fathomless smile. A bottle that looked like whiskey was being passed from hand to hand, its contents increasingly depleted.

The good men and women reached me around the middle of the thoroughfare. We started up some idle chitchat. Where we came from, where we were headed, that kind of thing. They had gone to celebrate something momentous for some student—that was pretty much it. Even so, I laughed at things they said, and they laughed at things I said. Those out-of-sync laughing voices, those irregular whispers. This polyhedral mass of high spirits took wing and vanished into the starless night, leaving only a faint twenty-watt trace of light.

The bottle of whiskey had somehow found its way into my hands. That was my first sip of Bourbon. In theory, the most delightful Bourbon I have tasted in my whole life. That was pretty much it.

We had been talking about loving cities when the talk turned to human beings. Takeda Tetsuya had crooned that one can love only another *human* soul. On a giddy night like this, one feels like easily agreeing, and yet, I wonder if it is true.

Smitten by someone who swore against instant coffee, I became a coffee enthusiast.

Then, smitten by someone who could quaff shots of whiskey, I became a whiskey fancier.

Their faces are forgotten, but I continue to drink coffee and Bourbon.

Are material objects more powerful than people?

Mama, what is it like to be head over heels in love with another person?

3. Feigned Madness and Drunken Caprice

The village was just like my family: everyone pretty much knew about one another. Strangers were rare, just the Bear Lady from Nishiyama and the Akasaka nut.

(Upon being asked if she was referring to the Akasaka district in Tokyo) *No, no. Akasaka was probably his last name. Yeah, I think that may have been it. He came from a good family in a distant village—-that's what I heard af-*

terward anyway. He was mad enough to be called a nut. At least, the children were convinced that he was. He would paint his face a chalky white, and then with the scraped black char from pan bottoms, he would give himself a small, pursed mouth. Splotchy white too, his face was. His red undershirt ruffled at the collar. Several layers of garishly patterned kimonos thrown over that. And a beggar's bag hanging from his neck.

Yeah, he was mad, but he never behaved violently. Always well behaved. (How old, you ask?) *The children couldn't tell how old he was. Come to think of it, he didn't seem to have that many wrinkles on his face. He walked around from house to house asking for alms. Some people dropped him a penny, and some emptied an entire bowl of rice into his bag. He may have done good business that way. They say, you know, that with teaching and begging, you do it for three days and you're in for a lifetime. Some of the adults said he was mad, and others that he was a smart fellow, just slightly off-kilter, that's all. All in all, he had a good racket going. Walking around all day on a sunny day, he must have raked in quite a lot.* (Where am I going with this story?) *That's all.*

Bear Lady and the Akasaka nut came very rarely. They would come just when people had started to forget about them. So the children would look at them with great curiosity.

Now Bear Lady from Nishiyama was gigantic—you know, the kind of person who walks around with her kimono gaping open. She always wore a short, pinstriped cotton kimono the color of red-bean jelly. With the hem riding a little high. And thick feet sticking out. Thump-thump like a drumbeat, that's how she walked, with her thighs and toes turned outward. She had a bundle wrapped in a large kerchieflike thing that was tied over the shoulder and slung across the back. Well, I guess they call that a handbag these days. And for some strange reason, she carried a stick. She loped about town with the stick in hand, not really using it as a walking stick. Looking back, I think that she may have been a young woman. I was really young, maybe in elementary school. For someone of that age, she was a formidable old woman.

I wonder what she was. A beggar perhaps? Then again, I don't really remember her walking from house to house panhandling. (What was she then, she is asked. She hangs her head down thoughtfully for a moment, and then with sudden purpose, she says) *I don't know. But whenever the woman came to town, all the children gathered around. Bear Lady is here, the Bear Lady is here! Everyone would come running to that call. Turning to her, we would shout,*

"*Bear Lady! Bear Lady!*"

She would chase after the kids swinging her stick. The kids would run, scattering like baby spiders. In any case, she was a good diversion for us.

And here's something I heard. She went into town to eat at a restaurant in the Mitsukoshi Department Store. The waitress there asked her, "Are you carrying money?" She flew into a rage, reached into the beggar's bag, and . . . What, wasn't she carrying a kerchief bundle on her back, you ask? No, no, you're getting it all wrong. She also carried a beggar's bag in addition to the kerchief bundle. She gadded about in that short kimono of hers, a bunch of dangly things hanging off her body. The Akasaka nut was more droopy-saggy, and he looked more like seaweed. Well, she wasn't as bad as the Akasaka nut, but she definitely had that straggly look. That's right, now I remember: she did have a beggar's bag too. She turned it upside down, swung it around, and sent its contents smashing to the floor. Fifty sen coins, ten sen coins rolled around the floor. Fifty sen is a good sum of money, you know. Of course, there must have been plenty of one sen coins as well. Wait, something else is coming back to me. The village had two buses. There was a stool in the bus depot, where she was perched. The bus came backing to the shed and the driver found her. He asked her to flash him. He said he would give her one sen if she would. That's what I heard, anyway. Now, I can't remember whether she did or didn't flash him. Anyway, the pile of coins on the floor must have had a few of those one sen coins as well. What happened, you ask, after she had dashed the coins to the floor? She dashed them to the floor, that's all there is to the story. That's all I heard, that she threw them to the floor.

Mama says, *"You know, there are no beggars around anymore,"* and slurps her tea with her small head hung low. Her eyes narrow as they gaze upon the drooping plum tree in the garden, and she sighs at the realization that the weeds are overgrown.

I am drinking plum and kelp tea, as I always do mornings after I have had too much to drink. What is the worst thing in the world? The worst thing is when your stomach can't even hold down coffee. What is a hangover? . . . I had spent my anger in rubbing out the entry for hangover in our dictionary till it was black. The stomach is one's dearest partner in life. If one can't nurture it with good wines and delicacies, then I would wish, at least, for an undefeated, resilient gut like the homeless guy's in P.

For the homeless guy in P., a bottle of the cheap red is like a necktie to the white-collar worker: the two cannot be separated.

The homeless guy in P. was a descendant of Diogenes. A whole day spent with leaden eyes and cheap alcohol, and he still would show no signs of a hangover. Like a stone unconcerned with passing traffic, and still to the world like a frozen Bodhidharma, he would glare imperiously at the world below him, all the while ruminating on his vagrant philosophy, or indeed, the vagrancy of philosophy itself.

The street corner takes on a new expression when the homeless old man dressed in a concrete-colored overcoat settles down on his bench, with a bottle in hand and a stroller full of his possessions parked beside him. On the surface, P. has the soft and meticulously maintained face of a high-class prostitute. The red lip gloss of "art" and the eye shadow of "culture" shine beautifully against the luxurious foundation of "history." When P. breaks into a smile, currency from the world over dances on her streets, and the easy money from tourism comes pouring in. But place the homeless old man next to her, and her supple skin turns leathery—it is then that the first real human expression devoid of makeup is born.

The protagonists of P.'s underside are beggars, vagrants, pickpockets, street thieves, Gypsies who also do begging and thieving, Gypsies with more responsible professions, students working part-time as street performers, full-time street performers, alcoholics who stagger around train platforms shouting, "I see a rat!" and transients with Middle Eastern and Asian accents.

A meek "foreigner with an Asian accent" in P., I spent my days nervously, watching the other protagonists perform their attacks and retreats. I was hit by a pickpocket once, and fended off a street thief another time. I developed the habit of lowering my eyes and breaking into a run the moment I saw a Gypsy with a middle-age belly, a sheet of paper with a sob story in one hand, and a baby of uncertain parentage slung over the other shoulder. Surprise panhandling became a trend: some of these folks would thrust out their hand at an unsuspecting passerby, asking for a hundred yen. Asked once for a hundred yen in this fashion, I turned around to look at the fellow and found him in a better state than I. It was pitiful.

I learned to pass my days in this fashion. Man can somehow survive as long as he learns to throw out his possessions and stiffen his resolve. When I am feeling distressed, I often think: if it gets worse, I can always hit the streets and panhandle, asking for a hundred yen.

Or, I could sit on the sidewalk holding my knees; buildings to my back and an empty can in front. If it got too embarrassing, I could always burrow my face between my knees. I could place a piece of cardboard beside me with the words "I am hungry" dashed off in large lettering. Alternatively, I could pick up a dog and have the cardboard read instead, "The two of us are hungry."

I could buy some colored chalk and draw on the sidewalk, pictures of flowers, Christ, and clowns. I might even leave a can with a hundred-yen coin in it near the pictures.

I could find a companion who was able to sing, and we could move from one subway compartment to another performing. After each song, we could smile and thrust out hats to the passengers. We can neither be too good nor too bad at singing; nor can the hat be too big or small.

But in the end, it is the hobo cradling a bottle that takes the cake. He is neither helpful nor a hindrance. He never shaves and owns only one pair of shoes and one set of clothes. There are oil stains on his clothes, and grime as well. In places, the grime has a coating of oil over it, upon which another layer of grime has settled. Over time, the oil and grime bind together, becoming thicker than the cloth beneath, and the old man's face, awash in rain and filth, becomes leathery like parchment.

On winter nights, the old man lays a sheet of paper over the subway vents and settles down for the night in his clothes. On most nights, he sleeps as if dead to the world. Sometimes, he does die in his sleep like that. The year that a record-breaking cold front hit the city of P., the park fountains froze into a giant icicle, and the tangerines we had left out iced up. The entire town advanced from being a natural refrigerator to a natural freezer. This is how many of the old men died.

It is strange to have one's feet bump into sleeping people when one is walking about. There is the vertical self, and then there is the horizontal old man. The moving self and the immobile old man. Passing by the sleeping figure at death's door, I feel momentarily as if I have touched with my bare hands something that I should not have. My heart is laid bare, naked. I think about returning to the dawn of mankind, when there were neither good things nor bad things.

4. The Fox, the Dog, and the Cat

Shiro had a plot of land across from the temple, but over to the side. What's that you say? When I say across but to the side, I mean across but to the side. Look here, here's this, and here's that (drawing a diagram). *Oh I see, you call that diagonally across, do you? Okay, so it is to the right. Not that it matters whether it is to the right or left.*

Shiro believed that wheat fields do well as long as you have plenty of fertilizer. Sure enough, his wheat stalks grew taller and thicker than those in other fields. (Holding her arms open wide in demonstration) *They were this tall and they would fall when the wind blew. So Shiro got worried and placed stakes around the plot and strung some rope all around the wheat stalks. What's that? Look, here's the way it was.* (A diagram. Four stakes for each furrow, two at each edge. Two lengths of rope strung in a way that they ran parallel to the furrows.) *All around the field, mind you. Each furrow with its own rope. And the wheat stalks stopped falling after that. That far, everything was fine. But it was a strange thing to see. People walking by always stopped to look. They thought it looked odd because they had never seen anything like it.*

When they started bringing the harvest in, the crop was really small in comparison. You know what I think? The stalks and the leaves took up all the nourishment and there wasn't enough to go around to the berries.

As the fourth son, Shiro had to leave the family home and set up his own branch line. He moved out to a small, no, more like a medium-size house. His family built him a proper house, with his own fields to farm. And naturally, he got himself a beautiful and considerate wife. Shiro was something of a dreamer—you know, he went to work for the railroad company, but didn't get further than a janitor's post. People say that he swept the platforms for a living, and is still at the same job. But he got himself that wife because of the land and the house, that's how it was back in those days too. He used to tie up worn brooms with frayed ends into a neat big bunch. Knowing that he would be scolded by his wife, he would first leave it leaning against the temple fence in a spot no one would see. He would go home with a nonchalant look on his face. Later, he would quietly steal it into the storage closet in his house. That's what Shiro told someone else, I hear.

What did he do with the broomsticks, you ask? He must have used them for that, I bet—as the stake for the rope to put around the wheat fields.

Shiro's family, like everyone in the area, farmed. The men held day jobs in banks, schools, but mostly on the railroad. They had jobs, sure, but everyone at home got together and farmed. The father-in-law, the mother-in-law, and the bride. Subsistence farming, I believe they call it—you know, making just enough for the single family to eat.

Shiro would return from the night shift at the railroad, and the guy next door would be over massaging his wife's shoulders. The old guy was often over at Shiro's house. He had a face like a dwarf and his back was slouched, to be sure. But he was sensible and wise. Shiro said to my grandmother, "The old man next door is very kind, you know. When I came home from work, he was massaging my wife's shoulders."

All the neighbors were gossiping about the unusual relationship between Shiro's wife and the guy next door. The only one who didn't know was Shiro himself. Shiro, you know, was a good soul.

"I myself don't know how to use money. But my wife puts it to good use."

He wasn't being sarcastic, he really meant it. He was simply a really good man. He was blessed that way.

He was always quite healthy and energetic. That's right, now it is coming back to me. Shiro, who had never once fallen sick, apparently once said to my grandmother, "I may look this way, but there is something wrong with me."

I don't know why, but Shiro adopted a child along the way when he couldn't have one of his own. They lavished love on the kid, both of them. The kid,

strangely enough, grew to resemble the wife more and more. Everyone talked about it. "Kids start to look like their mothers over time, don't they?"
(When asked whether the wife had given birth to that child) *No, you've got it wrong. It can't be right. I feel certain about it. Think about it, we would have heard about it if her belly had gotten big and she had had to go home to her parents. People in the village know these things.*

Of course, there were people whose bellies never got big but were gone for long periods of time, only to return with an "adopted" child. Yes, there was one woman like that, who lived in the same village but at its outskirts. Our house was also at the edge of the village, but her house was further out. The young woman in that family got herself operated on, for a retroverted uterus. That was after many years of trying. Soon after the surgery, her husband got called up for military duty. After waiting around a few months, the girl went back to her birth home. When she came back, she had a child in tow. All the villagers knew that the child was a "gramp baby." A gramp baby is a kid that . . . well, keep listening and you will catch on.

The young woman was a beauty—her face made up with powder and her sash always neatly tied. Her father-in-law was a bit handsome too—he had a keen eye and always liked things to look good. Their doorstep was always neat, with no more than two wooden clogs sitting out. When it was their turn to clean the tombstones, the tombstones would be clean enough to lick. The old lady of the house was always touring the neighborhood, hair tightly pulled back in a bun, and dressed in a deep-indigo kimono tied with a boyish sash. She only went home during mealtimes, that's what people used to say. Of course, a beautiful bride and a good-looking father-in-law are bound to get along well. Everyone agrees on this. (Asked what the husband was like) *How am I supposed to know? I never saw him. He probably looked rumpled like his mother.* (Asked what happened to the husband when he came home from the war) *I don't know. The old lady would carry the baby on her back around the neighborhood, I heard. A happy ending, to be sure.*

The old man, it is said, had something going in the past with the girl's mother. After all, he was quite handsome. The girl's mother had chosen the groom herself. She set him up with her daughter. All ended well, as they say. Things don't turn out this way in novels, do they?

You want to know what happened to Shiro?
Years later, after the children were all happily settled, Shiro retired from the railroad with a pension. The neighbors gossiped that the girl was taking really good care of Shiro—you know, to make sure that Shiro lived a long life. The pension is good only as long as the pensioner is alive, you know. The girl was smart that way.

If Shiro had not died, he would still be around. A happy ending, to be sure.

(I began speaking in Kansai dialect.) This is about something that happened much longer ago, in the Sasayama area of Tanba province. One of the young men in the village had a big black hunting dog. Ugly as a demon, he was. All the kids in the village were quite afraid of him.

One day, the young man went into the forest with his dog. Somewhere along the narrow mountain path, the dog ran into an enormous fox. The startled fox fell backward and began trembling like a leaf. The dog too was frozen to the spot in surprise. The two faced each other, their eyes locked. It may be funny to you now, but it wasn't anything to laugh about back then. Glued to the spot they stared at each other, refusing to either blink or growl. The fox didn't scamper away, and the dog didn't chase after him. Neither of them moved, prolonging their stares. They glared at each other for so long that it appeared that their eyes would fall out of their sockets.

The young man, alarmed that the two weren't moving in the slightest, went to take a closer look. He found both of them with their eyes hanging down from their sockets.

I could call this one of the seven wonders of Tanba or the story of the eyeless fox. But it would be an outright lie, as red a lie as they come. Red is the color of shame but it is also the color of lies, no? I actually read about this in a Western story about strange occurrences. What do you think? Isn't my Kansai accent pretty good?

"Your Kansai accent is pretty good. But your stories, I can't understand. They all seem so fake."

"They are quite tasteful, don't you think, these Renaissance tales performed in a Kansai accent?"

"I couldn't care less about whether they seem sweet or sour. But what does all this amount to? You know what they say, life is stranger than fiction. You haven't seen tough times in life, that's the problem. That is why you spend all your time spinning fabulous tales. If you have the time to waste, why don't you do something worthwhile, like weeding the garden?"

"Sorry for not being more useful around the house. But who are you to complain? You have been sitting around drinking tea and telling strange stories."

"They are not strange stories. They are all real. You, on the other hand, abandon yourself to the pursuit of these incomprehensible stories, leaving me stuck with all the housework. Well, I am certainly entitled to my cup of tea when I get tired. Strongly brewed tea is not just delightful, it is a work of art."

"If you go that far, let me say my share as well. It is offensive to see you drinking 'high art' out of a mug, so stop doing it."

(I resumed my writing.) Mama was in the habit of drinking strongly brewed green tea in a mug illustrated with bears, large enough to easily hold a bottle and a half of milk.

When she went into the kitchen with her empty mug, she found Hanatarō and Otama and their mother at the back door. They were, as always, starved.

"Help us out, will you," they whined. Incidentally, Mama and I are human, but Hanatarō and Otama are cats.

When she first appeared at our door at that retiring age of eighteen, with that dark face of one who has turned her back to mankind, we could not have known that we would come to care for not just her but also her family of two kittens.

Her perverse pride in her past street life ensured that she never got close to us. She would scratch the hands that fed her with a deft left uppercut. She had scratched me twice, and Mama five times. This turned our daily ritual of pouring the special dried cat food (which rather resembled rat droppings) into the mother cat's can into quite a thrilling encounter.

First, we would kick the mother cat away. In the two to five seconds that it took her to return, we would swiftly pour a handful of food into the can. She would then start picking at the food as if it were awful. As always, Hanatarō would get his hand in there. Rather, I mean his face. He would send restless yowls into the air, this surprisingly loquacious child of a taciturn mother. And then, kicking his mother away, he would dive with his head into the can. So perfect was his wide face that it neatly filled the opening—with all of his face stuck in the can. It was an appalling way to eat! A thoroughly ill-bred cat, I would think to myself. But really, my mother and I were responsible for his bad manners. The mother cat was not one to be left out either. Using her special left uppercut swing, she would deliver a stout blow to Hanatarō's head. She would show no mercy—she really gave the swing all she had. Hanatarō would scamper away. Otama, who had bulbous eyes because of a gland disorder, would stare blankly at the two. Mama too would direct her vacant gaze at them.

"Once the object of zealous nurturing, they are now deadly enemies competing for food. Beasts, that's what they are (sigh). I wonder why animals are like this. Why do they nurture their infants at all?"

Mama's back wore an expression somewhere between a laugh and a sob. It occurred to me that she had aged—her backbone looked frail. Her back seemed to be saying to me, "You are making me grow old." When she did turn around, my mother's words were horribly prosaic.

"What should we make for dinner tonight?"

5. Tenacious Attachments and Resigned Acceptance

Kimchi pickles, pollack roe dressed with red pepper, wasabi preserved in rice lees, salted pickled radish, salted opossum shrimp, and salted guts of cod.

To hell with natural foods and a low-salt diet! Some evenings you eat knowing that you deserve to get up the next morning with a bleeding nose and acute high blood pressure. You eat one salty food after another and chase it down with alcohol to neutralize it. Your stomach becomes a Salty Dog, a Red Pepper Stomach, if you will.

Whenever storms come lapping toward the Japanese archipelago, our whole house becomes a low-pressure zone, saturated with air that is unpleasant in every way—humid, slimy, and sticky. My mother starts to feel "reptilian." She lies on the floor like a gigantic lizard, able to flap her eyelids but incapable of any other kind of movement. I slither by her side like a snake that failed to molt successfully and is about to be hanged. I roll around the floor wondering absently to myself how hanging a snake would involve knowing where its neck began and ended. When the night arrives, neither the snake nor the lizard has any desire to cook. On days like this, white rice is glaring to the eye. The fingers of the reptile reach for kimchi, pollack, and cup noodles—processed foods that have a bit of a shadow about them. Yes, there are some nights when you yearn, as if for a childhood home, for the utterly listless taste of MSG in the grounds of dried soup for ramen noodles.

The reptile and the snake sip at the cold sake. They appear to gasp for breath as before.

"Back when I was living in P., things were great. The air in P. was never this humid."

Snakes, apparently, like to complain when they have a little alcohol in their system.

"The winters in P. were pretty humid, as I recall."

The lizard casually slapped the snake with the tail of conscience.

"I insist, P. was just a much better place. Sure, the place is full of pickpockets, rife with terrorism, and the toilets are filthy. People curse at you if you don't speak the language, the great teachers are crafty, and the men and women about town have eyes that rove in search of profit. Daily life was full of tension, and yet the town was redolent with the air of freedom."

"You were a foreigner in P., you had no ties to bind you there. That is all there was to it."

"But you know P. was really wonderful. I could drink cheap wine by the cask. The drink was great and the girls were beautiful."

"You called home from P., wailing that you missed Japanese sake and wanted to eat fermented soybeans."

Mama's memory of "those days" just didn't overlap with my own image of that time. Our memories were pointing in different directions, to the point that they were facing away from each other. Yet we faced each other as we chewed on the kimchi and sipped on the sake. We were two people separated by a generation facing each other over drink. Since she *was* my mother, I suppose it can't be helped that there lay so many years between us. I thought to myself how interesting things would be if parents grew younger as their children grew up. We should just swap our ages with our parents when we turn thirty. It would be quite fascinating—some people would have parents of the same age, and others would be older than their parents. The silly coincidences of age, sex, and geography bring two horribly unlike beings together while preventing two souls meant for each other from ever meeting. God has a perverse way of doing things. After bearing the brunt of the dastardly workings of coincidence, I decided that I would continue to believe in God.

What would have happened if Mama and I had met purely as strangers of the same age? We might have walked past each other, struck by the other's weirdness. I bet that is what would have happened. As I played in my mind with these dangerous thoughts, Mama, who probably sensed something unnatural in the air, spoke up.

"You are my product."

The lizard's tail landed on me like a slap.

"You are the factory that produced me. Is that what you want to say?"

"Those words are blasphemous! You were given to me by God and I raised you. To call you a product was profane. I take back my earlier words."

"You got stuck with a tough one from God, didn't you?"

"There is a saying that goes like this. If you want to gaze at a fool, look at a parent. Parents everywhere think to themselves that they should not have had children at all. Even so, one has to become a parent."

"Why?"

"Because that is the way things are, no particular reason why."

Her voice was suddenly raised. I fell silent. In the same way that parents will always be older than their children, the logic of parents cannot be contested.

When the "present" that two people share slips into memories of "those days," do people always face away from each other? They may share an evening, drink the same sake, and nibble at the same salted foods. But, in the end, two people always have separate dregs of memory.

"Ah, how oddly distressing it all is!"[2]

"What's that you said just now?"

"I said the pairing of a parent and child is an odd thing."

"Why would you call that odd?"

"Parents and their children, husbands and their wives, even friends—it has always seemed odd to me, the coupling of people. There is nothing inevitable about it."
"That is too cynical. Don't be thinking too much about this."
"This pollack is 'distressingly' spicy."
"Touché, my dear. Perhaps I should say that I am 'frightened' by tea.[3] Pour me some, there's a dear."
There goes my mother again, drinking tea.

They laid the highways when I was in third grade. The bus started passing through our town only after the highway was built. (Asked whether it got easier getting around with the buses) *That's right.* (After a pause) *Nobody got on the bus. When I glanced at a passing bus, I would see only two or three people on board.*

They built a little bus stop at the corner of the highway crossing. The guy who ran the nursery built a house right in front of the stop. You know, the sort of home you live in after retirement. The old man and his wife lived there. We called him the "old man from the nursery" even though he had long since quit working there. They lived simply, selling bus tickets and cheap candy. His son would send miso and rice from the main house, so all they had to earn was pocket money. They lived a leisurely life.

Every summer, you would see the old lady in a kimono so crisply starched it looked rectangular. When it was hot, she would walk around with her kimono down to her waist, practically naked. The linen chemise she wore under her clothes would be starched stiff too, mind you. And the kimono she had slipped off would hang by her waist making loud crinkly crumply sounds. Her clothes looked stiff, like on a scarecrow. Normally, kimonos drape around the shape of the body, right? She, on the other hand, had used so much starch that the cloth pulled away from her body. You know, sort of the way kimonos look when they are hung on a rack. I wonder now whether underneath the clothes she was a thin, wiry woman. In any case, it looked like a kimono had walked off its rack and was ambling about.

The old lady was always working with her back bent over something. Probably doing laundry or cleaning the house, now that I think about it. She always looked busy.

As for the old man, he was what you call really still. He was always anchored to a spot. He would look at each person who walked by while stroking his rheumatic arm. Not one person escaped his look.

Sometimes a stranger would walk into the village. Most of the time, they were usually there to "inquire." To "inquire" is to look further into a match. Back in those days, marriages were decided with the help of intermediaries.

The parents would usually travel to the village of the prospective to confirm what the intermediary had said. That's why we called it an "inquiry." The house that the old man of the nursery lived in was right next to the bus stop, and it thus sat at the entrance to the village. Most people would rest their tired feet there. What do you think the old man did? He ruined all the matches. He interfered in every marriage proposal that passed his way. I wonder what he said—how he came up with all the stories. But basically, he finished them off. (Didn't that mean that people in the village couldn't get married?) Luckily, some people would enter the village from the other side.

Many years later, someone came by to inquire about his own grandson. And he broke that off as well. His son and his daughter-in-law were furious. It was quite a scene, I am told.

Unlike the old man, the son and his wife were good people. Many years after the old couple died, the young woman happened to stop by their place. She let some fresh air into the house, which had essentially been closed since the death of the older couple. A truck veered off the highway lanes and ran right into the house. The young woman died on the spot.

Retribution, the village gossips used to say, sometimes skips the sinner and strikes much later, at blameless individuals.

That's the way it is.

The next story is not about retribution but about death, about people who die in a strange fashion.

Hiraku of the Mountaintop—now, I don't mean the summit of a mountain, but a flat area that was known by the name Mountaintop—he was found a whole week after his death. They found him in a large empty house with a mosquito net hanging from the ceiling and the fan still running. This was a long time ago, mind you. Very few people owned a fan. It was not just the fan; it appeared he had been cooking rice on his electric stove, because they found some leftovers. It was quite a rare sight, you know. Most people cooked with firewood and straw. Hiraku's family was a big landowning family. But most landowners didn't use these things. Hiraku was quite enlightened.

Hiraku was single his whole life. His life was not long by any means—I seem to remember that he was not quite fifty when he died. His sister was married to a novelist who wrote books that wouldn't sell. She seems to have come back home frequently to ask for money. Their parents had died young, and though I don't know how it all came about, Hiraku ended up living by himself. He never worked a day in his life, and his room was scattered with books. His whole life had been devoted to nothing but books. Because he never worked, he eked out an existence slowly selling away parcels of land that had been in his family for generations. People commented on how even big landowners like him could be reduced to such pitiable means. I personally feel like he lived his life as he wished, and that should be just fine.

What? You want to know what Hiraku's father did for a living? I already told you, he was a landowner. They were a landowning family. Landowners do not do farmwork. I don't know if landowning can be called an "occupation," as you put it. They lived off the rent paid by the tenant farmers. What's that? The father, like Hiraku, never worked either, you say? There are lots of administrative things to take care of; he must have been busy. I couldn't tell you what tasks kept him busy. A tenant here, a tenant there—there are matters to be dealt with. The yield from every paddy varied. He would have to decide the volume of rice they owed him in tax. As the representative of all the households working under him, he had to deal with the Buddhist temple to which they all belonged. He had to look after the people of the village as well. Village chief, you say? No, we never called him village chief.

Hiraku didn't do those things for the village. He spent all his time with books. What kind of books, I couldn't say. Mostly novels, I would imagine. After all, he sent his sister to be married to a novelist. But word has it that he acquired all kinds of licenses. I have no idea what these licenses allowed him to do, and I have never heard of a time when he did use a license. He lived for himself, when all is said and done. He died surrounded by a mosquito net, a fan, and an electric stove. Cause of death? He probably died of reading too many books, I imagine.

You, my dear, should watch out.

Notes

1. This and the quotations in the last two paragraphs of this chapter about "alone and just being" echo the opening section and section 75, respectively, of *Tsurezuregusa* (Essays in Idleness [1330–31]) by Priest Kenkō (ca. 1283-ca. 1352).

2. The narrator quotes a phrase from the opening section of *Tsurezuregusa*, where the author says, "How oddly distressing it is when I think about how I have spent whole days in idleness before this inkstone writing down whatever thoughts have come into my head."

3. The playful banter between the two about being scared of tea is a reference to a *rakugo* (comic-storytelling) piece called *Manjū kowai* (Afraid of Dumplings). A group of friends are discussing things that they fear. Whereas most of the participants bring up truly scary things like snakes, one man says that he is afraid of dumplings. As a gag, the others decided to gang up on him and throw a mountain of dumplings into his room. When they peep in on the shrieking "manjūphobe," they see that he has consumed all the dumplings with great relish. To rub it in for his peeved friends, the man gleefully tells his friends that what he really fears is "green tea," the drink that will help him wash down his dumplings.

11

Transit

Ogawa Yōko

It was completely dark outside by the time I arrived at Hong Kong's Kai Tak International Airport. Following the signs, I proceeded along the route for passengers on connecting flights, passed through baggage inspection, and went upstairs to the second floor departures lobby.

The lobby was a tasteless, long, and narrow space, stains noticeable on the floor and ceiling. The restaurants, duty-free shops, and money exchanges were filled with bustling crowds.

I wasted no time in finding a chair. Although I should have been tired of sitting after the more than thirteen-hour flight from Paris, I could not think of anything better to do. There were still two hours and fifty minutes until my flight to Narita.

The lights of the planes outside the windows continuously blinked. That orange glow made the planes seem drenched in the darkness that covered the night sky. I pulled my boarding pass out of the inner pocket of my bag and double-checked the gate number. Gate 29. Since I was sitting in front of gate 18, gate 29 was further down to the right.

Although gate 18 had not yet opened, a line was forming in front. It seemed that the flight to Manila would soon begin boarding. I put the ticket back in my bag and carefully closed the fastener.

"Where are you going?"

Upon suddenly hearing a man's voice, it took me a moment to realize

---

"Toranjitto," from Ogawa Yōko, *Shishū suru shōjo* (The Embroidery Girl) (Tokyo: Kadokawa Shoten, 1996). Copyright 1996 by Yoko Ogawa. Translated by Alisa Freedman with the permission of the author, by arrangement through the Japan Foreign Rights Centre and Anna Stein/Aitken Alexander Associates LLC. This translation first appeared in *Review of Japanese Culture and Society,* XV, Josai University, December 2003. Translation copyright 2004 by Josai University.

that the question had been directed at me. Although he did not ask in an overly friendly tone, the man seemed to mutter in English without caution, casually letting words spill out of his mouth. It probably just sounded this way because his speech was inflected with a peculiar accent, for he seemed to falter.

Turning my head, I looked at the man and then answered, "Tokyo."

"Ah, Japan. I have never been there." He shook his head, as if to say that it was too bad. "But I know a little Japanese. Head, caterpillar, sick, study, horse . . ."

"Oh, those are difficult words." I replied. And certainly they were strange Japanese words for a foreigner to know. He smiled bashfully and began to aimlessly rub his hands against his knees. "I took care of a small business matter in Hong Kong, and I am now on my way back to Paris."

"Is that so? Until yesterday, I was on vacation in France." I remarked in spite of myself, although soon regretting having done so. The guidebooks warn to beware of people who indiscreetly strike up conversations in airports. Besides, I was just too tired to make conversation in my poor English with someone I was just meeting for the first time.

"I see. That's nice." But after having said that, the man sat quietly for a while, looking down at his fingertips.

The man had sat down beside me without my having noticed. I am sure that when I had taken a seat here, the chairs on both sides of me had been empty. When the man spoke to me, I turned to have a look, and that was the first time that I realized he was there.

The man was short and slender for a European, but the lines of his joints and shoulders were solid and firm. He had on well-worn cotton pants and a wrinkled check shirt. He seemed to be in his late fifties. His chestnut-colored hair was starting to recede, and his eyes, the same color as his hair, gave out a hint of deep thought. His lips were dry and chapped.

Yet the most noticeable thing about him was the large bundle lying at his feet. Because of its uneven and complicated contours and awkward shape, it seemed hard to manage, whether he were to lift it or wrap his arms around it, and it appeared very heavy. It was wrapped in a strong, plain cloth like a quilt cover, and a hemp cord was tied tightly around the top. It certainly did not look like the kind of thing often found in an airport lobby.

I glanced at the bundle, while wondering suspiciously why he had not left it at the baggage counter. There was no doubt that a very valuable object was inside. But isn't it against the rules to bring something so large onto an airplane?

"Why France?" he asked, rearranging his fingers on his knees.

"In mourning for my grandfather. . . ." After hesitating slightly, I decided to speak honestly. It surprised me that I did not just answer that I had gone there for sightseeing, which would have put an end to the conversation, and I could have then moved to another seat. None of the man's questions were pushy or intrusive, as if he were trying to get closer to me. Instead, he seemed to speak words—still warm from his body and wet with his saliva—into the palms of his hands and then present them to me one by one, which naturally made me relax my guard.

And besides, that unidentified bundle had caught hold of my imagination, and I was curious to find out what was inside.

"Oh." He sighed deeply in sympathy, and his face clouded over. "Was your grandfather French?"

"Yes, he came to Japan during the war, married a Japanese woman, and never once returned to France. And so after my grandfather's death, I thought that I would take the opportunity to visit the country where he was born."

"And so that's why you are wearing a black dress. May I ask how old he was?"

"Yes, he was eighty-five."

"Eighty-five. Well, well . . ." The man alternated between muttering sounds that did not form words and sighing. I really did not know if this were because he deeply sympathized with my grandfather's death or if he just could not find the right English words.

He then thrust his hand into the back pocket of his pants and pulled out a small bottle of mineral water. Excusing himself for having a drink, he poured the contents noiselessly into his mouth. It was an old bottle, dark with dirt and smudged with fingerprints. It was dirty enough to make me wonder whether the water inside had gone bad.

The large bundle, like a loyal servant, knelt beside his feet.

My grandfather on my mother's side died on a cold Sunday, three months ago. Since he was very frail from old age, every member of my family was prepared for his death. That winter evening as the powdery snow began to flurry, my grandfather quietly breathed his last in his own bed.

My grandfather worked as a pastry chef at a factory that manufactured Western-style desserts, but he had been retired ever since I could remember. Aside from being enlisted to work at the factory several days during the Christmas season, he occasionally baked cakes in our home kitchen for us to snack on.

I remember an afternoon my grandfather and I spent together when I was a child. "Grandpa, what's that?" I asked, pointing to my grandfather's left arm. "Someone's phone number? Lottery numbers? Or how much butter and sugar you need for some secret cake recipe?"

My grandfather gazed hard at his left arm as if he were also noticing those numbers for the first time and said, "This is a mark to show that I am me and can never be mistaken for anyone else."

I looked doubtful, not understanding what he meant.

"And even if my face gets all burned, all you have to do is look at my arm, and you'll know I'm really Grandpa."

Oh, so that's all, I thought, and that put my mind completely at ease.

"Can I touch it?"

"Sure. Go right ahead." My grandfather held out his arm before my eyes.

It was a skinny arm, covered in gold-colored hair. I could see his bones, blood vessels, and veins beneath his thin skin. His arm was a little rough to the touch.

193328.[1] Even now I clearly remember it. Uneven numbers written unskillfully. The 2 leaned to the right and seemed as if it were going to tip over. When I looked closely, I saw that the numbers were made of little holes, and deep darkness lurked within each of those little holes.

It was not until many years later that I learned that my grandfather was a Jew born in France and a survivor of a Nazi concentration camp.

"My grandfather was a pastry chef," I said to the man. The man leaned slightly toward me, his ears cocked toward my lips, and he had an expression on his face as if gazing intently at something rare and beautiful. "Cake making is good. Really very good. It makes everyone feel fulfilled." As he talked, the man carefully pronounced each word.

"Every time I hugged my grandfather, he smelled so sweet. His hair, cheeks, chest, arms . . ."

"What was your grandfather's specialty?"

"There were many. Tarts, chocolate cake, sherbet, and macaroons, those perfectly round cookies. He flavored them with vanilla, orange, and lemon, and they had little crispy cracks on top. But most of all . . . Well, of course, the best were his big, whole, fresh cream cakes. When he placed one in front of me, I felt just like a princess."

"Those blessed with the ability to create things are lucky. They leave traces in people's memories. This is so even though cakes are things that disappear as soon as you eat them."

"I often remember seeing my grandfather standing in the kitchen. That was usually on days like Brother's birthday or Doll's Day or sports day at school.[2] Various things were laid out on the kitchen table—bowls, wooden ladles, brushes, a marble chopping block, measures, eggbeaters, cookie sheets, little bottles of liquor and spices. . . . Skillfully as a magician, he slowly poured the liquid from those little bottles one drop at a time into the bowls. Glass bottles of various colors, so charmingly contoured and labeled with foreign names hard for a child to pronounce. Being very careful not to spill anything, I used to quietly nose in closer, and each time I smelled a faraway world I had never once set foot in. My grandfather very carefully replaced the bottle lids. His back was enveloped in a white smoke with a mix of flour, baking soda, and sugar."

Feeling as though I might be taking advantage of the man by talking so much, I paused and took a deep breath. English and Chinese announcements periodically streamed out of speakers so badly tuned that the words could not be understood.

The restaurants diagonally in front of the waiting area were as crowded as before, and there was a constant clatter of tableware. In the chair directly before me, a middle-aged Asian woman was asleep, using her handbag as a pillow. A deep, peaceful sleep. I could see the leg hairs sticking out of her stockings.

Without my having noticed, a cleaning woman with a mop had drawn near. She was painstakingly wiping the floor. I began to worry—what to do if she told the man that the bundle was in her way? Would it be better to pick it up? But the man appeared unconcerned by this and was waiting for what I would say next.

Silently reaching her mop until it was just about to touch the bundle, the cleaning woman wiped the floor around it and then went away.

"I am sorry I am talking so much about myself," I apologized, but the man sat up straighter and said, "No, please don't worry. Go on. Please talk to your heart's content. I still have much time until my flight."

The plane for Manila began to board, and the line slowly started to move. A woman dragging a torn shopping bag, a large man over six feet tall, a young girl in sandals, an elderly couple—both the man and woman holding on to canes—a baby being pushed in a carriage, a nun . . . They all disappeared behind gate 18.

No matter how insignificant the matter, any talk about my grandfather's time in France was strictly taboo in my family. As a child, at the dinner table or elsewhere when I asked, without any ulterior motive, a question about the war (for example: Who was Hitler? What does "informing" mean?), either my grandmother or my mother would quickly interject and change the topic. Showing no discomfort but rather with a composed look on his face, my grandfather would silently let the topic change.

My grandfather never talked about his past. I never heard him speak a word of French. He had no French friends, and relatives from there never visited. Airmail letters never came. All along, I thought my grandfather was Japanese like me.

Although he never spoke of it, one way or another, my grandmother knew well how my grandfather had been taken from the family that had hid him to a concentration camp and how he had been liberated after the war and had come to Japan.

Whenever we were faced with some small misfortune and things around the house became a little oppressive (when our cat died, when my brother was hospitalized because of an asthma attack, when my father's company went bankrupt), my mother and grandmother would lean in close and whisper about the past under their breath. They would say that Grandpa had to bear such great misfortune for all of us; it can't get worse than that. And, of course, this was something they discussed when my grandfather was not around.

At that time, Grandpa had just gotten married, my grandmother said. Of course not to me. To the daughter apparently of a man who owned a variety store. It was pretty easy to find a place for Grandpa to hide. Grandpa had met someone connected with an underground organization through a customer at the bakery where he worked. First was a sculptor's atelier in Paris, then a farmhouse shed, and last the attic of a private home in a small port town. By that time, Grandpa had already become separated from his wife. That way there was a better chance for at least one of them to survive. But for some reason—maybe because someone had informed, although to this day we don't know—early one morning, the police burst in. Grandpa hid in the burrow he had made in a wardrobe. He had made the burrow just for that purpose. But the police had seen through the trick. They opened the door without any hesitation. What happened next is even beyond Grandma's understanding. You have heard what the concentration camps were like. In the end, his wife was also captured, and she died in a different concentration camp. The person who had hidden Grandpa in his attic was a tailor. But he was not arrested because Grandpa bribed the police. Grandpa had kept a mink stole as a possible getaway fund. It seems Grandpa had also given the tailor's wife a diamond ring. She was pretty unhappy about protecting a Jew, and Grandpa had had to win her over. It is so awful that people had to give things to others just to stay alive. Maybe the tailor's wife informed on Grandpa because he had nothing left for her to take from him. But of course, this is just Grandma's opinion. Do you know what Grandpa's bad habit was? He would grasp his left shirt cuff and keep stretching it down. He seemed to do this without realizing it, because he did it even when he was wearing short sleeves.

I felt that I could not believe everything that my grandmother told me. Each time she told this story, a part of it was slightly different, and because my grandmother was the talkative type, when she told a long story, she often embellished the truth to suit her purposes.

Did my grandfather say nothing about the past because he truly did not want to talk about it? Or had he perhaps wished to put more of his memories into words? It crossed my mind that this might have been the case. But, in the end, my grandfather just continued to bake cakes in our kitchen.

"Carrying around such a large package must be very difficult." I took the opportunity to ask what I had been curious about from the start.

"No, it really does not seem that difficult when you master the best way to carry it. I hold it on my back, balancing the weight behind my neck and between my shoulders on three points, and then I walk slowly, letting my body naturally guide it as I move." He showed me by pretending to pick up the bundle and put it on his back, and then he gently swayed his shoulders.

"Is it something you need for work?"

"Yes, it is a rocking horse."

"A what?" I thought that I must not have heard right, and I asked again to make sure.

"R-o-c-k-i-n-g h-o-r-s-e." The man leaned closer and enunciated the words, his mouth opened so widely that I could see his tongue. I could see the stubble on his chin and the grease around his nostrils. "I work at a rocking horse museum in Paris. I travel around the world collecting old rocking horses, and then classify, repair, exhibit, and preserve them."

"For example, where do you look for them?"

"There are old rocking horses, those made in the seventeenth and eighteenth centuries and passed down through aristocratic families. These are the ones children play on. Then there are horses from amusement park merry-go-rounds. And I collect just the bodies of horses, removed from stage props."

"I didn't know that rocking horses were so valuable."

"Oh, thank you for your kind words, but our museum is not just for valuable things. Of course, we have a horse with sapphire eyes and a gold saddle that once belonged to the Habsburg family, but the others are just horse-shaped toys."

"Did you come across anything good in Hong Kong?"

"Fortunately, I did. A neighborhood amusement park had been closed, and we inherited one of the horses from their merry-go-round. It is our first horse from Hong Kong. Its legs are a little wider than those of European horses, and the narrow part of its back is slightly more arched. And the pattern painted on its body seems somehow Asian."

The man explained enthusiastically. I must have become used to his English because, by this time, I had come to understand him without a problem.

The woman directly in front of me was still asleep. A Japanese man was trying to cram the bottles of liquor he had bought at a duty-free shop into one shopping bag. An airport worker holding a transceiver passed in front of me. A group of flight attendants silently followed him. Nobody seemed to notice the man, me, or the large bundle kneeling at his feet.

"Your grandfather probably rode a rocking horse somewhere, sometime," said the man, as if expressing his condolences.

"I wonder. Although I don't remember ever having gone to an amusement park with my grandfather, maybe in his distant past unknown to me, perhaps in some small park in Paris, he rode a traveling merry-go-round or something like that."

"Whenever I see a rocking horse, I think about the countless strangers who rode on its back. Resting my palms on the slight indentation on the horse's back, I think of the people who, for just a moment, had placed their bodies in the horse's care, and then got off, never to return and ride again."

I imagined my grandfather astride a horse on a merry-go-round. My grandfather's long legs bent, his back hunched as if cramped, his hair fluttering in the wind. Although the horse is rather old, the pattern decorating its body is bright. My grandfather's arm is tightly wrapped around the support as if he could be thrown off the horse if he even slightly relaxed his guard. Because the light is so dazzling, even if you look closely, you can't tell whether 193328 is still there.

To tell the truth, the reason I went to France was not that profound. Of course it had to do with my grandfather's death, but I had had no specific goal. It just happened unexpectedly because of some vague lead. I was very surprised that, after arriving in Paris, I came up with the idea of visiting the seaside house where my grandfather had hidden.

I bought a ticket at Montparnasse Station, rode a train for about three hours, and arrived at my destination more easily than I had expected. Since I did not know the address, I was not sure if I would be able to find the house. And so I started to walk down the seaside road and to go where my mood led me.

The town was busier than I had imagined it would be. Cozy restaurants and inns had been built along the U-shaped curve of the road, and crowds of tourists were wandering here and there. Castle walls and ruins remained at the bottom of the U. The weather was wonderful, the sea beautiful, and the gleam of the white paint on the tourist boats moored at the pier was dazzling.

According to my grandmother, from the windows of the house, my grandfather could see a dolphin-shaped island, on which a yacht-repair factory had been located, in the sea directly in front of him.

And there it was. Yet to see it from the front, I had to walk quite a distance. As I walked further, the people became fewer, and the castle walls receded into the distance.

But I just kept walking without giving it much thought.

Without my having noticed, all around me had grown quiet. I heard only the sound of the waves. I unintentionally stopped in my tracks—there was a men's tailor shop.

When I came across the shop, I realized that I had not yet considered what I would do next. Should I take a picture and then leave? Should I thank the head of the household? Or should I go recover the diamond ring?

In the shop window stood a mannequin dressed in a dark-gray suit, surrounded by many button-down shirts and neckties. I could just about catch a glimpse of the work area, irons, and machines inside the shop. Although the shop appeared to be neatly in order, it seemed to have seen better days. The letters on the signboard had faded, and the patterns on the neckties were outdated.

"Welcome. Please come in." Suddenly the owner of the shop appeared, holding the door wide open and smiling at me. Actually, because he spoke in such rapid French, I did not really understand him. But judging from his appearance, I could only imagine that this is what he had said.

"Please, come in. Come in."

No, no, I shook my head. I had considered that I needed to have some kind of excuse for visiting the place, but I had not at all expected to be spoken to. I lost my composure and could not think of the right words. And far worse, the shop owner's smile had been so full of goodwill that I went in just as I had been invited to do.

Inside, the ceiling was high, and different kinds of cloth were closely aligned on the shelves along one wall. A woman, who appeared to be the shop owner's wife, got up from a chair in the corner, where she had been reading a book.

"I did not come to have a suit made." I tried to tell them the truth. "Because my grandfather was hidden here during the war, I thought that I would have a look."

Since the couple did not seem to understand English, we exchanged looks and sighed.

"Grandfather, a Jew, from the Nazis, hidden here, the attic room, fifty years ago . . ." I listed as many French words as I knew, and, seeming to understand the general situation, the shop owner and his wife raised their arms and, while emitting words of surprise, they patted my shoulders and grasped my hands.

In fear of overdoing things, I tried several times to excuse myself and leave, but they would not hear of it and instead swiftly ushered me into the second-floor living room.

Through an exchange of body and hand gestures, I learned that the wife, who seemed to be in her late thirties, was the granddaughter of the shop owner who had helped my grandfather, and the current shop owner had married into the family.

The living room was as tidy as the shop, and the window facing the sea was open, letting bright sunshine stream in. The flower box beneath the window was overflowing with small white and yellow blossoms.

After briefly introducing ourselves, we did not know what best to say. There were many things we wanted to tell one another but lacked the words to do so. As we gazed out at the sea, tapped on the table, and shifted our legs, we sometimes made eye contact and smiled awkwardly. With the creak of the chairs and the clearing of throats, we tried to deflect the silence.

The woman had soft blond hair and blue eyes. Her eyes were so clear and bright that they hardly seemed to be like those of other humans like me. The man sat modestly at her side.

"Thank you very much." At any rate, I thought that I should thank them. "Thanks to your grandfather's help, my grandfather's life was spared, and he was able to live to be eighty-five."

"My grandfather died. When I was ten. He talked to me many times about the war. He was proud to have been able to help your grandfather."

The woman gave the gist of the story in her faltering English. When she could not think of the way to say something in English, she peered into her husband's face, and then the two of them together struggled to squeeze out the right word. Then silence again descended. For a while, we listened to the sound of the sea.

"Could I see the attic room?" I wished to break the silence that controlled the three of us and to advance the situation forward, even by a little.

"What a good idea. I wonder why I did not think of it myself. Please. Come along. Now it's a storage room. But all is the same as in the past."

We followed her lead, our bodies leaning close together as we ascended the narrow stairway and entered the attic room.

"The bed was here."

"And the desk here."

"That is where the washstand was."

"Shutters were on the window."

The woman pointed to different aspects of the room and explained how things had looked in the past. Now wooden boxes, cardboard cartons, and cloth spools were heaped in disarray, and none of the furniture from my grandfather's time remained.

I walked around the room. The shop owner and his wife followed silently behind. The floor creaked—*eeee, eeee*—beneath our feet. From time to time, I placed my hand on the moss-green painted walls, but they felt only pleasantly cool to the touch. Just as my grandmother had said, an island and yachts could be seen from the two windows. The tide had ebbed before I had realized it.

The woman suddenly remarked, "Oh, I must go get something. Something very important. Please have a look at it." Then she hurried downstairs and came back with something that seemed very soft and fluffy. It was a mink stole.

"Your grandfather gave it to my grandmother. In gratitude. My grandmother said it was not necessary to thank her. She told him to use it when he really needed money. But he would not take no for an answer. He pressed it into my grandmother's hand. She always wore it when she was invited out for the evening. When she wore it around her shoulders, she always explained why she used it. She told me that an expression of someone's thanks is deeply significant. She took very, very good care of this stole. The last time she wore it was on my wedding day. I have it as a keepsake of my grandmother. A keepsake of your grandfather."

I slowly extended my fingers and took the stole into my hand. Although it was certainly old, it retained much of its warmth and gloss. Depending on how the sun shone on it, it seemed to shimmer silver or gray.

My grandmother had been wrong. My grandfather had not given the tailor's wife a diamond ring but a mink stole.

"I am happy that your grandfather expressed his thanks to us. I feel I'm the one to express my thanks to you."

She looked at the stole in my hands, with affection for this delicate object showing in her blue eyes. Looking satisfied, her husband nodded several times in agreement.

"I should really be going." And I grasped the handle of my bag.

"Is it that time already?" The man muttered.

"Yes, I have to go to gate 29."

"That is the furthest one on the west end."

"And you?"

"I still have to wait a while."

The man glanced at the lights of the airplanes that were slowly shifting outside the window.

"I am sorry to have bored you with my story."

"It was no bother at all. And I am sorry to have detained you."

"If it wouldn't be any trouble," I asked, gathering my courage to ask this last request, "may I take a look at the rocking horse?"

"Yes, of course." The man bent down, untied the hemp cord, and opened the top of the bundle. There was indeed a horse's head peering out from inside. Although the paint was coming off and half the decorations on the horse's head were missing, the face was dignified. The slightly lonely eyes seemed deep in thought, lost in some faraway time.

"Thank you very much."

"It was no problem." The man tied the cord tighter than it had been before.

"Please take care."

"You too."

We shook hands good-bye.

"If you ever visit France again, be sure to come to our museum. We might just have a rocking horse that your grandfather rode."

He continued to wave good-bye. The rocking horse silently sat close to his feet.

Notes

1. The number 193328 can perhaps be read allegorically. Hitler gained greater power in Germany after the February 27, 1933, burning of the Reichstag building and the subsequent February 28 emergency decree, imposed purportedly for the protection of the people and state and in effect marking the end of constitutional rights remaining from the former Weimar Republic.

2. Doll's Day (Hinamatsuri) is a festival celebrated on March 3. Dolls in tenth-century court dress representing the emperor, empress, and their attendants are placed on a tiered stand, and diamond-shaped Japanese sweets (*hishimochi*), not Western cakes, are traditionally eaten.

12

The Tidal Hour

Yū Miri

There wasn't a shadow in sight. The cabbage butterfly that was fluttering around the school yard looked like it was trapped inside a television picture tube. How did you count cabbage butterflies? Did you use *ippiki* or *ichiwa*?[1] For a swallowtail butterfly you'd use *ichiwa*, but for a cabbage butterfly *ippiki* seemed like a better fit. What was it doing all by itself on the athletic field anyway? A butterfly should be with other butterflies flying around a flower garden. Mayumi shut her eyes and pictured a flock of butterflies. She must have been about five then.

From the way its wings moved, the butterfly appeared to be struggling. She picked up a stone and threw it. Even when it nearly hit its mark, the butterfly showed no signs of flying off. Go back where you came from! She took aim again and was about to let the stone fly when a shout came from behind her. "Mayumi, don't throw rocks at butterflies! Why do you do things like that?" It was her mother. Mayumi wanted to explain that she was trying to chase it back to the flower garden, but she couldn't find the right words. "But . . . but . . ." That's as far as she got. Even now, thinking back to that moment filled her with rage.

A hot air balloon's going to come out of the sky. She looked expectantly out the classroom window, but all she saw was sky that was the color they used to paint swimming pools. There wasn't a single cloud in it. What she was talking about wasn't some dumb kid's idea of a UFO. There were balloons in the sky on a day like today, and a school yard during class was the perfect place for one to land and take a break. It would create a scene if it were to

---

"Shioai" (1996), from Yū Miri, *Kazoku shinema* (Family Cinema) (Tokyo: Kōdansha, Kōdansha Bunko), 1999. Copyright 1999 by Yū Miri. Translated by Robert Steen with the permission of the author. Translation copyright 2011 by Robert Steen.

arrive during recess. That's what *I'd* do if *I* were the pilot. Mayumi slammed both hands down on the desk out of a feeling of abandonment and betrayal.

"What? What happened?" Kaori, who sat in the desk in front of hers, turned around to see what was going on. Mayumi couldn't stand the way she made a fuss over everything when she was so *ugly*. She stretched out her legs and pushed Kaori's chair away.

"Hey, cut it out. That hurts, Mā-chan. Stop it!" Mayumi stopped pushing and laughed. What was so funny? She didn't even know if she was really laughing. It felt like someone had taken her by the shoulders and was shaking her back and forth. Who's doing that? Stop shaking me. She was about to yell, "Cut it out!" when the laughing died down. Shake her any more and she'd have overinflated and blown up.

There wasn't a shadow in sight. How strange that there were none around the drinking fountain, or the trees, or the jungle gym, even though the midsummer sun filled the school yard like spilled cooking oil. Some stray slippers lying on the ground looked as though they were about to start floating any moment. Rina was being led by Mr. Tanaka, the homeroom teacher of sixth grade, class 2. They'd just met with the principal, who'd assured her that it wouldn't be long before she'd made lots of friends. As they passed through the walkway to the classroom building she looked out at the school yard. The glare of the sun made her head spin. She cocked her head to one side, wondering if there hadn't been another time that she'd seen a place without any shadows like this one.

"Yasuda, what's wrong?" Tanaka stopped and looked at her. She didn't know if he was angry or if maybe he thought she was feeling faint. She herself wasn't sure if she was about to fall over or not. It's nothing, she tried to say, but the words wouldn't come out.

The moment she saw the girl enter the classroom behind Tanaka, attendance book in hand, Mayumi knew she was a transfer student. Her hair was in a bob with a ribbon on each of two side braids. Instead of a balloon, a transfer student had arrived. It had looked like it was going to be a miserable day, but this was a promising turn of events. When the class was told to stand she noticed that the new girl was trembling in front of the blackboard. When Mayumi had been in fourth grade, a transfer student tried to crack a joke when he was up there. This enraged her, and she had made a point of ignoring him. But she liked what she saw standing up there now looking like a scared rabbit. It might be worth befriending her.

Tanaka clenched his hands together and looked at the students. "Al-l-right everybody, this is our new transfer student from Ōyama Elementary in Ōta Ward." He picked up the chalk and wrote on the board:

Yasuda Rina

Mayumi quickly tried to remember if there had ever been a comic book heroine named Rina, but none came to mind.

"O-o-kay. Have you all learned her name? She's new to class 2, so if there's anything she doesn't understand, be nice and explain it to her. Alri-i-ght?"

Mayumi wanted to tell the teacher that she wouldn't mind if Rina sat next to her. She was about to raise her hand when Tanaka again clenched his hands together. "We-e-l-ll," he drawled, "for the time being, please sit in the back row, oka-a-y?" Jun'ichi, whose seat was next to hers, was absent today, she clucked in chagrin. If he'd just let the new girl sit where he sat, she'd be more than happy to help her get settled. Expressionless, Rina sat down on the hallway side in the back. Hinako, who sat in the seat in front of her, immediately started jabbering away to her. Hinako wanted everyone to like her and was always acting like Little Miss Sweetheart. Mayumi wanted to give her a good pinch. She had that feeling you get when you suddenly swallow a piece of ice. She began rubbing her chest. Kaori turned around and gave her a look as if to say, "She's cute, isn't she?" But Mayumi was not so sure that the transfer student was cute. Even after stealing looks a number of times during first period social studies class, she couldn't bring herself to think of her as cute in the way that, say, Yoshikawa Hinano or Tomosaka Rie was cute. Rina's face was skinny, with narrow eyes, small lips, and a nose too long. Her complexion was so white it made you sick just looking at it. Mayumi tried drawing a portrait of her in her notebook, but the face turned out so badly she had to erase it.

Mayumi noticed a change in the way the boys were acting between second and third periods. They want to talk to Rina. They want her to pay attention to them. They want to do whatever it takes to get her respect. She scowled. What's so special about a transfer student? It'd be different if she'd transferred from Hokkaido or Okinawa. Or, even better, if she were American. Then Mayumi could get her to teach her English. If she came over to the house, her mother would like her. Everybody would be impressed when they saw her holding hands and walking around with an American girl. Hey, they'd turn around and mumble to themselves, that girl is friends with an American. She can speak English. She gets along with foreigners. That girl is really something! Mayumi knew she could be a real friend to her. Just because Kaori and Tomoe were playing with her didn't make them her friends.

Mayumi pursed her lips and thumbed through her textbook.

Science class began. She felt sluggish. She didn't want to think about Rina anymore. Could refusing to talk to anybody be a strategy on Rina's part to attract attention? What would Mayumi do if she were her? She'd probably make a point of going up to everybody and making conversation. She'd pick one of the class leaders and ask them to be friends with her. Glancing out at the school yard, she noted that the shadow of a cloud had moved slowly from the north classroom building to the sandpit.

"Hey, there's a UFO," she cried to herself. "Huh? Where?" asked Kaori, expressing interest. Mayumi hadn't thought it was worth a poke of the pencil to get her attention. She was feeling sluggish. Didn't feel like lifting a finger. How good would it feel to jump out the window right now? She was about to scream any second from the anxiety and irritability she'd woken up with that morning.

Last night had been the worst, she thought as she started to shred an eraser between the fingernails of her thumb and forefinger. The sound of her mother's voice was making her temples pound. "What are we going to do about Mayumi? Don't you feel sorry for her?" She had no idea how many times her mother had used her name unnecessarily. I will not stand for your excessive use of my name! Mayumi didn't know why they didn't just separate. What she couldn't stand was watching them become more and more ugly and nasty toward each other. It had already been a month since she had stopped looking at their faces. The father that she had so adored had become a filthy old man with ticks. Get closer than six feet and you'd catch them yourself. Remembering how she couldn't stand the itchiness when her father's hand brushed up against her bottom as they'd passed each other in front of the changing room yesterday, she rubbed her bottom against the seat. Come to think of it, maybe the rumors were true about Jun'ichi being infected with *E. coli*. Just today she'd been talking to Kaori before class about whether or not to ask Tanaka to change their seats when he got back. Then Chinami, in the seat behind her, asked what if it really wasn't *E. coli*? Licking her lip, she deliberated. I should take it upon myself to resolve the issue. It might be necessary to ask for absolute proof that it was not *E. coli*.

During the next break she would try to make conversation with Rina. That would take her mind off things, and if she found out what kind of girl Rina was, she'd be able to tell everybody. Then again it might seem odd for her to make the first move. Rina should be the one to initiate the conversation. Mayumi turned her head again, this time nearly choking at the sight of Rina smiling and nodding to Minoru. What was this? The Rina of just a minute ago had changed into what could only be called a perfectly lovely lady. Mayumi frantically looked back toward the blackboard, but was unable to get control of her racing heart. She couldn't make sense of the distress that had taken hold of her. All she knew was that Rina brought something utterly disgusting, some form of trouble that was going to make her sick. The hubbub she was causing among the boys wasn't just because of the fact that she was a transfer student; it was because she stood out! What if she was a model? She was certainly pretty enough. That's why she was acting so prissy. Mayumi was incensed when it dawned on her that the reason Tanaka had been fiddling with his hands was that he had been taken by her beauty. When she realized there was a possibility that he might nonchalantly allow his hand to brush up against her chest or her bottom the way he sometimes did with her, she felt as if all the blood in her body had rushed to her head.

She slowly swung her gaze over the entire classroom row by row, beginning with the seat in the front nearest the window. She felt dejected, as if the tide had gone down and the craggy rocks beneath were left exposed. What's the point of transferring during the spring semester when they were about to graduate in six more months? No doubt she was a selfish little brat who had done something wrong at her other school and was made to transfer.

As soon as third period was over Mayumi moved to the seat next to Rina.

"Where do you live?"

When Rina said nothing and just looked down, nodded, and smiled, Mayumi was not quite sure how to respond. But she reasoned that if she could get Rina to open up just to her, her popularity among her classmates would rise. Besides, if she was really a model there was no question that the right thing to do was to get on her good side.

Rina snuck a quick glance at Mayumi and lowered her face. Mayumi, noticing what appeared to be a smile on Rina's face, felt as though a part of her chest had been hollowed out. She began to lose her composure and asked again, "Where do you live?"

Mayumi decided that she would wait ten seconds for an answer. Six, seven, eight, nine . . . is she not going to answer me? . . . ten. "Hey, everybody, the new transfer doesn't feel like talking to us. Why do you think that is?" Her voice was so shrill she felt like holding her own ears. "She thinks we're all idiots, that's why. She's thinks she's so smart and beautiful she doesn't have to talk to us!"

"It's probably because she just transferred," Tatsuya mumbled.

"Why can't you talk if you transfer?"

"I don't know. It's none of my business anyway," he stammered on his way out of the room.

"Seems like the first thing you'd do when you came to a new school is try to talk to people. And who in class 2 wears ribbons anyway? You think you're so cute. Ribbons? Give me a break. Take them off. Now!"

She couldn't help thinking that Rina was taking the ribbons off intentionally slowly, but the fact was that Rina's fingers were so numb she could barely move them.

"If you don't like to I'll do it for you." Mayumi grabbed a knot along with the braided hair and gave it a yank. When the knot didn't come out, she grew impatient and pulled even harder. She could hear the sound of hair coming loose in the palm of her hand, but the knot stayed put.

"Hurry up and take the ribbon out!" she said, letting go roughly. Rina reached up again for the ribbon. For both of them it felt as though time had come to a standstill.

"You moved to a new house, right? So tell me where you live."

"I . . . I don't know."

For a moment Mayumi wasn't sure she'd heard her correctly. Then she burst out laughing. Maybe this girl is retarded. Who doesn't know where her own house is? If that were the case, how would she get home? She started to feel ridiculous trying to have a conversation, but she couldn't stop now. The whole class was looking. She had to prevail. "What, you're homeless?" She meant it as a clever joke, but it didn't get the laughs she expected.

"You have a telephone, don't you?"

Rina leaned her head to one side. Oddly, the sight of her doing this each time she was spoken to gave Mayumi goose bumps. She couldn't stand it when people were unclear, or slow to move. How could she explain this to her?

"All right, why don't you draw me a map," Mayumi suggested, opening the notebook on Rina's desk and taking a pencil out of her pencil box. She may not remember the address, but she could surely draw a map.

Rina stared at the notebook, gripping the pencil tightly. She could visualize the route from the house she'd moved into three days ago to the school, but she didn't feel like drawing it. Besides, she wasn't sure she could fit it all on the page. Even if she had the whole school yard to draw on, it probably wouldn't fit. But even though she might not be able to draw a map, she knew the way home. That's why she and her mother had walked to school and back yesterday.

The school had long since closed for the day and the front gate was shut. Her mother had looked through the gate at the school yard and said that it looked like a nice school. Mama has a good feeling about it, she'd said; she didn't sound convincing. It was like a bottle of soda with all the fizz gone. You'll be able to come perfectly well by yourself, right? I mean, Mama will come with you tomorrow, but . . . Coming by herself would be simple, Rina thought. It was the "perfectly well" part that bothered her. That's what her mother didn't understand.

I might as well try to draw the picture. She was just starting to move the pencil when she heard "You can't even draw a map?" She thought she'd been hit by something. That's how loud the ringing in her ears was.

The bell rang. The one that was relieved was Mayumi. She grabbed the pencil from Rina's hand and dug it into the notebook with all her might. It made a dull sound when it snapped.

"You make Mayumi mad, you're dead meat," said Hirokazu, but nobody laughed. He had made it known that his dream was to join the Yoshimoto comedy troupe. That's why he was always talking in a strange version of Kansai dialect.

"If you're gonna commit suicide, don't bother putting me in your last will and testament. I mean it."

It was lunch break. "Let's play running bases! Come on, Tatchan." Hinako was yelling before they'd even finished cleaning up.

"No, let's play cops and robbers." Tatsuya flew out of the classroom.

Mayumi took Hinako by the arm and, casting a sidelong glance at Rina, headed out of the classroom. Everyone had to leave the classroom and play in the yard during lunch break. She wondered who would bring Rina out. Mayumi always ran straight for the shoe racks, but today she walked slowly down the hall, arm in arm with Hinako.

Hinako wondered why Mayumi, who was friends with Kaori and Tomoe, was walking arm in arm with her. She had been about to invite the transfer student to come and play when she'd been led out into the hallway by Mayumi. Hinako quickly calculated that it was to her advantage to get into the group going out to play. If she became friends with the new girl, she could end up being shunned.

"Wanna play running bases?"

"No. Do you?"

"Not really. What do you want to do?"

Without replying Mayumi changed her shoes and checked the hallway. There was no sign of Rina. When they started walking over to the ring wheel, Kaori, Tomoe, and Chinami had joined them. The three of them always latched on to Mayumi at lunch and after school. Half of class 2 had begun playing cops and robbers. Tatsuya and Hirokazu were doing rock-paper-scissors to divide the group up. Come on, said Hirokazu to Mayumi, trying to pull her over, but Mayumi ignored him and grabbed the steel rings of the wheel. The four other girls hurriedly grabbed a pair of rings. Kaori started to kick the wheel into motion, but Mayumi dug her feet into the ground and swung her head around, looking for Rina.

"You know that girl? The one named Yasuda Rina?" she asked casually. "Do you want to let her in?" The four of them felt like they were in secret deliberations to decide the fate of Rina, which hung in the balance at this very moment. They understood that the real meaning of Mayumi's question was whether Rina would be recognized as their classmate. It also served the crucial function of reaffirming their solidarity as a group.

When all five of them let go of the rings and formed a circle, they all felt the tension. The playful voices of the other students drifted away like the receding tide. Mayumi loved the tension so much she could hardly bear it. If someone were to ask why, she wouldn't know the answer. It was something like the feeling she got when she was riding the train and was being stared at intently by a boy from middle school or high school sitting in the seat across from her, but this feeling was even better. The joy that slowly filled her body was so intense that it made her tremble. She turned her face toward the others to ask what they thought.

"Kaori, how about you?"

"I don't know." She had no idea what to say, but she was afraid that if she didn't say more she'd be left out. "I mean, I really don't know what kind of girl she is, and I don't want to play with her if she turns out to be no good." She tried to read Mayumi's expression as she spoke, but Mayumi just gave her a blank stare.

Mayumi turned to Chinami.

"Mmm, I don't know, but why do you think she transferred anyway? I mean, it's already second semester. Seems like you'd just stay where you were until you graduate." Kaori and the others launched into a discussion of possible reasons for Rina's transfer. Though Mayumi wasn't pleased that they were straying from the point, she did think there was something odd about it. Just then she caught sight of Rina walking toward the gym with a book in her hands. The neckline of her white dress was trimmed with lace, and with the sunlight hitting her hair it looked brown. Surely she wasn't dying her hair. Look! She pointed at Rina and began walking over to her. As she got closer she could see Rina's silhouette and her underpants showing through her dress clearly in the sunlight.

"No way. Look. Do you see that?" said Mayumi, gesturing with her chin.

"Oh my God, you can see her underpants perfectly," shrieked Tomoe, using the back of her hand to wipe the perspiration from her nose.

"That little pervert," squealed Kaori. "Yasuda!" Mayumi yelled. Rina looked around the school yard to see who was calling her. Mayumi waved over Hirokazu and the kids playing cops and robbers.

"What happened? What's going on?" asked Hirokazu as six or seven of them ran over. Mayumi yelled again, "*Ya-su-da!*" By the time she'd whispered, "Take a look!" to Hirokazu, the rest of his friends had gathered at the scene.

"Whoa! You can see right through. You can see *everything*."

When the entire group burst into laughter, Rina finally realized that she was under observation by everyone in class 2. She knew that she should try to join in the game, but her body was too numb to move.

Under Mayumi's leadership the group surrounded Rina.

"You can see right thro-o-ugh!" Kaori drew out the ends of her sentences for maximum effect. They all joined in. "You can see right through! You can see your underpants!"

Rina anxiously lowered her eyes to her skirt. It didn't look like anything was showing through to her. She thought she heard a scream coming from far off. She kept her head down and strained to hear what it was. Pop! Something burst inside her head. The tide was rolling in and she'd certainly drown in it. She took a deep breath.

"You're not allowed to show your undies in class 2," somebody said. "What should the penalty be? Take them off!" The words had been spoken. *"Take Them Off! Take Them Off!"* They were clapping in unison now.

Only once before, just after the sixth grade classes had been rearranged, had there been a strip call. Tomoe had been the victim then, but she had been given a reprieve. When she started to cry, they let go of her panties as if relieved not to have to go through with it. Now, as Mayumi witnessed the very same Tomoe chanting rhythmically and louder than anyone else, *"Take Them Off! Hey! Take Them Off! Hey!"* she wanted to stop clapping and leave the line. At the same time, she felt as if she were being mocked by Rina, who stood rooted with a blank look on her face. Driven by an impulse to rip Rina's dress to pieces, Mayumi clapped till the palms of her hands hurt. She couldn't imagine how a person could have the nerve to just stand there and take it.

She thought of the trip she'd taken with her family to a hot spring last spring vacation. The chef had come to their room and prepared a live lobster right in front of them. Even after its torso had been cut off, the lobster had continued to writhe and struggle. Mayumi had been terrified by the lobster's head and had cried out. She'd taken the sea urchin from the wooden serving boat and thrown it at the chef, who had joined her father in laughing at her. He'd wiped off his face with the hand towel her mother had given him. "That was too much for a little girl to see, wasn't it?" he'd said. "Some children enjoy it, but you're too kindhearted for that." Her older brother by two years had laughed at that and said she was just a coward.

They had grown tired of the strip call and were looking at one another, none wishing to perform the act itself. Now Hirokazu began chanting, *"Ma-yu-mi,"* and then they all started saying it. *"Ma-yu-mi, Ma-yu-mi, Ma-yu-mi."* Mayumi was pushed slowly to the center of the circle as though being forced to proceed to the witness stand along with Rina. Mayumi, who wasn't really interested in making Rina take her underpants off, suddenly remembered the time she had fallen into the swimming pool with her clothes on in third grade. She had been so embarrassed she was unable to come to school for two days. So now she cried, "The pool. Let's make her swim in the pool!"

"But what if the teacher finds out?" Tatsuya queried.

"Okay, then *you* take her pants off," she shot back. Tatsuya immediately hid his face behind the back of another onlooker, but Mayumi knew that horny little Tatsuya probably *did* want to see Rina take her panties off. She therefore whispered to Rina in the sweetest voice she could muster, "You'd rather take a dip in the pool, wouldn't you?" and began walking in that direction with Rina in tow. The rest fell in line behind them. Swimming in the pool was prohibited, but it was kept filled year-round in case it was needed for fire prevention. Just once a year, in the first week of June before the swimming season opened, the pool was emptied and scrubbed clean by the students and filled with fresh water.

Amid the fallen leaves a pink pencil box floated on the surface.

"Jump in," said Mayumi casually. Keeping her eyes fixed on Mayumi's face, Rina allowed herself to fall backward into the pool. Covered from head to foot with droplets from the splash, Mayumi edged backward. As she bobbed above and below the surface, Rina neither attempted to swim nor called for help. As they maintained silence and gazed down at the pool the bell rang. Hirokazu bent down, reached out, and grabbed hold of Rina by the arm. A number of others lent a hand. Once Rina was out they all ran back to the classroom, leaving the two girls where they were. "How will I ever explain to Tanaka why we're soaked?" Mayumi grumbled.

"I just asked if you were going to jump in, and then you just went ahead and did it. Did your foot slip?"

Rina stood silently, letting the water drip off.

When they'd gotten as far as the door to the classroom, Tanaka stopped Rina in the hallway. "Yasuda! What's going on?" He was clearly upset.

"We were at the pool, and . . ." Mayumi got no further. She fumbled for a way to put things delicately, but nothing came to mind.

"You were at the pool and what? What've you two been up to?" He looked from one to the other. "She fell in?"

Mayumi nodded. "You people are hopeless," he muttered in disgust. "Well, first we need to get you to the infirmary. Mizuno, you get yourself back to the classroom," he said, placing his hand on Rina's shoulder as they set off for the infirmary. Could Tanaka possibly be planning on having Rina change out of her dress in the infirmary? This won't do, she thought. "Let's all go take a peek," Mayumi wanted to shout to the class, but if they were caught, Tanaka would find out that it was she who'd made Rina jump into the pool. She pictured Rina being made to strip down to her underpants, and felt a dryness in her mouth. Serves her right, she thought. On the other hand, it struck her as an injustice; it was as though something valuable were being stolen from her and all she could do was watch with her arms folded. "I can't stand it!" She wanted to scream. "Tanaka is stripping Rina naked in the infirmary."

The classroom was quiet again.

"Mr. Tanaka is making the new student change clothes in the infirmary," she announced to the class in a monotone, but the significance of this did not seem to register, for there was no response whatsoever. Mayumi was disappointed and debated whether or not to add that she was naked, but elected to keep her mouth shut and merely stare at the class in derision. She envisioned Rina's white dress hanging in the sunlight and blowing gently in the wind.

Rina returned to class in her gym suit. Mayumi abruptly turned away at the sight of Rina's long legs in shorts. She sensed that the entire class was under the spell of those white legs. A mixture of pain and anxiety welled up in the pit of her stomach. Rina was getting all the attention.

Tanaka looked around the classroom as though he had something to say, but all he could think of was to tell them "not to get too close to the pool." He then had them turn to page sixty-eight of their text.

She felt unbelievably sick. The class was looking upon Rina sympathetically. They had all made it back to shore, Mayumi thought, while she alone remained at sea. I'm the one who ended up a loser in all this. It wasn't the first time she had had this feeling. Her brother always got the better end of the deal. No matter how much he tormented her, her mother would never take her side. The thought of this brought tears to her eyes. She had promised herself that she would let absolutely no one get the better of her once she started grade school. She had learned from her brother that you lose because you are weak. No matter how hard you get beat up you couldn't tell on them to your teacher or your parents because they'd get back at you for it. All you could do is cry. You absolutely never showed your faults or your weak points. That's what she'd always told herself. So why was she so distraught? Everything started to go dark as she wondered why she had turned out to be such a weakling.

"I'm sick of this!" Mayumi stood up and ran out of the classroom.

"Mizuno, what's going on?" asked the flustered Tanaka as he rushed out into the hallway.

"I'm going to the infirmary. Is there something wrong with that? I'm sick." Tears were now running down her cheeks.

When the last class of the afternoon began, Mayumi was already in her seat. Kaori and Tomoe had come to the infirmary between classes looking worried. Mayumi had been so overcome with joy that she leaped from the bed to tell them she was fine, just fine! Back in the hallway Kaori and Tomoe stopped in their footsteps and exchanged glances as they watched Mayumi from behind skipping back to the classroom and gleefully exclaiming that everything was fine. By the time she was in the classroom the image she'd had while lying on her back of Rina playing cops and robbers and playing the middle in running bases had vanished. She was filled with a soothing feeling of well-being, and the doubts that had tormented her until just a few moments ago had fallen away. Friends are absolutely necessary. You must never lose them, she told herself.

Nevertheless, as class time approached she felt an ebb and flow of anxiety and joy. From around the beginning of summer vacation, this intense ebb and flow had begun to occur several times a day. Mayumi closed her eyes. If only somebody would hold her in their arms. Somebody . . . she tried to picture who it would be. Her mother came to mind but she immediately blocked her out. Tanaka, Kaori, Hirokazu, Chinami, Tatsuya—as she ran through the names as they occurred to her she began to giggle and put her hand to her mouth.

Mayumi decided to ignore Rina. She would call the group together after fifth class to discuss only the problem of Jun'ichi.

"If he's really negative for *E. coli*, we should have Tanaka certify it," she said with a smile on her face.

"How?" Hinako asked, glancing out the window.

"We'll have him give a stool sample!" Tomoe screamed, and the others nudged one another's shoulders and giggled.

"My dad said they used to make people put their pooh in a matchbox" Tomoe told them.

"No way! How'd they get it in the box? They must have squished it in."

"Gross!" said Kaori, throwing her head back in laughter. Tomoe squealed as she banged on her desk with both hands.

"Wait, wait. Who's gonna tell Tanaka we want the certification?" asked Hinako, spoiling the fun when she managed to stop laughing. Mayumi suddenly grew irritated. It would have been better not to include Hinako in the group. They were having such a good time, and then she had to go and say something like that. She wanted to pinch her.

"Hina should do it, don't you think?" Mayumi looked to her friends for agreement, but all she saw was Kaori's eyes growing bigger and bigger. She'd been expecting to be the one to get the nod and had been preparing for the worst.

Hinako panicked. "But how could he really be positive? We all eat the same lunches, so we'd be infected too, right?"

"You don't just get it from the lunches, stupid." And with that, Hinako's role was decided. Kaori was usually the one who went to buy things at the co-op, but Hinako should be the one to do it. "Oh, Hina, I don't have a notebook. Could you go to the co-op and get me one?" Without waiting for a reply, Mayumi took her coin purse out of her backpack and placed two one-hundred-yen coins on the palm of her hand. Hinako raised her eyebrows momentarily, but then, with a little sniff, reached out to pick up the coins. They slipped between Mayumi's fingers and rolled under the desk. "What a klutz," snickered Kaori as Hinako got down on her knees to retrieve them. In the blink of an eye she'd been released from the degradation of being the gofer. Mayumi's eyes met Kaori's. "See?" her expression said. "It wasn't such a bad idea to let Hinako in after all, was it?" "And don't forget the change," Kaori shouted at Hinako on her way out the door. Her voice echoed throughout the classroom.

"Now that would be a laugh," said Mayumi. "Jun'ichi taking a dump in a matchbox." But it didn't seem funny anymore. The members of the group went back to their seats.

"This is what you wanted, right?" When Hinako put the notebook and change on the desktop, Mayumi noted a look in her eyes that reflected anger, humiliation, and defeat. "What do you think I meant?" Mayumi contemplated throwing it back in her face, but decided not to provoke her any further. "Thanks," she said, managing a smile. "My, my," she muttered to herself as she watched Hinako return to her seat. Making a group certainly was difficult.

After classes had ended for the day Tanaka came into the classroom. "Yasuda, have you finished cleaning up? Good. Come up front. A seat in front is better for you, right? All right, now listen up." Starting with Kawakami, they all moved back one seat. "You, Matsumura, all the way in the back, move to where Yasuda was seated until now." "Okay," he said, clapping his hands, "let's go!" Why was Tanaka taking this step, and why was he getting so worked up about it? "And I'd just decided to ignore her," thought a dejected Mayumi as she glared at Tanaka and Rina, who, thanks to the move, were now right in her line of vision. If Tanaka had been paying attention to Rina the whole day, that meant she must be his new favorite. Now that she thought of it, it did seem as though Tanaka had been trying to avoid looking at Mayumi. Unforgivable! She felt as though something strong were pulling at her face. If this kept up, she'd end up with facial paralysis. Her face might end up bent out of shape.

When they had finished with the seat changes, Tanaka made some quick announcements and informed the class that "after-school play would end at 4:30 today." Then he waited for the "all rise" from the class representative.

The group encircled Mayumi, who was so lost in thought she hadn't stood up.

"What's wrong? You're not feeling well?"

"This sucks!" Without shifting her gaze, Mayumi raised her chin. "Tell the transfer student to meet us behind the gym. She's still here, right? You can still catch her if you run."

"Come here a minute. There's something we need to talk about," Hinako told Rina, who had just changed into her street shoes. "I'm going home." Rina managed to mumble the words, but they were barely audible. When she exited the door, Kaori was there waving her over. Rina was walked over to the gym sandwiched between the two girls. Out of the corner of her eye she could see the school yard baking in the sun. The students leaped about as if dancing across the surface of a hot frying pan. To Rina they looked like ants swarming around a lump of sugar. As she was trying to recall when and where she had seen a shadowless landscape like the one she'd seen that morning, Hinako pushed her from behind. She stumbled. A sense of fatigue robbed her of all thought. She wasn't afraid. She had known from the moment she walked through the school gate that morning that something like this would happen. As they turned into the corridor that led to the yard behind the gym, Rina went weak at the knees, and Hinako again pushed her hard from behind. Rina pitched forward, then looked up. Mayumi, Tomoe, and Chinami were all three leaning against the wall of the gym.

"If you want to join the class, you have to tell us the truth. Why'd you transfer? Give us the reason," Mayumi demanded as she crouched down and stared up at Rina from below. Unable to answer, Rina tilted her head.

"Tell us. Tell us why!" Mayumi took a step forward.

Rina had no intention of giving them the reason. She looked over at the vegetable garden. There were morning glories in the second graders' plot, and in the sixth graders' plot there were eggplants with five or six on each plant. They were so long and thin they could have been cucumbers.

Mayumi had turned red in the face. "Why don't you say something? There's got to be a reason. Maybe your father got transferred?" But if her father had been transferred, that would have meant that they'd come from another part of the country, so that was a dead end. At a loss, she tried something else. "Maybe your family built a house near here," she said, remembering students who had transferred in the second and fourth grades for this reason.

Rina shook her head and responded in a tiny voice, "We moved into an apartment."

"But why did you move here?" Tomoe shouted at Rina from behind. "That's what she's asking you. Is something wrong with your head?"

"We didn't like it anymore."

"But *why* did you not like it anymore? Why did you need to transfer? Something happened at your old school, didn't it?"

The smell of power and sweat coming from Mayumi made the inside of Rina's nose tingle. It was best not to give them the reason. They wouldn't let her go anyway. "Um-m-m," she mumbled, again tilting her head to the side.

"You caused some kind of trouble at your last school, didn't you? You stole some money, or the teacher saw you kissing a boy." Tomoe's voice was so shrill it tickled.

"Kiss? I bet she used her tongue. She's a devil-woman. Hey everybody,

Yasuda Rina pushed a guy over and kissed him." She put her hands together megaphone-style and bellowed the news for everyone to hear. "Pervert!" she screamed and lifted up Rina's skirt.

Watching Rina stand there looking straight ahead and showing no signs of crying, the hatred Mayumi felt toward Rina gradually went from something like the red trace of a scratch on the skin to something pleasant. It was as if the loneliness of the moment just before she fell asleep at night, when she had that creepy feeling of being buried in sand and would wonder if she might turn cold and die and never wake up, had been replaced by an entirely different feeling, a pleasant sensation of buoyancy in her hips and thighs. She couldn't suppress the joy that welled up inside her at the thought that she was sucking the warmth from Rina's body.

"In class 2 kissing is against the rules. Strictly prohibited! That's why we don't want you to transfer in. It's not just us. Everyone shares that opinion. Understand? Even the boys think so. So you have to promise that you won't transfer into this school." Mayumi felt full of determination, and inhaled deeply. "When you go home please make this clear to everyone in your family, okay? You aren't going to come to our school, no matter what. And another thing, you can't tell anyone about this. You don't want to come to school anyway, right? There's one in the fifth grade too, a kid who refuses to come to school. So just transfer to another school. Why aren't you saying anything? Answer me!"

Rina looked at Mayumi as she drew closer, and concluded that it wasn't worth trying to say something. She'd seen that look a million times before. No matter how many times she transferred, everyone wore the same face. She couldn't figure out why she alone looked different.

Every morning she would wake up not wanting to go to school. But there was not wanting to go and there was the fact that she had to go, and they were separated by a great distance. Right now, though, it seemed remarkably easy to decide to stop going to school once and for all, no matter what happened. Could she really do it? She thought about it. What if she were to stop eating? It was the same kind of thing. I don't feel like eating, so I don't eat. I can do that, can't I? I have to make it so that I don't have to go to school. She repeated this to herself like a mantra. As she did so the tension left her body and all her pain and suffering drifted away.

Rina nodded firmly and began to walk away.

The five girls were so taken aback that they could do nothing but watch as she took leave of them. She walked as though she were determined to disappear from the face of the earth.

"If she tells on us, what are we gonna do?" Prompted by Chinami's vague expression of concern, Mayumi dashed off, followed by the other four girls.

With the word "betrayal" running through her head, Mayumi grabbed Rina and shook her violently. *I won't forgive a traitor! How much is she going to make me suffer before she's satisfied?* "You're going to tell the teacher, aren't you? Say something to me. Why do you want to betray me?" Mayumi continued to shake Rina violently and threw her against the wall of the gymnasium. Rina's face showed no signs of emotion.

"What are you guys doing?" Hirokazu and Tatsuya came over dribbling a soccer ball.

"This little brat is going to tell on us," said Kaori.

"What for?"

As Kaori attempted to formulate a reply, Mayumi drove Rina into the wall and her head flew back and forth. "Hey, no fighting," said Tatsuya. He kicked the soccer ball as hard as he could against the wall. It rebounded at almost precisely the same moment that Mayumi slammed Rina's head back against the wall. Rina crumpled and slid to the ground.

The voices of the children playing in the school yard suddenly grew distant. Hirokazu crept toward Rina. Her legs were stretched out and blood dripped from her hair onto the nape of her neck.

Hirokazu gasped. "We're in for it now."

"What are we gonna do?" Tomoe appeared ready to break into tears.

"The hospital! Mr. Tanaka! We have to call Mr. Tanaka! I didn't have anything to do with this!" Tatsuya ran off toward the school yard. Breathing heavily, Mayumi watched the bloody stain spread across the front of Rina's white dress. It hadn't been a good day for her. She'd gone to a lot of trouble for nothing. The stain—it looked sort of like a lizard. . . .

"Is this a case of bullying, or is it not? Let us at least be clear on that point, Mr. Tanaka." The principal had decided to maintain a calm demeanor and give him the benefit of the doubt, but the exasperation was beginning to show on his face.

"I don't—I don't believe it is."

"I see. So there were no reports of bullying. But Mr. Tanaka, are you absolutely confident that Miss Yasuda's injury was not the result of bullying? *Was* there any bullying?"

Not only did Tanaka find the principal's manner of speech irritatingly slow, but his face appeared preternaturally large, and he was blinking excessively.

"I don't think there was. No, it wasn't bullying, I don't think so." What else could he say?

"You 'don't think'? This doesn't exactly inspire confidence, does it? But if you are convinced that it wasn't, it wasn't. In any case, make sure you calm the children down before sending them home. You'd better take Miss Yasuda to the hospital. And somehow you need to convince her mother that nothing else needs to be done. I'll stay here until I hear from you. I'll ask the other teachers not to go anywhere either. I'm just glad I have your word that there wasn't any bullying."

Tanaka did as the principal had instructed and asked Sugiyama, the head of class 1 to take Rina to the hospital. He then gathered the students, who'd remained at school, in the classroom. Unable to avoid the fear that events would spin out of control, Tanaka started to go a little shaky at the knees. Yasuda had turned out to be a problem child after all. He'd been sweet-talked into having her in his class by the vice principal, who'd told him that she'd transferred because she'd been bullied at her previous school and that things would go more smoothly if she were in the hands of a veteran like him instead of a greenhorn like Sugiyama. He now cursed himself for not thinking it over before deciding that, no, it wouldn't necessarily be a bad thing to give the students some guidance on how to prevent bullying. But it didn't make any difference, since he couldn't refuse anyway. What really worried him was that, when he had agreed to the request, the principal had told him that the mother had made a big deal about how she had agreed to the transfer at the last principal's request on the condition that the next time it happened she wouldn't put up with it, so please take good care of my child. And the principal had bowed his head to Tanaka and joked that all he asked was that we not end up on the evening news after a bullied kid killed herself, so please do take care of Miss Yasuda. Afterward the mother had come to introduce herself, and that was the last he'd seen of her. The fact that he'd just been informed by the principal that she was a naturalized Korean Japanese only added to his anxiety. Add discrimination to bullying, and even if she'd only been injured, you'd never hear the end of it when the media got hold of it.

Tanaka took a deep breath and walked into the classroom.

"The injury Yasuda received today was not the result of bullying. Now listen up, everybody. I spoke to Yasuda before she left for the hospital. She told me that she slipped and hit her head behind the gym. I wouldn't believe it if someone told me there was bullying going on in class 2. I can't stand bullying. I say it all the time, don't I? We all have to do our best to get along and . . ." He suddenly choked up and tears came to his eyes. While he was surprised at himself, he couldn't deny that he was growing emotional. He even thought he might be feeling the joy of teaching he hadn't known for some time.

The teacher is crying. Kaori looked around in shock at the other students. Some of them had started crying too! She tried to make herself cry, but she couldn't get herself to shed a tear. She'd break down at the drop of a hat during a sob scene on TV, but she couldn't manage it now no matter how hard she blinked. It was because the teacher was embarrassing himself. To see an adult making a fool of himself before her very eyes, and for that person to be the teacher! Seeing him like this was just plain laughable.

"What happened to Yasuda was an accident. But *if* a bullying incident were ever to occur in class 2, I would leave the school. I would give up teaching. I want to make this much absolutely clear." Tanaka took a handkerchief and turned toward the blackboard. He wiped his tears and blew his nose, then turned back and smiled.

I don't think anything like this will happen, but tomorrow if the wrong information gets out and TV reporters show up, I'd like you to either ignore them or send them to me. Okay? This was an accident. Everybody who thinks this was an accident, please raise their hand."

What is he crying for? Suppressing a vague sense of anger, Hirokazu cast a glance around the room. How could this be? They were all raising their hands. He shifted his eyes ever so slightly and glanced at the students who'd been behind the gym. Their hands were going up one after another. They were all doing it, Hirokazu thought, as he thrust his arm into the air.

"A-l-l-right, you can put your hands down now. Of course I'm upset about the accident, but I'm happy too. I'm happy that class 2 never lets me down. O-o-kay, you can go home now. But you all have to promise me something. As soon as you leave the classroom, you must all forget about this accident and not speak a word of it to anyone. Okay? Good. Class dismissed!"

As Kaori walked down the corridor she wondered what she would do if a reporter showed up. They'd be there for sure if the transfer died. It's so sad to die without leaving a last will and testament. If they asked her anything, she would just answer honestly. Mayumi is the one who did it. If they blurred her face and changed her voice the way they do on the news, no one would ever know it was her. I'll ask Mother. She'll know how to get in touch with the TV station. Kaori was unaware that a smile was spreading across her face.

Lying down on the back seat on the way to the hospital, Rina's consciousness expanded and contracted like an accordion, but it made no sound. The scene of the shadowless school yard was exactly the way it had looked in front of Sendai Station when she was five and she and her mother went on a trip, and Mother told her just to wait right there, and Mother disappeared and she waited a whole hour, but Mother didn't come back and she got lost looking for her. Why her mother left her alone that long and why her father hadn't come along with them was still a mystery to her. She'd given up trying to find out about things she really wanted to know because nobody ever had the answer. Nobody knew anything. Rina's consciousness contracted.

Mayumi was disappointed that the red stains on Rina's dress didn't look like roses. Grapes . . . leaves . . . bats . . . goldfish . . . clouds at sunset . . . they looked a little bit like a lot of things, but not like so much that it would make you say, "Wow, they look just like that!" Mr. Tanaka had taken her to the library and told her to wait for her mother, but it had been an hour and nobody had shown up. She felt sick. If someone said something to her right now she wouldn't be able to speak. How could she get her mother to understand that it hurt to the extent that she couldn't even speak? I bet it hurt so much that transfer student couldn't talk either. It didn't matter anyway. All she had to do was ignore her forever, just not talk to her. Once she'd made up her mind about this she began to grow sleepy.

You could see the school yard from the library window. There was nobody there. Just the climbing pole, the swings, and the jungle gym and the shadows they cast stretching on forever.

Note

1. In most cases, Japanese numerals do not quantify nouns by themselves but require accompanying counters. *Ippiki* is made, with a euphonic change, of *ichi* (one) and the counter *hiki*, which is for small animals, insects, and fish. The counter *wa* in *ichiwa* applies to birds. It is also commonly used to count butterflies, although the lexical counter for butterflies is *tō*.

13

The Tale of Wind and Water

Sakiyama Tami

Between buildings that look like casually erected matchboxes of different sizes, not too tall but stretching upward while precariously leaning, the sea wind rolls and rolls as it advances. It brushes upward against the pointed corners of many anchored ships such as large-size passenger boats, cargoes, and small-size fishing boats. It brushes the deserted wharf and passes by the roofs of the dark warehouses standing side by side. It moves toward the busy streets, now fast asleep but still enclosing the stuffy human air that thickly covered the steamy ground during the day.

Having reached there, the wind slowly makes its way into the town's residential area, which stands with its back rounded. At times, the wind does so for the purpose of rubbing the people's peaceful, deep sleep the wrong way.

In response to this moist feeler from the sea that carries the smell of the tide, a midnight awakening comes as if premeditated. Automatically I sit up in one heavy motion and, my consciousness still vacant, start to take off what I have on me. After twisting what I have taken off and tossing it to the side of my pillow, my hands stretch toward the wall of the small room and pull down jeans and a thin polo shirt from hangers.

About the time that I push my feet through the jeans and finish dressing, the action I am following finally surfaces to my consciousness.

As I left the bed, Sato, who was curled up by my side, quivered once. It was not the physical reaction of one awake. It was more like the unconscious instinct within the woman taking the form of a spasm to criticize me. Sato was breathing like one who had just fallen asleep. Leaving her curled body

---

"Fūsuitan" (1997). From *Okinawa bungakusen* (Selected Okinawan Literary Works) (Tokyo: Bensei Shuppan, 2003). Copyright 1997 by Sakiyama Tami. Translated by Kyoko Selden with the permission of the author. Translation copyright 2011 by Kyoko Selden.

tangled in the sheet, and enticed by the moist whispers of the wind outdoors, I was on my way to town past midnight.

Saturday night. Or more precisely, the time when the next day had already begun two hours earlier.

It takes only twelve or thirteen minutes on foot to get out of the urban area. The entrance to the bridge appears before the wharf is reached. It is the largest bridge in this area, over half a mile long, known for the use of the latest technology in its construction.[1] The steel object across the bay that eats into the land looms in the dark, empty sky, and, mingling with the fog, disappears into darkness halfway across. The view of the unobstructed, boundless space twisted and bulged in an odd manner.

The wind raged high in the sky over the town. The stretch of a pale-blue fog shook like silk thread.

It was the wind's wild dance. *Saa, saa, saa, soh, soh, soh*—as it reaches me, the dance turns into sounds that tickle the ears. I felt that the wind's voice passing overhead resembled the melody of *shimauta*[2] that Sato sometimes hums. Just like a refrain uttered in a muffled way and cast up afar: *saa, suurii*.

I continued to walk along a night road now devoid of cars. I was on the bridge that looked out to the open sea on one side and to the town lights on the other. When I stopped moving my legs, the wind's voice that had continued without a break till then scattered into the empty sky, and all fell into silence around me.

The soundless night sank in the dark.

Turning my back against the transient town lights that began to disappear, I looked down at the dark sea. What seemed to curl upward like torn intestines were rolling waves on the surface of the water in the fluttering wind. Standing above the deep, black water, I rested my jaw on the guardrail, which was sticky with seawater.

Suddenly the wind slackened. I was pulled into a pit within the warm wind that formed behind my back. Turning my head, I saw a woman drifting this way on the wind. I had no idea when she had approached; it was as if she had landed softly from somewhere unknown. Turning her eyes toward me with a slight smile, she approached as if nestling up little by little. Red lips showed clearly on her roundish, white face. The hair, casually let down, fluttered in the wind, lending an abnormal swell to the head. Sato—I barely held myself back before voicing the name. It could not be. I shook my head. Deserted by me, Sato should now be in the sea of deep sleep.

The woman halted. Her purpose came through clearly. Stepping back quietly, I shook my head once again, this time with a big gesture. The woman continued to smile, extending her swaying, slender white arms. I pressed my back tight to the railing. The moment I did so, the woman's smile became contorted. Looking down, she quietly turned her back toward me. The form of her body, thin at the waist, mingled with the dark.

Suddenly I became aware of a bottomless hollow by my feet. The sea Sato had watched at that time was this color too. The way she had stood had made me think she was gazing at the dark water endlessly pouring into the hollow that had opened within her.

I saw the form of a woman looking down at the sea from the dimly lit deck of a night boat that I had taken on the spur of the moment. Fighting against the streaming hair blown upward by the wind, the woman's upper body swayed as if falling forward from the railing. "Stop," I shouted loudly, and abruptly held the form tightly from behind. The woman's body momentarily stiffened, then reeled, and, as it were, thawed in my arms, which were more forceful than necessary. She collapsed just like that, and before I knew it I was caressing her hair, which was permeated with the smell of seawater. It was my turn to nearly fall onto the resistless, soft flesh of the woman, when she, still crouched, spat out words to me: "What an odd person you are." The young, cheerful voice made me realize I had guessed wrong. Confused, as I quickly let go of her, she laughed softly. "I wasn't thinking of dying," she said. The face she lifted then gave me a start. Her eyes were blue. The feline eyes wet in the dark shot out at me. That her face and the back of her neck loomed white in the dark, I realized, was not only because of the night lights. *Ainoko*.[3] This occurred to me, an expression that accompanies a damp, dull pain within me. It referred to children, frequently seen here, of white or black men and women of the island.

"You're Yamatu,[4] aren't you?" she asked abruptly. Not that there was a thorn in her tone, but despite myself I felt that what she had said pushed me, a Yamatu, off to a distance.

"How do you know?"

"There you go, that *munui*, the way you talk.[5] Nasal and smooth."

I was reminded of the fact that islanders here speak as if pelting the breath out at something. The exhaled breath itself brushes the listener's ear. I felt that this woman's aspirates were particularly strong.

"Going back to the island?" I asked.

"Yes. Or rather, Anna's[6] dying, so I'm going to see her for the last time. When things are finished, I mean to go back to town."

I later learned that her *anna*, grandma, was her only close blood relative and a foster mother for her. And that *anna* was the one who had named her blue-eyed granddaughter Sato. After giving birth to this child of an unidentifiable father, the mother had abandoned her.

"You always go to the island by night boat like this?" I asked. The woman laughed again, this time silently.

"People nowadays don't go anywhere by boat, but I don't have much money. Besides, the night boat keeps me from taking an extra day off from my daytime job." Her voice sounded friendly. The form of the woman looking down at the water surface with a smiling profile appeared to me somewhat sad, but I felt that this was just because of my sentimental view and that she was not particularly conscious of it. Her voice was straight and cheerful. I had an illusion that her voice reflected her entire heart, that its strange cheerfulness also connected somehow to the deepness of the sea.

It has been five years since I settled down in a city of the southwestern islands, which is called the Japanese archipelago's tail; if looked at, in fact they dot the sea that way. Originally I had nothing whatsoever to do with this area. The reason I am here is no more than that my job happened to post me here. I came as a reporter dispatched to a local area by a central newspaper with an information network throughout the country. Given the nature of my work, I was buried under overflowing information; but when I received the letter appointing me to this southern land, which was not necessarily where I had hoped to go, I held an image of these sun-scorched islands as an unknown, alien place, and this depressed me. But then I lacked the courage to decline the offer, and I came over, dragging, somewhere around me, a sentiment like that of an exile sent to an undeveloped land out at sea.

When I looked down from the descending aircraft at these islands between clouds, I was overwhelmed by the mass and expanse of the whirlpools that surrounded them. The forms I saw in a light state of hallucination floated on the water in swaying motions, faint and flat, in distorted ovals or zigzagging triangles and squares.

On landing, I found that the interior of the island was far from undeveloped. There were two or three small cities, no different from the heart of a mainland city, and perhaps to balance with the appearance of those cities, the residents looked quite sophisticated as they acted the roles of Japanese in general. Or perhaps they behaved as if the only way to live on this island was to turn their eyes away from the difficult questions of their unreasonable history. Seeing the carefree, unexpectedly refined expressions on their faces, my melancholy about the southern islands dissipated. At the same time the exoticism that I had secretly harbored was betrayed, and I began my island life with a sense of exhaustion from feeling bypassed.

Amid the rush of miscellaneous work at the branch office, where I had several roles to play by myself, occasionally I felt irritated by the rhythm of island life, somewhat slow in tempo and relaxed. But the two impulses found a place of compromise by the time a year had passed. The sweltering heat of midsummer that slowed down thinking was now like a piece of poetry conveying local color. The violent typhoons that raged in season, brilliantly colorful flowers, the expanse of the absolutely limpid sky and sea: all began to pass my eyes and body like daily life matters.

I frequently went out for drinks with local reporters I felt comfortable with, and most of my evening hours went to that. At the beginning, there was a purpose on my side, which was to exchange information, but that too eventually became a habit that made my heart heavy. Sometimes, without my so intending, conversations with reporter friends in the usual corner of a drinking place developed into arguments, and those intoxicated would distance me saying, "*Ittā, Yamatunchun, nūnu wakai ga*, you mainlanders, what do you know?." And that was the end of it. Their gaze seemed crushed under the weight of history, their words becoming locked up deep within.

There were times when, between reportage trips, I walked around along the main streets or back alleys of the city, or just dropped in on a small, remote island. I thought of this as part of my job. During those casual excursions, the islands began to shed their outer garments layer by layer. Eventually, I felt, they would bare their jet-black surface of the ground, exposing their original form. It was not that any special change had occurred to my gaze at the islands. The islanders' intonation, which seemed to adhere to my ears, dark eyebrows, and large, black eyes; the air that held heat all through the year; the diverse, odd annual events that were tirelessly repeated. It was not that these things made me feel what I felt either.

What happened is that the standpoints were reversed: the seeing and being seen. The island's eye had caught me. With an expression of a silent rock cave, the island stared at me. I was unable to escape this feeling.

Had I wished, I should have been able to return to the main office by the spring of the following year. In the summer of my second year, when I started to think that it was slowly coming to the limit for a man over forty to live alone in a local area away from family, Sato entered my heart as if to set up a stake in it.

It was at the end of that summer. Relieved by the sun, which had finally begun to soften, I set out for an overnight visit to a remote island. I chose M. Island,[7] relatively easily accessible, with four regular flights a day, as well as some passenger-boat services.

I wasn't aiming to cover anything in particular as a reporter. Nor was I, at this late point, planning to enjoy a sightseeing mood. The fact was that the continuous holiday time I spent alone, void of any plans, turned into a white space that stretched before my eyes and suddenly started to threaten me. Urged by something I didn't know, I hit upon the idea of going to the island. I had no guide for this first trip there, but I could get whatever information I wanted, so I carried out my idea immediately. Another thing that made me do so was that, all the various main events and festivals having ended, it was a good time for going on a trip alone with no fixed schedule.

Somehow I felt like seeing the ocean rather than the sky. I was fortunate enough to catch the evening boat at 8:00 on the day I thought of taking this trip. The boat would cross the sea during the night, arriving at the island port by dawn the following day.

Thinking of using the night wind to divert the seasickness from the unfamiliar sound of the engine that kept shaking at the bottom of the boat, I went up to the deck. It was then that I saw the swaying form of the woman with her body bent, leaning out over the dark sea.

The wind, which had slackened, soughed again: *saa saa saa, soh soh soh.*

When I happened to lower my eyes, I saw a pale image that swiftly drifted over the water. It abruptly swelled large, wriggled into a narrow, long shape, and rapidly sank to the water. "Hey." Startled, I let out a cry before thinking, my throat twitching with tension. My body moved back. I slowly exhaled. Must be an illusion, this thing, I thought. The motion of an immense form sliding down to the other side of the bridge cannot belong to a real human being. Without trying to see it, I saw it again. Saw the spirit, perhaps, of Sato wandering over the night sea.

The body that I had held tightly on the boat was an empty shell. The real Sato, after all, had fallen into that dark sea. On an evening like tonight when a tepid wind blows, this other Sato lures me. Taking the place of the physical Sato, who had fallen asleep after a deep embrace, the Sato wandering over the night sea, I thought, comes to wake me. I cannot get away from this idea. My postmidnight wandering too was a bad habit that I formed soon after I began seeing Sato.

The wind's singing overlapped Sato's voice.

It was an early evening in town three years ago.

I heard Sato's bursting voice in the downtown area. When I entered a *shimauta* folk song club with my usual group, a blue-eyed young woman was swinging a pair of drumsticks. *Saassa, saassa, ha, iya, ha, iyaiya,* she interjected crisp chants between the rhythms of the drum. Somehow I found something painful in the bottomless brightness of her raised voice. Sato's eyes, momentarily lit up, pierced my expression, which must have revealed such a thought. It was a chance reencounter. But somehow I was unable to brush it away as simply coincidental, and even as I felt something unmanageable about such a feeling, I approached Sato. During the day she worked part-time at a coffee shop, she explained during the intermission, and she performed here on weekday nights because her skills in traditional drumming, which she had begun for diversion's sake, came to be appreciated.

"The audience finds the colors of my eyes and my skin curious, and that's a factor too."

She added this in a carefree manner, and taking a look at a business card I offered, she said without hesitation, "You're a Yamatu reporter. No wonder."

What did she mean by no wonder, I asked. Sato pursed her lips slightly and lowered her eyes, which glistened again. No wonder what, I thought. Her lowered eyes caused me to ask again at a later moment during the chat. Looking annoyed by my persistent tone, she said in a low voice, "There's no special meaning." But then she continued, with her clear, blue eyes wide open, "You, you have eyes that stare at everything on the island. Eyes that defile islanders, who try to live quietly by themselves. Lately they've increased, those eyes. Here and there on the island, only eyeballs are hanging around, by day and by night."

I must have once again looked steadily with those staring eyes at Sato's powdered face with its clear-cut features. She was plainly aware of having hurt me, but sent back a faint, deep smile from across the table.

I was unable to leave just like that. I parted from my company of three and waited for Sato at the back entrance of the shop, which was nearing its closing time. It was past 2:00 AM. With a large, black bag hanging from her shoulder, she hurried out the door, tall, the makeup washed away, and ponytailed. I drew toward her so as to block her way. "*Ai*, you,"[8] she said surprised, but immediately softened her face, and, without saying anything, she fell in step with me. When I saw her up close, the woman's body that had seemed to thaw in my arms on the night boat two months earlier turned into the swell of a surging billow and swallowed me. This was a southern winter night, when cooler winds had finally started to blow.

After this, I habitually joined Sato at her small apartment on weekend nights. I repeatedly postponed my return to the main office, and, while being looked at with suspicion by people around me, I had broken a record by staying at the place of my new assignment for a fifth year. I had no excuse for my wife and two children, whom I had left at a newly bought mansion in the heart of the city, and my relationship with them had completely cooled. Perhaps I would no longer find any living space there.

It wasn't that Sato wanted to keep me on the island. She never demanded anything from me except for my company on weekend nights. She didn't even visit my room. So a commuting marriage, in which a man commutes to a woman's place, had already lasted three years. "A Yamatu," she said, "I think can better attain nirvana if he goes back to Yamato." Sato said this in a voice that contained a smile. "For one thing, though the colors of my skin and eyes are what they are, I'm a *shimanchu*,[9] so it's best for me to live on the island, and I won't chase after you either. By and by you should go back to where you'll eventually go back."

She didn't sound as if she forced herself to speak this way out of thoughtfulness for me, nor did she sound as if she had become tired of me. From the beginning she had something like resignation about men. When she said, "I won't do such a thing as follow you to Yamato," her words hinted at a hidden complex feeling about her mother, who had followed to the States the man who was a U.S. soldier stationed on the island. Something like a resolution not to repeat what her mother had done, I felt, supported the heart of this twenty-six-year-old woman who was trying to live by herself on this island, bereft of her grandmother and with nobody there to rely on or to be relied upon. Even so, it was hard to guess what she felt deep down, she who sometimes casually mentioned how free of care she felt for the reason, rather than despite, that she was all alone in the world. How would Sato, without leaning on a man, continue to shoulder the sense of emptiness that must spread in her heart?

"This is something like a keepsake that Anna left for me." With this introduction, Sato sometimes softly hums a *shimauta*. She told me it's called "Hana nu Kajimayā," flowery pinwheel. "*Hana nu kajimayā, ya, suri, kaji chiriti miguru, chintuntentun, manchintan* . . . , a lovely pinwheel is twirling in the wind, twirling around and around, it beckons the wind."[10] It's an old local song everyone knows here. Sato tells me that when she cried and cried without knowing what she cried for, her grandmother took the little granddaughter to the beach and sang this song while turning a pinwheel she had made of pandanus leaves from which the thorns had been removed.

"Anna was a little tone-deaf, and she wasn't at all good at *shimauta*. That was clear even to a child's ear. But when she sang this song, the wind really came and turned the pinwheel around and around. Really."

As if to tease herself about telling such a childish story, she burst into exaggerated laughter.

"It's okay to laugh at me, saying I'm like a *warabā*, a child."[11]

Invited by her rollicking laughter, I laughed back, but I wasn't laughing. I thought I saw at that moment the roots of what was innocent that was left within her. I felt that the bright southern wind that travels from a distant sea to the beach on a summer afternoon was always blowing within Sato. Why did I involuntarily superimpose it on the tepid wind howling over the dark sea that earlier night?

That person. This was how she sometimes started talking about her on the spur of something. "That person too wasn't able to manage her life over there and seems to have come back here right away, but never came to see me, her daughter with different-colored eyes whom she had abandoned at home in a state of sheer poverty. Oh, I'm not wanting to say I resent it, really, really," Sato said and added, "that person was desperate too, I'm sure, about living." Even when the topic turned to this sort of thing, Sato was almost unexpectedly innocent, with no gloom in her voice, while her facial expression turned oddly wise.

"At my age," this woman in her mid-twenties would start to say with her arms folded. "No matter what people say," she would go on, "sometimes I think that person's approach is impressive, though I know it's a little odd that an abandoned daughter say something like that." I hesitated to ask how she found a mother who had abandoned her daughter impressive. Looking up at me, Sato seemed to recall the face of the person whom she said she had never met, or perhaps some image occurred in her mind's eye, for her gaze suggested she thought of her mother living in a distant place; but then at the next moment her eyes were devoid of sentiment, as if having wiped off that image.

Without even clarifying who had fathered it, she thrust a child she had born upon her mother, a weakening war widow who'd had nothing but hardships throughout her life; and she continued to live without reflecting on what she had done: a southern woman with red flames of emotion burning straight upward. I imagined something like that. Sato might perhaps see within herself too the fire her mother carried. There were times when I felt that this was the source of energy with which Sato led her life. Unable to hold back the movement of my staring eyes, I once asked Sato about her thoughts of her foreign father, about whom she had been told nothing. It was a stupid question. "Someone not there's not there," she snapped at me, "it's as simple as that. Going after something that was not there from the very start," she added, "meant walking around looking for a lie. There're times when lies are important, but if I look for only things like that, I feel I'll lose something more important. That's even more painful for me. So, I don't do that." Sato's words came back at me with the resounding rhythm of the drum she beat.

Could it perhaps be that a sense of absence itself sometimes supported a human heart? Sato's articulate words allowed no space for my sentiment to squeeze in.

Hearing whispers, I turned around to find a few couples, shoulders close, here and there near the railing of the bridge. Lovers' cars were parked some distance from one another in the wind, which went *soh, soh, soh*. Quiet voices floated on the wind. Merry laughter also mingled with the voices. They belonged to those young couples. To the extent I could make this out, it was tranquil on the bridge. My vision swayed unsteadily, and the forms around me gradually receded into faint shadows. It was then.

"Hey, you."

I was stopped by a sugary voice with vibrato in it. I looked and saw that it was the woman I had seen just a while ago. Stretching her neck as much as possible, she was looking up at me. Although I hadn't thought much of it a few minutes ago, I was surprised by how petite she was. As a man, I am just slightly taller than average, so the woman whose head was way below my eyes looked like a young girl still waiting to mature rather than a grown woman. Indifferent to my confusion, she was looking up as if to cling to me, her deep-red lips just slightly parted. She would not change that posture. I was forced to look at her too, straining my eyes, which had begun to be dim. When I took a good look at her, I realized that she had appeared young just because of her height. Neither the chest, which was so rich that it was out of proportion and gave a sense of resilience while hovering around the stable-looking lower torso, or the languid expression on her face belonged to a young girl. She had something that made me think she was at least older than Sato.

I was looking down at her without being able to respond in any way. However, I was held by a premonition that I would not be able to turn away from the light lodged in the deep-sculpted eyes that were clearly those of a southern islander. It was after starting life on the island that I came to let myself be drawn into an ambience itself in this way. When exposed to the strong ambience of a person who suddenly springs out from an invisible, warped hollow hidden in the interior of the island, my gaze at reality becomes inflected, and my body is lured in that direction.

The woman's small, sad-looking head swayed as if in the wind. The swaying motion seemed to plead: hey, hey. I nodded. She smiled softly.

"I'm glad, you know, if it's you, there may be a chance, I thought, you know."

She spoke alluringly though in a halting manner that was almost painful to the ear. The moment she spoke she erased the smile from her face, turned her eyes toward me, in a prompting, if not gripping, manner, and started ahead.

The woman walked swaying along the centerline of the bridge. As if coaxed by a gust of wind, I followed her across the bridge. Toward the beach on the outskirts of the city, that is, in the opposite direction from which I had come.

We were walking on a street that ran along the beach, with a view of the bridge girders above. Considering the length of the bridge, I must have walked for quite a while. But my sense of time was lost while traveling between clouds, which was what it felt like to me to be walking behind the narrow-waisted woman across the bridge in or on that misty night.

The woman led the way to a neighborhood where shops lined up over the water in a disorderly fashion. Boats were afloat on the swaying water, moored close to the shore. Most were sex parlors. The noise of individual electric generators suggested that some parlors were still open at this late hour. Passing by a number of boats showing glimpses of human forms under restrained lights, the woman entered one not lit at all. A precarious-looking wooden ladder stretched over the water and creaked when she crossed it. Not at such a place, I thought and stopped, flinching despite myself. She turned around slowly and waved her small, thin wrist. Beckoned to, I too crept across the ladder, dragging my body, a floating substance no longer capable of declining the woman. A sliding door opened, and a light went on.

What the sooty, naked light bulb illuminated within the box was a closed room about the size of three tatami mats. Perhaps because of the way the light fell, the carpet looked dark orange. The woman pulled loose a spread that had been folded in one corner of the room. Lying on the unfolded spread as if having become part of it, she extended a hand toward me. I must have walked quite a long while after all. I was unable to feel anything like a center in my body. My feet slipped and I fell on my knees. The woman rose and stepped over to put her arm caringly around my shoulder. I pulled her arm away, which, though weightlessly soft, felt oddly sticky as it clung around my neck. Expressionless, she looked at me.

"To tell you the truth, I'm not much in need today. So, for a while I want to just sit like this."

Nodding, the woman sidled back on her knees, which were placed together, and pulled herself away. Her steady eyes made her even more difficult to figure out. I couldn't judge whether they expressed relief or pain. The simple outline of her thickly made-up, round, white face hinted some shade but no particular characteristics except for the eyes. It was hard to tell whether her expression belonged to one who was completely steeped in her line of work or was worn just temporarily. The discomfort of being in a small, closed room with a speechless woman increased the sense of confinement. The urgent expression on her face when she had addressed me was no longer visible; once she had picked me up, she was somewhat unfriendly. She didn't do anything like try to chat to make me feel relaxed, offer a drink, or provide an electric or paper fan. A look across the room was enough to reveal that this was not a place where service items could be prepared, but I began to perspire a bit after having been exposed to the wind all along the way here.

"*Achisan ya,* hot, isn't it?" the woman said apologetically. She rose and seemed to push part of the wall outward. When a prop was applied to the wooden door, I could see, while seated on the floor, the dark, swaying surface of the sea. I had thought of this as a floating structure when I saw it from the shore, but in fact the place was not apparently on a boat. It was only that the little hut, which let down its stays into the water, was itself eating into the water. The room never actually swayed.

The wind entering through the open sliding window caressed my perspiring skin. Little by little an expression surfaced on the woman's face, and she even grinned when her eyes met mine. From so close a distance, I still could not tell her age. I wondered to what age a woman could do this sort of work. On closer inspection, I noticed that the wrinkles that had collected on her neck were fairly deep. As if to smooth those wrinkles, she cocked her chin and steadily looked at me.

"Why did you follow me, when you weren't even in need."

"Why? But you approached me."

The woman's relatively large eyes moistened childishly, at odds with her tired face.

"You're right, I was persistent, but you could've turned me down."

"I could, but didn't. I suppose that isn't an acceptable explanation?"

"Acceptable or not, I'm not in a position to say so, you know."

I felt that her tone, now softened, somehow resembled Sato's. I even thought she might be from the same island as Sato; yet my inquisitive eyes, which tended to stare, didn't work on this woman any more than that.

It suffices just to sense the air, I've been thinking recently. As I live this way, cornered by no destination yet struggling to see the future, the rich ambience of the island suddenly comes wafting before my eyes. If I were to stay crouched inside that air, never turning my head, I would be able to perceive what flows into, and fills, my empty body. If so, could I not thaw in the fog, the island air, Sato's words that Yamatu could better attain nirvana by returning to Yamato? I try thinking this sort of thing. How a woman is here before me in this manner and what history she shoulders. I'll stop bringing up my consciousness, which had become part of my habit, and asking such questions to a woman. That should not be a story she would wish to tell. The presence of the woman, unfriendly and nonchalant after having been declined by a man she had managed to pick up, seemed to me at this moment to represent the history of the island itself.

As if watching the distant shade of a rocky stretch by the seashore where the sun had started to set, I was vacantly looking at the woman. Perhaps she was made uncomfortable even by such a pointless gaze, for she swayed, nearly twisting her body.

"I'm taking this off, it's hot."

So saying, the woman slipped out of the flared skirt that wrapped her lower body. Despite her petite build, the fullness of her resilient-looking thighs was obvious through her thin slip. She kept her sleeveless top on. Not that she was enticing me; she seemed indeed hot. After exhaling a long breath, she moved to the window side, her ankles thin and tight in proportion to her full hips and thighs. Then, with a twist of her waist, she said to me, "So you're okay, in such a place, doing nothing, just sitting still."

I suppressed a laugh that was about to burst. I couldn't quite say, you're the one who brought me to such a place.

"Yeah, it's really hot," I said instead as I rose to move toward the window. When I stood straight up, the top of my head almost went through the ceiling of the room. I walked slightly bending forward. Walk, I say, but it was a matter of three steps. I sat again, and peered through the window, hollowed out, so to speak, from the wall and provided with a sliding shade. I faced the swaying of the water, which contained black darkness. My face felt as if it had been smoothly brushed with a sticky, black liquid, so I lifted it, and to the side of my eye was the waist of the woman, who stood near me.

"There're many winds outside," she said.

A strange look drifted on the face of the woman as she, eyes relaxed, looked down at me. I still could not guess her age. The tone of her clumsy speech sounded quite young, but her languid face and the slow movement of her body suggested an age one or two dozen years older than mine. Trying to cut off my gaze, which once again started to pry, I extended my arms toward her waist. "*Ai*," she shouted, bending. Her petite body fit inside my crossed legs. Her torso leaned toward the windowsill, with her chin resting on it. It was no different from a young woman's pose. Because I had absolutely no intention of forcing anything on her, I decided to just slowly stroke her permed, reddish hair. Seeming to respond to the motion of my hand, the woman's torso began to sway. The fragrance of cheap shampoo wafted from her dry hair. Oddly, I began to have a feeling that I held Sato, whose build was far stronger than that of the woman on my lap.

"On a night like this, afterwards some jumped into the water from here."

The woman's muffled laugh fell to the water. That made me put out my head and look toward the water's surface. Crests of flickering reflections of the city lights far and near delicately showing the undulation, the curling water surface looked alluring, like a woman's belly.

Suddenly I heard a voice from that belly. "*Chin, tun, ten, tun . . . manchintan . . .*" I looked at the woman. She was just vacantly looking down at the water's surface; her mouth did not seem to be moving. But I certainly heard the tune. "*Chintuntentun . . .*" It was the refrain from the song "Flowery Kajimayā," which Anna used to sing for Sato. The lingering reverberation of the voice was not that of Sato's. Unmistakably, the voice came from underwater. If it was not Sato's voice, I sensed, it must be Anna's: the hesitant swaying of the water had carried toward me the song that she sang to comfort Sato. Why did I think that I heard just now the song that was sung long ago?

I was rocked by a certain thought. I shifted my legs from the woman, who crouched on my lap. Removing my hands, which were holding her, I started taking off what I wore. Jeans, shirt, underclothing, all. Twisting just her neck, the woman watched me. She seemed puzzled, because I looked as if possessed by something, but she didn't say anything. Perhaps she felt she had to do the same, for she took off what was left on her. Blocking each other's eyes, she and I tangled for a brief moment, after which I picked her up as if I were holding a pillow, bent myself, and took a large step out from the windowsill. There was a precarious verandah of one wooden board immersed in water. While still holding the woman, who seemed ready to fall from my hands if I loosened my hold even a little, I entered the water.

The woman slipped away from me. She was disappearing underwater. I followed her toward the bottom. It was too deep for my feet to reach. I couldn't stop the motion of my limbs. In the water, to which a light that shone from somewhere lent unexpected visibility, the woman's small body looked like a large jellyfish. As her limbs swayed this way and that, kicking the water, she was like a tremendously large mollusk. I drew near her. The moment I did, she pushed her torso upward. Even with her face above the water's surface, she did not look human. After shaking her wet hair once, she began swimming away from the shore. She was surprisingly fast. In haste I followed her. No consciousness functioned in me to make me think of anything. The reflexes alone, of my naked body kicking the water as I followed the jellyfish-woman, controlled me and pushed me forward. But my limbs felt the weight of layers of water encircling and oppressing me, and would not, no matter how I tried, reproduce her swiftness. She rode the current, as she liked, like a creature that had long inhabited the sea. I could not recognize anything in the dark sea in the direction she was heading. I felt that the single-minded swimming of the woman, who had instantly transformed into a fish in water, might have some hidden meaning. Distanced little by little, I continued to kick the water, trying not to lose sight of her.

Suddenly the woman was completely out of sight. Feeling a light numbness in my arms and lower body that I had been thrashing about in chase of her, I stopped moving forward to become aware of myself floating alone on the open sea. Where did she go? I made a circle, treading water, but there was no form like hers within the scope of my vision. It was as if the woman had not been there to begin with. Did she dive to the bottom of the sea again? It couldn't be that something had happened to her and she had drowned. Even if it were the case that she had hidden somewhere in the sea, motionlessly waiting to be found, no energy sprung up from within me to look around for her in this dark sea.

Once I stopped moving, the night sea became unusually smooth, forming a dark blue expanse around me. There certainly was wind, but over the water that held thick darkness, it was completely calm all the way into the distance. Farther out, the water slowly swelled, showing the white bellies of undulating waves. When I looked around again, my eyes caught, on the left, a large black boulder planted in the sea, and, on the right, the hazy flickering lights of the city.

I was by myself amid the silence, floating with my head out of the water.

I was neither scared nor lonely, but sudden sorrow filled me, welling up from somewhere I didn't know. As if the sea's liquid were made of the essence of sorrow, the sentiment seeped into all corners of my body. The weight of the sorrow that filled me, I thought, was going to drag me to the bottom of the dark water. Right then, a willpower started up, making me resist the water's lure from down below. Adding strength to my abdomen and bending backward, I slowly turned over on my back. Only the center of my abdomen and front half of my head were above the water. The seawater had enough buoyancy to keep me afloat. Gently spreading my limbs so as not to lose the delicate balance, I calmly opened my closed eyelids. It was an odd view. Or rather, nothing entered my view. The moon and even fragments of stars had disappeared from the sky, which had, before I knew it, become thickly covered by clouds. It was a dark night oppressed by a dull heaviness. There was no sound either. Immersed in the water, my ears caught no discernible sound. I had a feeling that, while I seemed to hear something, in fact I was not hearing anything. Where did it go, the voice of the wind that had beaten me so hard on the bridge?

But then, like the Sirens' song, something became audible: *chin, tun, tentun.* . . . The singing voice, hoarse like an old woman's yet carrying something pure and cheerful, reached my ears, which were still kept underwater. The refrain continued: *chintun . . . manchintan, unitarisunumee, umikakiree.* Was it Sato's, or Anna's? Between phrases of the refrain, strange sounds entered, which I could only call the sea's voice: *byurrr . . . kyurrr . . . hyurrr. . . .* The way those sounds reached me was as if they were blowing through the drift of sorrow that filled me. Just then, something grabbed my ankle. I sank underwater. The woman, I thought. She must have grown impatient since I didn't catch up with her however long she waited and returned to play a trick. My right ankle was in the grip of a soft-fleshed hand. After dragging me underwater, the hand suddenly twisted its wrist with great strength. It was terrifyingly powerful. I was swung around with force, and the seawater I instinctively swallowed choked my chest. I was in pain. Foaming, bending back, being swung around in the water, I writhed with suffocation, thrashed my legs about, and finally surfaced. The moment I took a breath, I was grabbed again around an ankle. The sound of the whirling water, which went *byuryuryu, kyuryuryu,* resembled the woman's giggle. Was it the woman's doing, or a water demon's prank? Probably this was a staged initiation rite, one for entering the perfect island community. The moment I thought so, my back, which bent backward from the tormenting play, trembled with an odd sense of pleasure. Pain alternating with pleasure, I was drawn to a wriggling sensation that made me wish to voluntarily enter the enigmatic world. Abruptly, I heard Sato's voice: *saassa, ha, iya iya iya.* In response to the rhythm, my legs kicked the water upward.

Upon surfacing, I found that the heavy, thick darkness had begun to fade, making the field of vision above the water somewhat lighter. Far and near, thin and thick mounting waves demonstrated an expanse of many layers. Calming my breath, I decided to wait a while for the woman to appear.

But she did not show herself no matter how long I waited. Possibly she had turned into a water creature, having lost her way for returning to human womanhood. This time, I was the one to be impatient. Physical exhaustion worried me. I suddenly feared the water. If I stayed in the water as I was, I would be at the mercy of the water demon.

Looking around, I was able to recognize the box-shaped hut on the water by the faint light leaking from its open window. I had felt that I had gone quite a long way from that area, but it wasn't perhaps so great a distance. I could see quite clearly the form of the box structure, which seemed about to float away yet sat still, as if clinging to the shore. In that direction, I moved my body.

The tide seemed full. The amount of water had increased before I had realized it, and it pushed me toward the window of the box room.

When I reached it, the woman, all wet, showed her white face from the window, though I had no idea when she had returned. I caught hold of the hands she extended. The strength with which she had swung me around in the water was nowhere to be seen, and the soft flesh of her hands caringly pressed against my hands. Had that really been the woman's act? Her face, lipstick now gone, was uniformly pale, the lingering hint of an aquatic animal still hovering. Because she pressed her wet body against me, we once again tangled around by way of, so to speak, parting words. Between those motions, she wiped the water from my hair and my back with the sheet she had pulled off the spread.

Even after I had put on all my clothes, she remained as she was. Exposing her white body of a plucked bird, she sat absentmindedly with no expression whatsoever. Aware of the awkwardness of doing so, yet out of a sense of duty, I pulled out my wallet from my jeans pocket, opened it, and placed all the bills I found there by the woman's side. I felt that she smiled faintly.

I thought I had to clarify something with the woman. But I wasn't myself sure what that was. The woman made no move. Since I had offered payment, I knew I should no longer stay by her side. I started to leave the hut, my back still bent.

"Hey, you."

So addressed, I was going to turn around. At that moment, something stuck to my back. Suddenly it rose to the back of my neck, gaining weight. My upper body felt stiff. I had no idea what was happening. It was not as if the muscles of my back, which had stayed bent to match the ceiling of the boxy room, had suddenly cramped. There was a deep sense that something had unexpectedly possessed my back. I tried to turn around but could not move my neck. I simply heard the woman's voice.

"Trusting you, I have something I want you to hear."

What directly leaned on my back did not necessarily seem to be the woman's spirit. Her voice reached me from the direction of a wall of the room, a little distance away. At any rate, the thing was heavy. What a sense of pressure. I waited for her next words, leaning further forward. Why was I forced to take this posture? And what did she wish to tell me at this moment just as I was leaving? But the woman did not easily continue. A murky interval of time surrounded me from behind. Then I was gripped by an oddly mysterious rumbling. It was a dissonance conveying a sense of disintegration. The sound stretched, shrank, and exploded in a discordant tone. She's breaking apart, I thought. The woman who started talking to me was shrieking, I felt, under attack. I thought I had to clarify the identity of the sound. While still bending my neck deeply downward, I thought of turning around just with the use of my legs, and tried to do so.

"Do-o-n't turn around."

The woman chantingly shouted with a fiercely vibrating voice. I stopped moving my legs.

"If you don't want to become a bubble."

Perhaps she was still the woman. Even as she spoke like that, her words sounded enticingly sad. I did not wish to become anything like a bubble, but I might become a bump on a rock or some other if I didn't do something. Besides, I also thought I needed to hear the story she wished to convey to me while she was still able to utter words that I could understand.

I bent my bent back further. I gradually moved my feet sideways until my legs were fully spread, and I looked through the space. Momentarily, the floor and the ceiling swayed and exchanged places. I wasn't sure if what turned upside down was the boxlike room or myself. A dissonant sound that exploded again made me spring up. I bumped against the wooden door. As it opened, I tumbled out onto the wooden ladder.

I raised my body from a crouching position on the cool ground. My feet were wobbly but the weight on my back had gone, and I was able without effort to turn around to see the shore. No light was lit any longer on any of the many waterborne shops clinging to the shore. They had blended into the night sea, and not even the outline of their forms came into sight.

The wind traveled through the sky above the sea.

The big bridge, over the sea at full tide, was clearly visible ahead of me. I wondered how much time there was before dawn. Wishing to arrive before Sato woke, I turned my feet to the entrance to the bridge.

Notes

1. A reference to the Tomari bridge in Naha, 3,668 feet long and Okinawa's fifth longest.
2. Traditional, local folk songs of the southwestern islands, particularly of Amami but more broadly including the Okinawan islands.
3. A Japanese expression, now considered derogatory, meaning a person of mixed ancestry.
4. An Okinawan word referring to Yamato, or mainland Japan, here meaning mainland Japanese.
5. *Munui* corresponds to the Japanese expression *monoii*, which means "the way one speaks" or "objection."
6. Anna means "grandma" in the Miyako dialect; *obā*, the main island's form, is now more common everywhere in Okinawa.
7. As the use of the word *anna* suggests, the author has Miyako in mind, approximately 200 miles southwest of Okinawa's main island.
8. *Ai* is an Okinawan interjection expressing surprise, annoyance, anger, and so forth in response to something counter to the speaker's expectation.
9. An islander, Okinawan, local person.
10. This is a children's song sung while twirling pinwheels, also used in celebrating the longevity of a ninety-seven-year-old. At that age, one is thought to return to childhood.
11. *Warabā* corresponds to Japanese *warawa*, an archaic expression meaning "child."

14

Stars Scintillating in My Eyes

Tawada Yōko

A Life Taker

The sky hints of a winter shower. By two o'clock both traffic noises and lunchtime smells of frying oil recede, and a moment of emptiness comes to Ottensen district's main street. Once a residential area for factory workers, in the eighties it attracted organic growers and mouse-loving green-haired youths who brought freshness to the place. In the nineties, major figures in educational circles, successful media reporters, and later even attorneys and businessmen, started buying houses. The price of land soared and the area became a target for investors. Still, the ghosts of the eighties had not disappeared. There were stores selling organic eggs from crested hens kept in backyards, and, around outdoor sculptures covered with graffiti, punks with their women congregated. In a little bookstore where I worked just a dozen steps down a narrow alley from that main street, all the customers happened to have left and the other clerks too were away. As I was killing time by looking outside, a graceful dog sat on its haunches behind the display window of the shoe store diagonally across the street—with an enchanting air as if it were a courtesan on display.

*

"Meboshi no hana chiromeite" (1996), from Tawada Yōko, *Hinagiku no ocha no baai* (When It's Chamomile) (Tokyo: Shinchōsha, 2000). Copyright 2000 by Yōko Tawada. Translated by Kyoko Selden with the permission of the author. This translation first appeared in *Review of Japanese Culture and Society,* XIII, Josai University, December 2001. Translation copyright 2001 by Josai University.

Suddenly a frightful-looking man rushed in. Seemingly in his mid-thirties, he wore a leather jacket over robust shoulders, wet bangs glued to his forehead. Stared at with sharp eyes that seemed ready to bite me, I asked a pointless question as if to dodge an attack: "Is it raining?" Not answering, he walked in long strides straight to the rear of the store and, his back rounded like that of a cat, began turning pages of books with zeal. Only illustrated children's books were on the shelves by which he stood. I felt dazzled by the thought that such a man too, perhaps, bought picture books for his children. After a fair amount of time he walked back toward the cash register. On seeing me, he hastily grabbed a thick Schopenhauer volume that happened to be on a shelf near his right hand, and with a thud placed it on the counter without even a look at its cover. Since my right hand was in a cast that month because of a broken bone, handling his bill took time. Noting the agitation with which he was looking outside the store, I thought perhaps he was in love with one of the clerks and was waiting for her return. "Are you looking for someone?" I asked. His eyes looked puzzled, then relaxed momentarily, showing a sparkle of playfulness. "No, but I left my wallet in my car; I'll get it right away. I would like the book gift wrapped in the meantime," he said and left the store. Then the sky cleared as though a curtain had rolled up, revealing a pure mallow blue of the northern European variety, and the stream of people on the street gathered speed. The man never returned. However, he had left the book behind. When we investigated together later, we found that nothing had been pilfered—a very strange, rare incident.

*

One day a year or so later, a letter arrived at the bookstore. Since it was addressed to "The Clerk Who Worked at the Store One Year Ago with a Cast on Her Hand," we knew that it was meant for me. We did not recognize the name of the writer. His address was the famous prison next to the botanical garden. "Dear clerk who wrapped a Schopenhauer for me that day. I had jumped into your bookstore since I was being chased by the police and had no place to hide. Thanks to you I got away without being spotted, or so I thought. I was arrested quite simply that night at Altona Station. There were various circumstances, but I should naturally be punished because I took another's life. This prison being a model institution that values human rights, there is a union to protect the rights of prisoners, there is a library, and we can take any courses we like. So, led by the goddess of fortune, I borrowed from the library and read Schopenhauer, and now I am even taking philosophy—of all things! This makes me laugh. While I was out in the world, I used to slight what philosophers said; but, as a prisoner in a solitary cell, I have learned to appreciate their books. It seems true that a human being can be wise in the true sense only when he lives alone by himself. I hope you will visit just once."

*

Their eyes shining, and breathing heavily, the other clerks insisted that I visit him. During the same week, there happened to be a television documentary on murderers. Stacks of love letters seemed to arrive at the jail from female strangers. Many even visited the jail and entreated lifers to marry them. Imprisoned murderers were the best lovers. One prisoner, the documentary said, has to spend the entire day opening envelopes and reading letters. Would it be the same with the man who wrote me? After much meandering thought, I decided to visit him, but I would like to leave that part of the story for another author.

A Visitor from the Past

Early in the morning, fragmenting my lingering dreams, the phone rang and a rusty male voice identified the caller. I did not recognize the name, but when he said he was calling from such and such machine manufacturing company, I recalled that factory on the wharf everyone knew and began to comprehend the situation. Hearing him say "I have a favor to ask you," however, I was on my guard, thinking, why me of all people? "Well, a very expensive late-model machine arrived from Japan several days ago, but perhaps due to an accident en route, a corner of the wooden box was broken and the machine won't start. Repair it, yes, but we are talking about a machine that is one of only three that exist in this world, and nobody knows anything about the mechanism inside it. We went to the considerable trouble of having a mechanic sent from Japan, and this man speaks nothing but Japanese, to our great distress. So, we would like you to interpret for him," the caller clarified the business after a long preface. As far as machines go,

I can't even handle a cuckoo clock. Thinking I would no way understand the mechanic's difficult language, I declined like one making a quick escape and hastily put down the receiver. I opened the window, drank my morning tea, and straightened my collar, then came another noisy ringing of the phone. The same pleading voice. He could not find an interpreter though he had done his best through all possible connections. There was no need to interpret difficult mechanical topics, for somehow the strange mechanic was able to spell out all technical terms in German. Yet he utterly failed to comprehend greeting terms and topics of food and lodging. So please, please do us a favor, the caller insisted. I nodded yes to the receiver—so regrettable.

*

I walked, hurried by the busy-looking movements of the beetle forklift-truck with its crane of iron crab scissors. Large Chinese ships slowly caught up with me on the other side of the red, green, and yellow containers covered with hangul. Chinese characters spoke to me with peculiar clarity from the rusting belly of the ship. From the dock came the constant sound of giant hammers pounding the earth. As instructed on the phone, I passed between red-brown brick warehouses to enter the colossal aluminum coffin from its rear entrance. A man in a suit jacket, which shone like sharkskin, met me and nodded again and again, saying thank god, thank god. Ushered in by Mr. Shark, I entered a bleak room. There was a dull-colored machine the size of a small car at the center, and from behind it, a Japanese man, still quite young, emerged vaguely like shimmering air but became clearer in outline with every breath. Seeing me, he straightened his body, then bent it in a bow. Hair, crew cut. Eyebrows, hairy caterpillars. Eyes, round brown Yamanashi grapes. Skin of a nursling. Short with a firm bone structure at the shoulders and waist and with no excess muscle.

Without a word, the man started to resume work right away. Prompted by Mr. Shark, I asked, "How about some lunch?" but was declined with determination: "No, thank you." "A sandwich, perhaps?" I tried to further encourage him, but his eyes blinked in perplexity, then, as if having had an afterthought, he shook his head violently right and left.

At a closer look, the machine in question was studded with lids here and there like pimples. The man opened them one at a time with a screwdriver, inserted a gauge, and scowled, and from time to time peered in, using a flashlight that illuminated the interior of the machine from its base. Would I receive my hourly payment for interpreting for one who never spoke? I wondered, born to be poor. Somehow I sensed that the man was avoiding my eyes. As I too was therefore letting my eyes wander about, his gaiters, the kind that soldiers used to wear during the war, suddenly struck my eyes. Impressed by the thought that such antique things could still be in fashion in Japan, I looked at the man's attire afresh. "The Pacific War"—these words surfaced from the innermost corner of my head. "What is that machine used for?" I asked aloud before thinking. "This was a machine manufactured for the purpose of determining whether magnetism was evenly distributed in the interior of a metallic object, but it was bombed in the course of its development, so the possibility of ascertaining if time is distributed evenly within space . . ." The words did not reach the inner chamber of my brain. Instead, separated in bits, they were sucked into the fog. After two rounds or so of going hazy, Mr. Shark came in again and asked which the man preferred, tea or coffee. When I interpreted, he replied with his cheeks flushed salmon, "Oh no, the likes of me has never had tea or coffee." His lip-sealed work resumed. Trying to kill time while thinking that nothing was as difficult as silent interpretation, I looked around the room and found portraits of catfish-whiskered generals on the walls. Such descriptions added under the names as "great German physicist" or "mechanical engineer who served the nation" struck me as odd. I checked the dates of birth and death, and they were in their prime during World War II. Shivers chiseled my back, sleepiness rising from around my stomach. I don't know how long I had drowsed when suddenly I was woken by the engineer's voice saying, "It's done." I went to get Mr. Shark, who nodded after taking a careful look at the machine, took from his pocket an amount of money that corresponded to eighty thousand yen, and extended it toward me. The bills were damp. I felt my face almost freeze. As if making an escape, I got out of the place together with the engineer. Looking at the harbor, just as I was thinking of walking him to his lodging, he shook his crew-cut head right and left like a child and said, "But no, excuse me because I have things to do." Then he saluted and disappeared into the red-light district, Reeperbahn.

*

The phone rings the following morning, and Mr. Shark sounds shrill as if with a fever. The real engineer has just arrived from Japan. He was delayed because he had had to spend a night in Moscow because of plane trouble. Which clarifies that yesterday's man was an imposter, but the machine is indeed repaired. Interpretation is necessary for explaining this complicated situation to the other party, the police, and the insurance company. Please come right away, he says.

A Wayfarer

Skyscrapers are gorgeous if they grow together as in Manhattan's primeval forest; but if they stand sparsely, they are painful to the eye because they look as if they repented the error of the seventies. Nobody calls Hamburg University's fourteen-story Philosophy Tower, which shoots up to the sky, beautiful. Not that there aren't some houses that suggest the modest pride of the Hansa around it, but even those are intermittent existences here and there, leaving a strangely spacious empty space, which is turf, rather than a park, that is there simply to conceal the emptiness. No sign of people; a monument saying Jews lived here long ago stands quite alone.

As I was looking down at the uncrowded, late Sunday morning street from the Philosophy Tower, one person after another began to gather. They were too far away for me to ascertain whether I knew them. I had been told, when I agreed to serve as a part-time receptionist for the conference, not to let in people without invitation cards. I sat at the table ready to do my job. In recent times there had been many lectures and conferences with guards posted. Often at lectures by authors critical of Islamic fundamentalism or conferences handling themes related to Judaism, ID's are requested, body checks proceed, and guards keep sharp-eyed vigil in various posts from beginning to end.

*

About the time the hall began to fill with participants, a greenish-complexioned man appeared as if out of nowhere. When my eyes met his, I detected a cat's eye in addition to his own in each of his eyeballs. I forgot to bring the invitation card, he confessed, his lips showing embarrassment. I've forgotten to bring my ID too, he said, looking at me as if coveting sympathy. Although he calmly waited for my decision, I was in distress. I would hate myself if I declined, because that would make me like a government official, yet I would have to take responsibility if I admitted him and anything occurred later. The man's accent suggested something outlandish, and the intensity of his shining eyes was as enticing as it was suspicious. I looked around hoping to find help from someone, when an acquaintance, a Literature Department assistant, happened to approach. Just as I tried to explain the situation, the two embraced each other's shoulders and exchanged intimate-sounding greetings, saying, "Haven't seen you for so long." This cleared the suspicion. When the first lecture began, the man, seated in a chair in the very back row, listened without taking notes, a teasing smile hovering about his lips. Distracted by the expression on his face, my eyes wandered stealthily that way from time to time. During the recess, the man appeared with the assistant and suggested that the three of us dine together at a nearby Turkish restaurant that evening. Conversation with yogurt-wet tongues and garlic breath revealed the man to be a thoroughly ordinary scholar, and my initial impression of him was oddly obscured.

*

Approximately one year later, I happened to come upon the same assistant at the same Turkish restaurant. Perhaps because I was tired I was less formal than usual when I inquired about how the man had been doing. Even you seem attracted by him, the assistant said. I was surprised to realize that he apparently was popular with the opposite sex. His life is such that a film version of it would be entertaining, so women easily fall for him, said the assistant, sounding as if I had fallen in love with the man. What kind of life, I asked and learned the following. The man, nicknamed Dark Angel, was an active member of a Moscow circus troupe, his name known all the way to the eastern end of Siberia for flying trapeze skills that supported him and his sisters, a family of five. But one day the rope broke. Sixteen years old at the time, the man known then by the stage name Bat was home with swollen knees because of a fever. His father, mother, older sister, and younger sister fell from a height and died instantly. It is still unknown today why the rope broke. One spectator later testified that a gigantic pair of sewing scissors was visible in the sky just before the rope broke. Bat escaped from a reformatory for boys and young men, crossed

Poland on foot, and reached Germany. Finding refuge with remote relatives, he polished whatever skills he could, from swiftness of bodily movement to manual dexterity, to ingenuity with words, to superb memory. With his unusual intuitive power and flair, he grasped the knack of dealing in academic circles and now lives by selling PhD dissertations. He accepts any theme in the area of humanities. Teasing open the wallets of those who yearn for the PhD title, if nothing else to succeed as politicians or businessmen, he writes dissertations for them. He brandishes his pen, producing lines and lines of lies. However, lies that are polished through and through are more magically powerful than overstewed vegetables. The results are always As, yet he has no PhD himself. As I was wondering how this serious and simpleminded assistant had come to know such a dangerous secret, he proudly told me that the man had confided in him alone and no others.

*

A while later, I came across a photo of the man's face in the newspaper. "A refugee poet who represents Hungary dies young in an airplane accident," it said. "Having exiled himself in the sixties to Germany with his parents, who were doctors, he remained active as an author in this country ever since." This background too may be fiction, and if so, I would hope that his death too might be fiction.

A Panhandler

A stream of people files out of the Central Station. Busy-looking workers. Travelers carrying a lot of luggage on their backs. They gain speed on their own ankles and move away into the distance. In the area shaded from the sun before the station, which should be no more than a passageway for those people, several remain, reeling. They are gaunt, pockmarked youths. Lifting their heavy foreheads from time to time and narrowing their eyes to the thinness of a hypodermic needle, they look around—apparently searching for a black-market drug dealer.

Leaving the station, I transferred to a bus line. I worked as a part-timer then at a furniture export company. Its ordering section had six people altogether. The section head, Herr Hocker, who had just recently joined the company, was still in his midthirties. He liked talking about fiction, mixed here and there in his sentences the kind of humor not intended for any material gain, and sometimes stealthily wore under his cuff a bracelet a young woman would wear. His parents were immigrant factory workers. He was a college graduate who had majored in world history. He had a star-shaped scar at the corner of each eye. That morning, on entering the room, Herr Hocker looked around and inquired if anyone wanted a baby crocodile. A good friend had asked him to find a taker. A disconcerted silence surrounded Herr Hocker. Frau Komode, a graceful person with her retirement coming up the following year, scowled. Perhaps disappointed that the young man she had attempted to train as an ideal section head had deviated from the right path, she sipped her tea as if sipping something bitter. Frau Zesser, cheerfully plump, asked in a tone of scolding her seven-year-old daughter: where did he pick up such an odd thing? Fraülein Schlank, a new employee, turned her back with a flat response: dirty. Herr Estisch, a music-loving, big man, merely shrugged his shoulders. "How large is the baby crocodile," I asked, the only one who felt excited imagining the reptile's armorlike skin, wet and shiny. Grateful like a child who had found a surrogate parent, Herr Hocker came over to my seat and urged me, saying that the beast was still the size of a banana, I should see it, and if I saw it I would want it. I promised to visit the owner of the crocodile on Friday afternoon after work. I want to be a crocodile, I so want to be a crocodile. This was a desire not yet revealed to anyone. I want to be a crocodile. Discarding a human body that was drying out little by little, job after job, I wanted to take on instead a body that swelled, expanded, spilled, bulged out, till nothing could be done—the body of a beast that might have crawled out of an illustrated book I had read long ago.

*

Getting off at Star-Shaped Fort Station, Herr Hocker, in his suit jacket, and I passed an alley filled with the smell of döner kebab, a storefront with a display of secondhand radios and records from the sixties, an ice cream shop, and a locksmith's. Stared at by young women who were seated on the steps of the front entrance of a building, deep in talk and smoking with necks tucked turtlelike, we climbed breathlessly all the way up the dark staircase of the apartment with rusty mailboxes. There was no doorbell. When Herr Hocker kicked the door with his foot several times, abruptly there appeared a punk with a stubble of beard. Embracing Herr

Hocker's suited shoulders, and saying, welcome, welcome, he kissed him on his lips by way of greeting. Then the host ushered us into a space without furniture. There was one bathtub in the room, no, two, three, four bathtubs, and in one, fish swam shimmering. They were piranha. I looked, though for nothing in particular, and saw an ink-colored mouse running about smoothly inside the cupboard, stopping from time to time thoughtfully to eat a nut with a graceful movement of its hands. The punk guided us to the innermost bathtub and pointed inside proudly. In a Japanese garden he had made with rocks and water, a fine crocodile posed like an ornament. It was about the size of a piece of dried bonito. It was such a mysterious sight that one almost felt like kneeling there and worshipping. In comparison, how miserable we humans look: limp, pale skin, two tottering legs that alone support the body, short nails, stuffy noses, nearsighted eyes, fragile teeth, blankly smooth foreheads. What a wretched form. Informed that there was no telling how large the crocodile would grow, I felt partly scared, partly excited. It would be impossible to keep it in an apartment.

For some reason, it was decided that Herr Hocker, not I, would take it home in a bucket as an adopted child.

A number of days later, after a stormy day, Herr Hocker stayed away from work without leave. He appeared neither the following day nor the day after, nor did he call. I happened to see the company president, his face boiling, tell his secretary to call him at home. According to a rumor I heard later, his wife answered the phone and said, "This isn't the first time that crackpot has disappeared; he'll turn up sometime." She sounded as if she were talking of a lost article, and the secretary had no words to say in return. Sure enough he appeared after two weeks, looking innocent. He told nobody where he had been during the interval. Asked about the crocodile, he simply grinned without answering. Several days later, he again stayed away from work without leave. "It's not as if he were an elementary school kid." The president lost patience and said, "I can't give him another chance to reform." The man never again appeared at the company.

*

Several months later, as I got off the train at the Star-Shaped Fort Station again after a long time, a female beggar was singing in a husky voice in front of the station. It just can't be, I thought, but it was the song of a crocodile. Tangled hair playfully hung over unnaturally large breasts, thick makeup was starting to melt with perspiration, and the legs revealed from under the skirt were a man's. Moistening my eyebrows to make sure I saw properly, I looked again at his face. There was a star-shaped scar at the corner of each eye. Just as I feared. My vision growing dark, stars scintillating in my eyes, reeling, I was swallowed up by the throng of people.

15

Fiction Within Fiction: "Shōno Yoriko, Fiction"

Shōno Yoriko

For over a year, starting soon after she had moved into her new place, Shōno had been tortured by the change of the one in charge.[1] It's true that her original god was, according to official history,[2] a god of transportation, construction, courses, and directions. For her, however, it was the sun deity itself.[3] One might say that the sun and the snake come as a set,[4] and she wouldn't argue, but the question is which is more important. It could be argued, for example, that the sun is the supreme deity, while the snake is a water deity, in other words, the sun's vassal.

For Shōno, her original shrine, located in an area where she had lived until graduating from high school,[5] was such that she was able to reproduce, whether in her mind or on her skin, everything, from the route from her parents' home to the shrine, the surrounding scenery, the shadows of the trees in the shrine precincts, the amount of water in the pond, the tactile sense of the gravel, to the gentle draping of the purple curtains at the worship hall. Moreover, there was absolutely no need to clap her hands as a gesture of worship, and even if she kept away from official history, in her dreams that deity had a certain reality. It was easy to imagine it as a dwelling place of the soul. In the first place, no matter where one is, if one worships "the sun's rays that fall from up above," a mental attitude emerges making one wish to behave "so as not to feel ashamed before one's deity." The heretical book[6] refers to the relationship between the original one in charge and the snake, but no matter what one says,

---

From Shōno Yoriko, *S-kura meimō tsūshin* (Illusory Communication from S-kura) (Tokyo: Shūeisha, 2002). Copyright 2002 by Yoriko Shono Translated by Kyoko Selden with the permission of the author, arranged through Sakai Chosakuken Sentā. Translation copyright 2011 by Kyoko Selden.

the original guardian is a shiny god of the region where the sun rises from the sea. In other words, the deity is sunlike. As one would find if one turned the pages of sources on the Izumo-tradition myths, the foreign god who newly came over belongs to the water-deity line. This foreign god is connected to grains and wine, in other words more soil-like than sunlike.

According to a book called *Izumo Mythology*,[7] gods who approached from the sea had something in common with the local water deities, and in many cases each became one with an indigenous variety. Or, in some cases, a god from the sea ended up becoming a local water deity. Either way, in the end Shōno's new god belonged to the snake line. "It's different from before," she thought, and this was her concern. As long as there was nothing that helped her visualize its shrine in her present area, or even in any major location of her hometown, Ise,[8] there was nothing she could do. While not a major location, Shiomisaki Point, to which her family made a trip together in her teens, is the only place, of all those she ever visited, where this new god is enshrined.[9] Nor does the god reside at the place of her grandfather on the paternal side, who was a Shinto official. Generations of relatives on her maternal side lived in a house with a steep rafter roof around Muro'o village in Nara. In its vicinity was only an Esoteric Buddhist temple, and the only myth found there was a legend that the sacred crow Yatagarasu[10] had come flying out of the mountain there. A major shrine stands adjacent to a famous temple nearby, but, if one looks at its roots, it is no more than a Buddhist dragon-deity.

The small god was hard to make out.[11] For one thing, even in a large shrine, this deity was enshrined much later in history (in other words, he was "new"), or enshrined just to make some sense. And on the other hand, he is not enshrined in any privileged location within the most famous shrine reserved for the representative Izumo-line deities, with whom he is supposed to be a set. (According to sources, the shrine that is supposed to be there was torn apart and replaced by another dedicated to a sea deity, who is said to be one of the many wives of the principal deity.) Shōno thought that the pressure from, or embellishment for the sake of, official history was on this small god. For he "returned to eternity" while remaining a heretic through and through.

Anyway, she thought at least once that there was nothing else to do but to go to the seashore of Ibaraki prefecture, where a major shrine dedicated to him was located.[12] The reason was that this small god who appeared at that place is said to have manifested himself through an old salt maker during his trance and said, "I have returned, having united with the Izumo god." That sort of deity, who appeared (or seemed to have appeared) as if in a wild fantasy, betraying the proper interpretation of official history, was attractive to the left-wing Shintoist that Shōno is. She wanted to pray where prayers were disconnected from the imperial household. A research source indicated that squirrels and grapes appearing in a dream pointed to that shrine. However, she had had no dreams of either (she had had a number of dreams suggestive of her original god: a different shrine, which is dedicated to the same god, a frog by the sea, a winged black figure in white, and so forth), which means that this particular deity was not really connected to her dreams or fantasies. Even so, there was relief in the fact that he "manifested himself in an individual's dream." In other words, although the small god claimed to have returned, to her he seemed to be a new god, and one who was created out of a fantasy of the socially weak.

Still, the small god and the Izumo god, who had later, in the old man's dream, unreasonably achieved perfect union in defiance of official history, were, after all, artificially enshrined in two separate shrines and reenshrined as a proper set at each of the two places.[13] She had to therefore study and pursue that background again. She also had to find out the social background of the old man's dream. But if she actually went there and grasped the feeling of the sea and the shrine, she guessed that she might be able to get a new mental locale for prayers. On the other hand, she also had some lingering hope that the old god in charge might somehow return. For the new god was unreliable at any rate.

The body so small that a palm can hold it; the carefree, delinquent nature that made him disobey his parent and fall from the parental hand to the land of humans; the odd childishness that, when the Izumo-line representative god put him on his palm because he looked so cute, made him jump up at his cheek; the irresponsibility that made him hide on so many occasions under leaves and whatnot and, in the end, disappear by springing from a millet stalk . . . in the first place, where was she to locate the little body? She found it hard to grasp the physical sensation of praying.

—To imagine the god being held in her hand; keep him on her shoulder; ask with her eyes turned up, "Please help mother, okay?" (Shōno has no plan to become a mother[14])—after all she abandoned all those ideas before trying any. They had no connection to her past lifestyle. Even so, because she knew that some of her dreams accurately reflected her psychology and physical condition, it was impossible for her to evade that fact and continue to offer prayers to her original god. During the one year without a "god," she endured the coldness at S-kura by means of "cursing." And, after all, she found her way out of that situation by psychological solutions, or her own psychological interpretations, rather than handling it as an issue of religious faith. The process was as usual like a wild fantasy, however—

"The original one in charge," who had been away starting on August 3 two years ago, once returned (in other words appeared in her dream) on October 7, and on the tenth she received an award from Kanazawa city, one that has perhaps the proudest tradition among literary prizes offered by local governments. The prize, named after the novelist of fantasy worlds, whom she had loved in her youth and whose grave she visited while living in Zōshigaya in Tokyo, was the one that Mori Mari had been awarded earlier.[15] Moreover the piece chosen was a critical biography of Mori. Shōno was delighted, feeling as if she had become part of the lineage of that fantastic author and of Mori Mari. Until the very day she had not even been informed of having been nominated, and thus she had no (at least no conscious) expectations. She had forgotten that each of her former awards had followed a dream about a shrine. When she had received the phone call about this new award, she had momentarily hesitated. The reason was that she would be unable to attend the ceremony unless she found someone to take care of her cats.

Dora, if left at a pet hotel, would experience closure of the urethra because of the shock, and that might threaten her life. That is why Shōno, when going home at the time of her father's major operation, had gone so far as to undergo a required interview (for the potential sitter to see if there was an affinity between the sitter and the cats so as to determine whether care would be possible) before being able to obtain the assistance of a famed cat sitter. It was uneventful at that time, for the cat was friendly toward the sitter and behaved like a "paragon child." But then a few days later, the cat was in critical condition because of dehydration. The veterinarian diagnosed the case as one of mental shock. Shōno has so far declined all invitations to overseas lectures and literary-exchange opportunities. Not only that, even for a memorial for the dead, she had made only a ten-hour day trip. If she was to attend the award ceremony this time, she had to think of an overnight trip. Given that it was "god's will," she thought at least at that moment that it might somehow work out.

One might suggest asking an acquaintance to help, but Shōno had no so-called ordinary "lovely little cats." It was even more disconcerting to try an unfamiliar business place she might find in the phone directory. Unexpectedly, the plan of the husband-and-wife veterinarian team kindly visiting her home materialized. She felt reassured, thinking that "she should be able to be awarded a prize as long as she had had such a dream." Though the arrangement was a rare luxury, she was able to attend the ceremony without event.

She had the dream when she had barely managed to publish the second part of the present novel, which had gone with difficulty because she had had the problematic task of making confessions in it about her *petit* faith. She did not even recall that each of her awards had followed a dream, but anyway she was happy that the original "one in charge" had returned. Also, when she won the award, there had been no warped, illusory joy from thinking, "It might after all have been a precognitive dream." She felt that the simulation that had occurred subconsciously five times in the past twenty years had by chance turned out to be a reality. Moreover, after having kept a dream diary for over twenty years, she knew that even if a dream looked like a precognition, it could miss the target at some point.

In the first place, expectation brought into a dream would dull the simulation, and a prophetic dream can be a mere coincidence. However, to be able to avoid fearing the future, if just for a moment, proved to be a positive mental effect of "precognitive dreams."

Are dreams absurd then? No, Shōno was struck by "the coherent sense of reality within the dream" when she experienced the true-to-life quality of that dream that had revisited her after twenty years.

One year before her literary debut, in her early twenties she saw the "god" just once in her dream. He looked like a distinguished, scary, omnipotent mature male who was concerned about her future. For over twenty years, even though items suggestive of his shrine and its symbols had appeared in her dreams, he had never showed himself again. When he reappeared in her dream after more than twenty years, he did not look older at all, and, moreover, he revealed his weaknesses in the same way as did other human beings she met (no matter who it was, she had the habit of finding a striking flaw in style, appearance, or a mole when seeing the same person for the second time). "Oh, an ordinary type, and moreover he looks mean, like an out-and-out believer in efficiency," she thought. The only thing is that his countenance was "not at all changed," though only from the memory of one who found it hard to remember people's faces. In this dream, quite unlike the usual image of a god, there was something petty about him, something that made her feel hesitant about telling people about him.

In this dream, after a series of occurrences, like the text of the history of Japanese literature she had used at a cram school coming out in shredded form in gradual stages and an ornamental frog abruptly turning into a real one and jumping up, there was a sense of a shrine though with no vision of concrete actions for showing respect (which was of course not scientific, because hers was not a precise premonitory dream leading to a fixed result under fixed conditions, but in the dream in which she had first met him, before the award on her debut piece, the point was his face rather than his shrine, though it too appeared), and a straightforward, metallic sound unlike a human voice rang and rang in her ears. Then—

"I have gone out of my way, even skipping a conference, to come here to see how you are doing. And look at you, giving up yourself to laziness," he chided, as if chiding a company employee, in language so unexpected from a god. He spoke one-sidedly without feeling, in a tone that can only be described as merciless. Spoke? Or rather, the voice "came," or "was produced," or "sounded competent." Despite the fact that she had heard a "divine voice" for the first time, it recalled that of an energetic young editor hurrying up an author. Moreover, despite the fact that it was the same face as the one she had seen at age twenty-four, his face was now strangely smooth, fuller around the cheekbones than before. "It's just that you've added on to your own age," he said. "How unreliable can you be, aren't you like a child." When she woke, she could not for a while believe that the god had returned. She was struck dumb by surprise, and then little by little joy reemerged. He has kindly returned, she felt, because she had somehow continued to write some things while being busily occupied with the work of playing the part of a master.[16] That made her think that she had to write no matter what, even if her work was somewhat flawed, or even if rejected by literary magazines. While understanding thus, she could not refrain from bursting into laughter because the dream was so odd. In the first place, his mention of something about a conference suggested an editorial meeting on the table of contents, as she became instantly aware. She didn't from the beginning believe in such a thing as the mysteriousness of dreams. But even so—

"Skipped a conference? Oh, of course, this is the Godless Month.[17] The gods are gathered at Izumo," she laughed loudly.

Shōno also felt relieved about the cool distance between her dream and herself. What if she had been of a predisposition conducive to having only grandiose dreams in which martial gods appeared, or if she had not continued to keep a dream diary for decades and not worked on concretely reflecting on her dreams—

She was well received at Kanazawa. She flew on an airplane for the first time in her life, saw the Sea of Japan also for the first time, was able to see authors she liked, and ate with her father, who had appeared for the ceremony. The editor who attended for congratulations' sake handled, on this single occasion, both the delayed celebration of five earlier publications and the launching of this new serialization. When Shōno returned with a pack of mackerel sushi for herself and bean bags, one thousand yen each, wrapped in Kaga crepe, for little siblings in the neighborhood (just two sets of four, the one rabbit shaped and the other cat shaped), both purchased at airport shops, she found Dora in good health. Rather, the one that had suffered from her absence was Guido. Whatever had finally calmed down over one year had restarted, and he made a racket. Making apologies, she closed the storm doors just past eight o'clock. With the precision of a machine or a primitive creature, however, "On a Cat I Stepped"[18] instantly started again. Unlike before, this time it was persistent, perhaps intentionally so.

"Has she obtained the right to step on a cat?" Summer nighttime piano had been the source of complaints in the neighborhood, and requests had reached Shōno, who lived close to the house, to indirectly express complaints about the piano and the dog. But the opponent, it was clear, wagered on the single point: cats. The piano piece was so noisy that it reached her ears from behind the closed windows, and even the cats knew it was not practice playing. Yet, as long as a child was playing, one could not really go to the extent of pointing that out. Whether Shōno opened her bay window or started the vacuum cleaner as a gesture, the music continued endlessly. She had been trying not to have to hear it, but it had suddenly begun. Perhaps because she was exhausted from the trip and Guido's care, her heart pounded noisily as if a whole portable refrigerator sat on her back, and she held her head in both hands in her living room, groaning. There was no deference or considerateness in the abruptness, and it was quite vehement even though something like this might be expected of children in general. "Right, when I snapped and yelled earlier once, the playing stopped. But this time it has reached the point where that kind of reaction is no longer sufficient to make it stop. How am I to handle this persistence and lack of reason?" Although she herself claimed to love children, and although she made efforts to be friends with the neighborhood children, Shōno was not in fact used to creatures called children. Or rather, she was most afraid of those who had lacked reason—this was how simple she was at heart. Well, she had so far been able to get by because her cats, though they may have lacked reason, used their instincts more or less as natural restraints.

Shōno's animosity was rising when she happened to look aside and found Guido had stopped crying, seemingly having recovered his senses for the moment, and was sitting up with his eyes turned her way. "Everyone" was frightened, Shōno thought. "Did Mother scare you, I'm all right now," she said in a fluster and quickly held Guido's head in both hands. With his moist reddish brown nose almost stupidly lustrous, the cat raised his chin like a Kabuki actor playing a female role. He was the kind of cat who calmed down for a minute or so if caressed, even when he snapped and mewed. But this method was inefficient when repeated. "Indirectly" expressing complaints to the neighbor was not the way to go. She would now speak clearly, Shōno thought.

She opened the window facing the piano. For one year since having moved into this place, for fear of their complaints, Shōno had opened this window for a total of less than five minutes, and she had been careful enough to open even the curtains no more than several times. When vacuuming the bay window too, she always kept it locked. But now, through the screen door, she said in a loud voice, "I'm sorry but that piece is disturbing to my ears. Please stop." The piano stopped. For the rest of the day there was no sound, almost to the extent that it was scary.

For a number of days after that, when it was sunny, especially in the afternoon, she opened just the cloth curtains to let the sunlight in through the lace behind them. Hers was a house with many windows and she had experienced no inconvenience, but she was surprised to find how open and pleasant it felt when the bay window was covered only by lace. The neighbors' bay window, which faced hers, was always covered only by lace. Shōno had held back from doing the same, because one time when she had tentatively opened her curtains, the neighbor's cloth curtains had closed with a snap.

Soon after that, she had spoken for the first time in one and a half years with the member of that palatial residence who was the most difficult to deal with, the very one who had said right away when they had first met, "Cats smell. I hate it, I hate your moving in. Everyone dislikes you, so don't move here."

On the day they had spoken for the second time, construction work had been going on at the house since noon, altering their yard so the family could feed wild birds. Some say that attracting wild birds negatively affects the natural environment, and besides, Shōno had just a month before washed away with water a large quantity of bird droppings that had accumulated on her verandah.

She recalled the news about someone who, under suspicion for a series of murders (though he was eventually proved innocent), was arrested on a separate charge of cruelty to cats. A bird lover, he shot cats with arrows because they caught birds. Dogs, pianos, children, and birds are welcome but out with cats—this disgusted her. With Shōno's broom, Shōno began sweeping Shōno's driveway, which was cluttered with leaves and twigs from the trees in the garden of the palatial residence, branches that had broken as a result of the palatial residence's alteration work. Then the person in question had called out in a very polite tone, "Ma'am, ma'am." How could she have forgotten that Shōno had said at their first meeting that she was going to live by herself. This neighbor probably no longer remembered what she herself had said one and a half years ago. Even so, her attitude was quite different from that of before.

The neighbor kept her very polite tone and demonstrated her thoughtfulness to the extent that she requested, "I was just thinking of sweeping your driveway, so please leave it as is." However, because she had not one word of apology for the construction noise and scattering of branches, her way of thinking seemed somewhat self-centered. Earlier, when Shōno had had some work done to her own house, the worker had first gone over to apologize. Even so, the neighbor had said disagreeable things. But anyway Shōno responded with, "Please don't worry, I'm just sweeping at my own convenience." It was late autumn, but somehow the conversation developed to a summer topic.

The neighbor's dog was leashed close to the border between the two houses, so when Shōno stood near the edge of her yard, it barked. It had once playfully sprung on her worker over the fence. Thus, when it came to the border area between the houses, Shōno made it a rule to weed when the dog was taken out for a walk. On one such occasion, noticing a few tall stalks of grass on her side having been pulled out, her understanding was this: "I see, they are annoyed. The pulled grass is deliberately left on my side, meaning I had better take notice." What the neighbor brought up was in fact that matter. "In the summer, you see, it's a problem, you know, ma'am, ma'am, ma'am."

What the neighbor had to convey was that she wanted Shōno to say one word to her before weeding because she would then leash her dog elsewhere. Something was odd, Shōno felt. She had weeded at least a number of times. Still—

"I'll try to weed when your dog is out for a walk," Shōno responded, because she thought the topic did not call for a candid reply like, "Why on earth do I have to report to you before entering my own garden? It's the other way around. When you see me weeding, figure out what you should do, then rush to leash your dog elsewhere." The neighbor noticed nothing, and said even more politely, "But the dog's walk finishes so quickly you can't carefully weed to your satisfaction, you see. Ma'am, I use care to pull out and throw away tall grass in the summer. I beg of you, won't you please understand?"

"I see, I am terribly sorry about that. I accept your kind offer then," Shōno apologized, too lazy to switch from the politeness mode to another. Having done that, she instantly and on the spot began feeling resentful of things, including earlier ones as she traced the time backward. "This is not at all to my taste, what does she mean, telling me to leave it alone when I was sweeping my own place? A few blades of grass versus so many dustpanfuls of fallen leaves per year." So, she was finally ready.

Okay, let me say something about the piano. Oh, but before then, I should first say, "That sort of brief walk is a cruelty to a dog." Shōno was about to change her stance in that manner, but then—

"People in this area don't like children," the neighbor lied again, like one and a half years ago. The first time around it was possibly a lighthearted, irresponsible comment. But persisting in it seemed pernicious. A young couple's child and his friends were noisy, so her dog barked, the neighbor said, at least her reasoning shifting from cats to children. Her voice sounded half teary, and Shōno might have felt sympathetic if she had been listening in ordinary circumstances. The woman said she was asking children, "though for selfish reasons," not to play on the street, for it was painful when her dog barked. "But that one there is the family that really disliked children and spoke harassingly to the young couple," she said, pointing at a house, the same one she had pointed to earlier. In that house, however, lived a tidy, mild-natured family. Where were reason, aesthetics, morality—this was what Shōno thought, seemingly unaware of her own limitations.

With nothing else to do, Shōno responded in a voice indicative of slight pain and sounding even more polite than before, "Which house is it? Is it that house? This house? The so-and-so family? The so-and-so-and-so family? All of them are fond of children, and they are nice people." In short, she wanted to say that a lie exactly identical to the one from one and a half years ago would not work.

The situation had developed since that first encounter, and Shōno had become friends with the members of the houses she pointed at as well as the young couple next door to her. Or, to put it more accurately, she had joined their consumer co-op. The one who used to wince at the very word co-op had somehow adapted herself to S-kura (would the Shirakaba school be furious if they heard this?).[19]

At the beginning she had declined to join because, needlessly, she had thought it bothersome and also felt repulsed by the photograph of a housewife on the pamphlet. But the person with whom the young couple had teamed and who was originally from this area had quit without a word "to team with old locals after all." The abandoned couple was in a bind, partly because there was a delivery charge for individual purchasers. Well then, newcomers could team up by themselves, Shōno thought, and joined. As a group, delivery was free and it was convenient for getting, for example, *kyōgen*[20] tickets. And against the expectation that co-op meant intimate socializing, she had found that she did not even need to appear at the door when the delivery arrived.

The expression "Which house?" and the proper nouns Shōno used made the other party falter in her speech. And moreover, an urgent matter happened to occur (this was true) concerning that person, so that Shōno was released. Right away a neighbor rushed over to her place and comforted her: "Poor you, what did she say to you?" "She seems to be thoughtful at least about her dog," Shōno replied, protective only of the dog, and thus firmly conveying the fact that the woman had spoken disagreeably.

"Thank you very much. I am out of cat food (this was true), so I'll go buy some," she said and parted with the neighbor. While walking the fifteen-minute distance along the main road in the mountains to the home center, she could not refrain from thinking as follows:

"A kind person comforting me—it's really like a noontime TV drama. But a noontime drama employs marketing skills to research and adapt this sort of common situation so that it gives a sense of familiarity to the audience, and furthermore earns program ratings with vulgarity and hyperbole, as well as dramatically introducing grandiose stories of easy-to-understand conflicts between good and evil, cause and effect, self-pity, or the Yomiuri Giants' dominance. Oh yes, there was one among the old tales related to a beautiful, good princess and a plain-looking, wicked princess in which, possibly to appeal to the listeners at large, one of them is put to work in the kitchen—unrealistic even in a fairy tale. Noontime drama is perhaps such a fairy tale. A fairy tale is a piece of adult rumor, to which the narrator adds on episodes as he likes, so said a book called *Deep Structure of Märchen*.[21] Oh well, given the present situation, perhaps it's more uneventful if I remain being bullied. But—

"If she persists," Shōno continued, "I'll bring the piano problem to the public nuisance section or something at city hall and have them build a large wall between us at her expense and on her lot. In terms of how that might block the view and so forth, I won't be the least inconvenienced, because my house has nineteen windows, while, no matter how many windows they may have, the majority face this way (a chuckle). Okay, that being the case, I don't mind contributing just a little to the cost, if that allows me to not see her face for thirty years. Before then, though, I might send certification-of-contents mail or something to force her to switch to a silent piano. No, no, patience is best. I see her only once or so a year, and besides, it may be a fairly good thing for her to be resented without her knowledge for thirty years running," and so on. Shōno was fond of Tokyo but was beginning to be aware that she liked the country too. "It would be a lifetime *vacance* if I had plenty of free time in addition," she sometimes said to herself on her way out to enjoy leisurely walks along a mountain path. The only thing was—

Having been called "ma'am" oddly weighed on her mind. The reason was that, for her, the truth of myths was petty, mass media reports were tales, and ghost stories were nothing but a compilation of realities. Connecting at once the meaning of the word "Mrs." to her *petit* myth, she was once again starting to be in a difficult frame of mind. The reason was that—

Although she had forgotten under the pressure of work, when she lived in Tokyo, each time she entered a coffee shop or a restaurant, she was greeted, "For two?" despite the fact that she was obviously by herself. When a few people came to interview her at a coffee shop, sometimes the waiter brought one too many glasses of water than the number of people. "I may have always been walking around looking carefree as if I had been with someone," she thought. Whether in Tokyo or anywhere else, traditionally speaking, it may have been bizarre for a woman to enter an eating place and order, eat, and drink quite at ease and at her own convenience. Was it better to look miserable and busy? But it was when she had a full purse or her writing was proceeding well that she ate out. She may have appeared happy, as if she had someone with her. Once she was told she was with a long-haired woman. "What does she look like?" she asked. The person apologized profusely, saying, "I take it back, lack of sleep must have made me see things." It was totally impossible that "the other person who had walked with me" was the former god in charge or an ancestor. Perhaps under the influence of that "incident," once in her dreams Shōno saw that person who reportedly walked with her. It was a tall, stylish person of an unknown gender who rather resembled a certain woman writer.

It is true that Shōno did not forcibly resist being called "Mrs.," which had been her appellation since her twenties. But this time she was called "Mrs." despite the fact that she had mentioned the first time they had met that she was going to live by herself.

At S-kura too, married women walked together. Shōno ate out by herself as before. But since moving to Chiba prefecture, a glass of water for her companion no longer came (although the frequency of dining out dropped sharply as well). That is to say—did she perhaps now appear insecure and guilty as she ate? In other words, did she no longer cause restaurant people to have an illusion (hallucination) because she looked like "a sneaky Mrs."? Had she been defeated by the world? Shōno felt insecure. Later, with a truly trite thing as a starting point, she began worrying about this matter.

The cause of her anxiety was one of the passersby who took a look at her cat fence.

When Shōno was weeding inside the fence, this woman of about her age addressed her: "These pussies are so tame." The moment she was spoken to, Shōno stiffened, suspicious of a sales or insurance solicitor. "They know me by my face," the woman continued. "Whenever I stand here, every one of them meows a hello." "You are wrong, that cannot be," Shōno thought but did not say this. She already knew that trying to speak with precision in daily life led others to think of the speaker as queer (she had learned this at age thirty-eight), so she answered, "Oh." Then, with even greater friendliness the woman said, "I hear your husband is a famous novelist. I saw him on TV. Let me catch a glimpse of him, please? Doesn't he come here much any longer?"

A while earlier Shōno had appeared on television, which she rarely did. But she had appeared in *female form*. When she went to the studio, an attendant there had done things like put lipstick on her. There was no way she had looked like her husband.

When she was called by her correct pen name at the cash register of the home center where she bought cat food, she almost went insane. It was a subscriber, rare in this area, to a non-Giants newspaper,[22] who had read an essay Shōno had published in it right after moving here. How the subscriber could tell from the small photograph of her with a different hairstyle was a riddle to her. It's said that no one knows novelists by their faces, and naturally most people don't know them at all. But an odd politeness that sometimes alerted Shōno led her to realize that there were those who knew her but kindly said nothing. "Keep it to yourself," she had asked the cashier. After that the person treated her with pretended innocence, so that whatever she wrote, she thought she should be able to live uneventfully for the time being. But—

Had rumor reached this place? If so, at that time the woman author herself would turn out to be the author's wife. At any rate, she was aghast. Of course it was easier not to be identified, but at least she wished to be mistaken for the author's younger sister or manager. As she was thinking this way, a phrase fell from heaven itself, or rather from episodes that had accumulated in overabundance since her move to this area of a suburban empire intended for married couples (although the store, mentioned in the second installment, that only handled menus for couples had recently finally changed its entire menu to accommodate single orders): "an evil consequence of the presence of a husband who is not there." In other words—

"When a single woman purchases a house, it turns out to be one that her husband, who is not there, has bought; when a woman writes a book, it turns out to be one that her husband, who is not there, has written; I am cursed by a husband who does not exist; okay, I will call this the evil consequence of the presence of a husband who is not there; so now I know the whole meaning behind the change of the one in charge; I have long thought of it, but finally it flashed just now."

This was her first, if somewhat tentative, "reading." Shōno thought, and was threatened by the idea that there was a reality that was like a common, societal hallucination shared by all villagers about the incomprehensible presence called "the husband who is not there," and felt almost stumped by the curse of a community. No matter what she did, what she did was ascribed to her husband. She could exist only through her husband who was not there.

Shōno was threatened because she had been researching the Izumo myths only halfway. In other words, she had misapprehended the "husband who does not exist" as the essence of her dream about the little god.

To explain further, in quest of the ground for the sensation and meaning of the little god who appeared in her dreams, what Shōno first took note of in mythological commentary books for general readers was a theory that "the representative Izumo-line deity was in fact female." There is a theory that this deity is a collective entity of all Izumo gods and great Izumo mediums worshipped by local people who had been conquered by the gods of the imperial line. As proof of this, it has been pointed out among other things that there were many empresses from this region and that their episodes were all too human.

According to the theory claiming the deity to be a woman, it was a female and, moreover, "a mountain god who supervised hunting and a mother god of the land who favored young men." When Shōno learned of this, the expression "snake medium" suddenly descended on her from above her head. For, in the *great* mythology, the mountain god[23] "seemed popular," while Shōno was unpopular. Suppose, tentatively, Shōno *arbitrarily* favored young men, then what—the hypothesis evoked the image of the "snake medium." A heterosexual who, pressed to live alone, went insane. Although thinking of herself as plain looking, Shōno lived quietly without *much* attachment to men. But what if her dream suggested something that might interrupt that calmness? Would she turn into a snake medium at S-kura here?

An insane, one might say uncanny, woman, dark and full of inner resentment, who experiences visions as a result of asceticism, who is a medium for the very reason that she was ostracized from the community, and whose uncanny nature offensively dismantled society with an avant-garde, evil intention—characterizing her so would sound rather smart, but in this case it was not accurate. Someone who is close-minded and surrendered to solitude for the reason that she has no man was, in short, the image the expression "snake medium" carried. Well, maybe the problem was that, around the time she had moved to this place, Shōno had been somewhat gloomy because of her fear of the couple-oriented culture, and that, during that period, the small god had entered her dream as "the husband." In the first place, it was a husband chosen by the mother earth deity, who was fond of young men (in fact, the female author Y. T.,[24] for example, had asked Shōno if she liked young men; but recently she had more often been mistaken for a lesbian).

In the heretical book, which called the small god a sperm deity, it was written that many Japanese mediums assumed they married snakes and brought up baby snakes (of course the ones they caught in the hills and fields) as their own children. In the *great* myth the marriage of a beauty and a snake-god is the conclusion. But the *petit* myth is for those who are likely to be obsessed by a suspicious religion. The expression "husband who is not there," naturally, linked beautifully with the expression "snake medium." Moreover, Shōno knew another mythic episode, which made her fret.

Below is that episode, recorded with a slightly changed nuance. That the Izumo god was female was on her mind, and thus she reread the story in the following manner.

After the small god jumped from a millet ear to return to the world of permanence, the Izumo god became lonely and depressed and lost interest in ruling the land. One day, the sea from where the small god had come shone, and a new god came ashore. "If you enshrine me as the god of Mount Miwa, I will rule this land with you," that god proposed. The Izumo god enshrined him in Mount Miwa. The new god stayed in Japan as the great god of the mountain, and the scar on the Izumo god's heart healed.

In Miwa, three giant boulders are enshrined. They are said to be the Izumo god X-okuninushi, the small god X-kunahikona, and the great god X-omononushi.[25] However, Shōno also read a theory holding that myths had been organized this way in a relatively recent period. If the Izumo god represented the entirety of the indigenous, conquered deities, Shōno thought, the female Izumo god alone could not be expected to cover all Izumo myths. However, the mountain god that she associated with this deity (this was an amateur's arbitrariness; or rather, because Shōno was following a reading of her dreams in order to find a solution in her own heart, she had no choice but to follow myths using her own associations, and the solution thus obtained was, rather than being historically or psychologically *correct*, something for convincing the individual's inner mind) was one who often appeared in old Japanese tales, according to which she was pleased when stonefish was offered, realizing that there was "someone uglier than herself," and who was so jealously fond of male hunters that she did not let women in the mountains. Not only that, she was unpopular. In other words, suppose it was a hunter-god who was a virgin (a suspicious term even in a myth), it was not a beautiful, boyish girl Artemis. Of course if a female god is a female god, the unseemly appearance and fondness for men are her attributes as a god and can be accepted as quite natural. But if the female god were to fall, she would turn out to be a petty "snake medium" who did not enjoy solitude, did not fight, and had neither logical language nor spirituality.

The small god, Shōno interpreted, was the "husband who is not there" who existed in that mountain god's long solitary life. And the great god who appeared when she realized that "he" was ultimately not there, not even found in the shade of leaves no matter how she searched, was the doppelgänger of the female god herself (unintentionally Shōno read the story in this way for the time being). She interpreted the myth in an easy-to-understand way, by applying the genders in her dreams to those in actuality. Upon that premise— the myths say that the Mount Miwa deity was a god who visited a woman by night. If one who lives by oneself in modern society turns out to be that way, would it not be like the "Peony Lantern" with the genders reversed?[26] In other words, it probably meant going insane from excessive solitude. The perception of "not there" and unreliable was still all right. If she can get by with the idea of "present, life-size, visits at night" as no more than supreme self-love (that too was in fact scary), then that was acceptable but—

Again, if one read with this perspective, one would certainly understand the reason that the original sun god appeared in her dream even though (in myths and documents) he has no real point of contact with the small god. The "original one in charge" then falls together with the father image that Shōno had in mind. When aware that one is becoming independent from one's father, one turns into a "snake medium" because one cannot bear that independence. However, Shōno had already decided to live alone in a distant place, having bought a house for her cats. Because her father lived alone, she had made preparations and plans to return for long periods to look after him. But, however far into the future, the time would come when she would have to part with him. Her self-image that emerged from this sort of interpretation of dreams was too wretched, infantile, and undependable for her to even want to look at it. But more important, if she was unable to withstand independence, fell into a ghastly situation like that of the "Peony Lantern" with the genders reversed, and went insane, what would happen to her close relatives and her cats?

If she interpreted the myth with a single focus on the small god as a foreigner, her dreams could be seen as a return to the indigenous serpentine medium that had sloughed off its foreign faith. However, both gods approached from the sea alike, and in any case they eventually assimilated with older, indigenous gods. When her own idea that "a god who appears before an individual belongs to that individual" linked to this, she was threatened by the unnaturalness of the conduct of the female god in the mountains calling to the sea god (despite the fact that Shōno herself arbitrarily connected the two). The sea was no more than an imaginary foreign world, and precisely because the female god of Izumo is a mountain god, Shōno thought, she might have chosen as her partner the god of Mount Miwa, who was an old, great power (in short, just as an *imaginative* woman, who claimed that the he who is not there is present, set him up as a celebrity). Like the image of the "snake medium," the concept of a "husband who is not there" too flowed out from around her at a petty, daily-life level.

After that there had been no problem with the family in question, and so this time she began thinking about the effectiveness of the "husband who is not there." While her mind seemed to roll in different directions, her dreams too were changing during this interval. It may be, Shōno thought, that the luxury-residence woman behaved politely to her after a fashion, or a passerby praised her cats after a fashion, possibly because they envisioned her "husband who is not there" as did Tokyo waiters who noticed her "company." One reason for her thinking this way was that the little god had somehow returned in one month or so following the award ceremony. "Oh no, twice I unintentionally picked up what had drifted from the sea," she thought to herself. "In the first place, I had a dream on the same day about having been to Awaji Island, and the highly educated right-winger who appeared in that dream declined to go with me. So it was definitely a dream of the Izumo-line gods." The original one in charge seemed to have departed, for Shōno had difficulty again in writing the third installment.

Later, after about two weeks, Guido calmed down, but as usual he sometimes returned to his loud meowing. While she was telling the cat to stop it, there came into her covered driveway the resident of the luxury residence, with knowledge (most probably) that Shōno was home. The neighbor was being so thoughtful as to sweep the scattered leaves fallen from her place.

"Don't enter as you please. When you had the impudence to tell me I should greet my neighbors before entering my own yard, why don't you say a word before entering my lot as you please after the nuisance you caused? Even a child says may I get my ball?" Shōno could have said this but did not. Somehow she was in a conciliatory mood, gradually coming to think that the neighbors were not bad people, just clumsy. Their dog started "smiling amicably" at her. But before long—

"Am I to settle down in my dream as a bad-looking, insane mountain god who fell and turned into a monster? Somehow this is disagreeable, unpleasant. I swear I haven't gone to Izumo at all," Shōno found herself muttering on the autumn mountain road that was already dark despite the number of cars still speeding by. As she walked carrying on one side of her body things like ten cans of cat food, which Dora had suddenly craved so she had hurriedly gone to buy, she was feeling the moisture of the marsh, which was beginning to grow dark. "Myths are petty, fairly tales are vulgar, mass media reports are tales, one must start a narrative from one's daily life," she continued to talk to herself, taking advantage of the gloom, as she, though somewhat depressed, walked energetically by fallen giant trees and depthless bamboo thickets. Having a realistic sense of the mountains, she felt all the more this way.

"Around here, if you go three hundred feet closer to the mountains, you feel so much colder," she had been told at a curry shop by the mountain highway. She had had a terrible experience the year before, so before winter came, she had bought an odorless electric heater each for the toilet and the shower room and, in her study, where no air conditioner could be installed without going through the family in question, placed a small domestic oil stove.

The oil stove was quiet and comfortable. But when she thought of getting to work, Dora would enter and sit on her computer or her chair. Last year what had happened was that Shōno had gotten hit by the cold of the northern Bōsō Peninsula. She had finally understood then that, although part of the generally warm Chiba prefecture, this was perhaps a spot where people battled against the cold. Having come from the seashore, she did not know the mountains. "So it's cold in the mountains," she realized. She had not yet been accustomed to this new bodily sensation. (Moreover, the entrance way, built in the blow-through style, which she had thought stylish, was really cold.) It was true winter had been particularly severe for the past two consecutive years, but at any rate the temperature was such that this Mie prefecture person brought up in a warm climate found it hard to cope. In a residential area to which the cold air of the mountains crept up, Shōno tried to live so as not to go insane, while oscillating between the choices of "husband not there" and "reverse 'Peony Lantern.' "

Another interpretation fell from heaven precisely following the first day of spring. Having no wish to keep up her fight against going insane, Shōno reread her voluminous dream diary. Of course this was because she decided to somehow grope for a way out, and although it was too much to check all twenty years' worth of it, she somehow managed to trace back ten or so years. That was because she had not yet been keeping a dream diary around the time of her first dream of the shrine (thus she had a clear memory of it even if all other dreams had been effaced) and that the next shrine dream appeared ten years ago. Amid this work she noticed that she had misunderstood one thing. While also inspecting every item in her old business-card case, she grasped one fact that had led to that misunderstanding.

The third prize awarded to Shōno was one named after the author who had raided Ichigaya, who had held an ideological position close to worshipping the Great Shrine, and who tended to have rightist support.[27] At that point, because she was aware of the "fated connection" between herself and the other shrine that her original one in charge belonged to, she had hesitated somewhat when accepting the award. Or rather, she had believed she would definitely fail. On that day, though it was almost time for the press interview, she had not yet even washed her face and had been thinking of calling for a large pizza and a cola after the news of a failure. So she was hungry at the time of the interview. And that was because the dream she had had just before this was of visiting the Great Shrine. She had interpreted this to mean she had missed the award. Somehow she ended up being selected, but at that point she—what did she do?—changed her dream interpretation for the moment. In other words, despite the fact that a specific shrine was the target of "precognition," she had involuntarily created a system of "fantasy" that included other shrines. She attributed, for example, a rightistlike award to the Great Shrine, and the others to the shrine of the former one in charge. In other words, she made the mistake of making coherent a "divination" that had gone wrong (yet it was logical enough and helped clarify her political and mythological standpoints). So, in an essay she wrote around that time, she referred only to a dream about visiting a shrine (even though she might have rephrased it by error when she published it in a book). In those days, even while she was just vaguely aware of being a Shintoist left-winger, she was indeed convinced of the fact that "a loser god was the god of literature." So she hesitated about what to do with this award that did not belong to her original shrine as she thought of herself as leaning toward the left. And at that point, a scene occurred, from a series of myths, of her original one in charge serving as a guide for a Great Shrine–line god.

To begin with, the place at which her grandfather had consecrated archery and music was the Great Shrine.

She would state her "mythological standpoint" in her speech at the ceremony, she concluded, which would enable her to accept this award. "In trying to dig out the buried myths of the earth, I am a heretic and something like a misshapen black pearl," she said in the speech. But after that, she visited in her dream the original shrine in charge before a fourth national-level prize she was chosen for. Therefore (again subjectively), in her speech she said that if there was a god of literature, she wished to thank him. At that ceremony she met a person who was spoken of in the area as a descendant of her original one in charge. There, something occurred that exerted a decisive influence on the interpretation of her dreams.

The first time it was Shōno's error, and even I thought him the director of a museum of Japanese literature, but a look into the business-card case revealed that that person to whom she had handed the manuscript of the prizewinning story was the head of the materials department. Generations of the manuscripts awarded this fourth prize were normally kept in that museum. But it was twenty years ago that she had chosen the original one in charge for her *petit* faith, and she could not be expected to have known the name of the head of the materials department. When she learned that he was from her hometown, the conversation became lively, and she promised to donate her manuscript. When she thought about this later, that person's rare family name turned out to be stamped right on the very shrine's amulet. Moreover, that shrine was located on the site of his ancestors' house. The only thing is that she knew that even those affiliated with that shrine (despite the fact that it enshrined a god of transportation) sometimes were involved in traffic accidents, and so it was after all *petit* faith rather than faith (there might be another error about this because of the lack of records). In short, she unknowingly assumed that she had "offered" her manuscript to the god of literature. So—

Several years later, when she was asked to read a piece aloud and leave the video as a record for the museum, she chose a short story she had written, with Akutagawa's name included in the title, on the theme of a certain dispute.[28] Not only that, she announced before the audience when reading it, "I dedicate this to Akutagawa no matter how he may object." An acquaintance was surprised that Shōno, a first-time reader, was not at all nervous. But, though she of course knew this was not scientific, she operated on the assumption that she offered the reading in the same way as dances and sumo matches are offered in the precincts of a shrine (she was remunerated but thought it the same as when her grandfather had been repaid at the shrine with wine and other things initially offered to the god). In other words, she took the occasion as a place of special connection, so she thought of further relying on her *petit* faith. That means to say that the "*petit* faith" part was intentional. Even if a *simulation* happened to succeed a few times in a row, it was still a conscious "*petit* faith." For, at some point, she had *interpreted* her dream on her own.

It may be bizarre to talk in contemporary times of "consecration" to a shrine, but her grandfather had served as the sole Shinto official for the village tutelary shrine just for the transportation fees of five hundred yen, or the cost for wooden clogs. Although the family went by Buddhism for funerals, Shōno was taken to his shrine for the first ritual visit after birth, and her parents' house stood on the lot where her grandfather performed the building ceremony. In pursuing fiction not as a game but in earnest while thinking of the societal character of literature, it was necessary to have something that regulated her from outside, or that drew power from deep down. Shōno had never learned about faith at school (in the first place it is nothing that should be taught at public schools), but she had something she wished to follow, and that was where myths and dedications inadvertently came in. The reason that the original one in charge was handsome may have been that her grandfather in his official attire had happened to be good-looking (though he was short and an irresponsible playboy). Her *petit* faith continued because it was necessary though self-generated. However, interpretations of dreams could change, and, she thought for a moment, she had been changing them for the sake of "faith."

Again, the record of her dream when she apologetically declined to be a nominee for a prize awarded by a Kansai local government to women alone caused her to change her interpretations. She rarely had dreams of a shrine. Even if she did, she classified those about shrines of nonlocal, unknown origins together with other miscellaneous dreams. In her diary, dreams of a locally specified shrine were limited to just a few occasions. When she was to miss a prize, she never had any dreams of any shrine. Even if a shrine might occur to her mind out of wishful thinking, it never appeared in her dreams. That was the case with all three occasions she had missed a prize. But at the time of the potential Kansai award, a concrete, local shrine consecrating a female god had appeared with too realistic a presence.

It was very warm, with a feeling similar to that of spring rain, and the trail gently wound. The groves were almost all oak trees. While an elementary school child, she had often picked acorns there. This was a place generally associated in myths with Yamato Takeru's aunt,[29] but judging from the feel of the historical site and the handling of the myths, Shōno in her fantasy suspected a connection with a male god of the conquered line. This female god, in her interpretation, was a result of rewriting history, and it in fact meant oppression (some exponents of American feminism seem to worship an indigenous female god, but Shōno thought to herself, "One may be taken in unless one does research." Moreover, it is an illusion that ethnic minorities do not, simply because they are minorities, belittle women). In her dream, however, the shrine at least represented a genuinely good, great female.

The shrine that looked so gentle that it almost had laugh lines on its face seemed to be in the water of a slow stream, and in that water trees densely grew with bending foliage. Yet when she tried to get to that inviting place, she felt afraid because the path threatened to curve. As long as she was passing by a shrine she would like to pay some respects, thought Shōno in her dream, but in the end she retraced the path without going through the torii. When she was nominated for the award, she declined with proper apologies. Regardless of whether or not she could win, if she, the author of *Restless Dreams*, who had perpetual complaints, won, she thought people might say that women were at an advantage so it was fine to discriminate against them. And again—

Not only that. The dream in which she failed to visit the shrine represented a "divine will" for her at that point. When she visited, in her dream, a shrine dedicated to the female god of the imperial ancestral line, at any rate she went through the gateway and showed her respect. As long as there was a manifestation in her dreams, she thought she should accept what came to her. For that reason, as long as she had a dream about not entering the female god's shrine, she considered that she should not accept this award. An award was basically a divine manifestation. As long as she did not find it hard to make a living, she should not accept what her dreams did not allow. She did not particularly wish to judge other people receiving awards or the reasons for their awards by bringing them under this category of "divine will," and even if she sometimes thought that something was "a wrong decision, despite the fact it was divine will," such was her understanding about her own case.

Thanks to having carefully reread her dream diary, Shōno was made aware of having forgotten her usual basic question as to what gender meant for gods. Gods in her dreams, those in myths—

"Me within the myths, me within my dreams, me as a male in my dream, my dream about a male," she was, before long, whispering this when taking a bath. She grew up brainwashed by Princess Knight.[30] Whether or not there was a gender difference in her soul was the question she finally woke to. The body itself aside, she did not take her eyes away from the bodily gender difference. Yet she averted her eyes from the spiritual gender difference.

While she did have grounds for thinking of herself heterosexual, there had been many occasions in today's social system when she had no choice but to basically hate men. She always thought that there was absolutely no need to think seriously about men as any concern of hers. But—

When she tentatively hypothesized that perhaps within herself "there was another self, something like an existence that might be called a male self, and perhaps she had a feeling that she was already living with this man," she felt that this pointed to one aspect within herself even if it were not 100 percent accurate.

A male god should be a great presence that overwhelmed her, and if it became less great even by a little, then he could no longer be worshipped. But wasn't it in fact something that always competed, as it coexisted, with the male gender within her? The reason that the "guiding male" god was necessary for her and that her god was always male was not that she was physically a woman and needed a husband. In this gendered modern world, the part of her that had no other choice but to appear in a dream in male form, or the part of her that had no choice but to take the form of a man even if tentatively, she suspected, was what made her invoke a male god as her leader. Moreover, although Shōno assumed that she was probably nearly all heterosexual, she also wondered if there was anyone who was 100 percent heterosexual. She may have had the potential to experience love that was like being drawn to a man as a man. She recalled in passing that, when examining as a judge some pieces nominated for a new author's prize, she almost shed tears despite herself while reading a study of Minakata Kumagusu[31] that was based on the viewpoint of fellow communion between men.

Naming it "male gender" sounded outdated, but she thought that she would tentatively call by that name what stuck out beyond female roles and was not allowed in the old-fashioned areas where she grew up, and call her "male self" what might in terms of gender be male (even if, as is the case with the author of the "The Principles of Yaoi,"[32] spiritually she and that other self might be male gays). In the first place, if a god is treated as a "female god because of having been conquered," expressions like "a great woman" or "women are great" become useless and the meanings deteriorate. Again, no matter how powerful the female god of a shrine, if a "husband" guides her, that would be poor.

Shin'i, will of the gods, is also *shin'i*, true meaning, and, she decided to think, it symbolizes understanding between her and her "male self" that exists in her dreams and in her spirit. In her spirit there is a man. She also thought that that man is good-looking not because he is of the opposite sex but because he is the product of her narcissism. It was common, she thought, for a woman to imagine herself to be a man, or rather in her fantasy to give a beautiful form to the male gender within herself, or to its friend or lover of the same sex.

Shōno also thought that what resided in her body might be a hard-to-deal-with macho figure. She began to be aware of her "male self," who, while she herself was thought of as a feminist, sometimes said terribly discriminating things to, or thought endearingly of, those women who trusted her, that is, just her plain "male self," neither a lesbian, which it was impossible for her to be, nor transgender.

But no matter how macho he is, as long as he is within a woman's body, what exists is "a macho man who is discriminated against as a woman." If he were able to have awareness of the fact that "he might be macho," this could be called a new, minority-type potential. For the majority of the rest are female to begin with.

He of the spirit, or one's self as a man, cannot be a husband. By how one faces this, one changes. He is a rival of the great male god. Suppress, or recognize, the male nature within oneself?

She decided to think that the fact that the small god was announced in her dream as being a "husband" represented the curse of the noise from the external world, or, of the suburban empire.

To use the language of the old age when gender roles were clearly defined, Shōno felt, a medium might have at once been male or female. Of course, in an era when being "an individual, total and human" was not allowed, there may have been numerous taboos; it might have been difficult to explore such a possibility. But when transforming sexual energy into the power of a visual hallucination or of a curse, that is at least an act of trying to transgress gender and physical differences.

Scholars who, about her work, cheerfully attached labels like daughter's feminism (in fact it was son's feminism!) or old resentment feminism (better to call it patriarchal feminism!) would never, Shōno thought, go down to the depths of "lowest people." It was possibly like the kind of things said by a cheaply constructed shrine just built in a deserted place with no worshippers and no object of worship. Again, she thought it odd if there were people who said that the spirit of a medium was equipped with bisexuality. A sensation welled from the bottom of her heart. She found it somewhat wrong to talk about "androgynouness" or "bisexuality." For in the case of men and women in her dreams, roles called manlike or womanlike in society were quite often interchangeable. To her, talking specifically of "bisexual" or "androgynous" about characters in fiction sounded as if saying "this is strawberry milk containing both strawberries and milk, it's queer." Shōno thought that eventually she would improve such expressions as "male self" or "male gender" to something more accurate (this was the best she could say for now).

When the second spring approached at S-kura, Shōno was thinking of buying a synthesizer drum. The moment she mentioned it on the phone, it turned out that she could inherit the drum that a vocalist from the jazz club from her university had been made to buy from a senior member. She also mail-ordered a foreign cosmetic item, foreign meaning without having done useless animal experiments, advertised as previously unsold in the country. She had given up the drum because it was impossible both in terms of physical strength and talent. She also thought that given power drummers Cindy Blackman and Terri Lyne Carrington, there was no need for her to drum. But, to use an old-fashioned expression, her thought was that her "male self" wished to drum, so she would allow him to at least practice drumming, and that both her male self and female self would undoubtedly wish to apply cosmetics.

From time to time she suddenly felt angry as if she had gone insane. She felt that she had arbitrarily forbade herself everything. It was odd that "what women do" was held in contempt, and there was no need for her to go insane, because, within herself, the male god who guided her "male self" became greater or smaller. For there was another "self that was male" within her. In short, in an attempt to thus believe, she kicked and struggled.

One night near the first day of spring, there was a powerful thunderstorm in S-kura. In her dream, she was walking hand in hand with a man her height. His face was too vague to figure out, but as an impression he did not much resemble the original sun god. Although he somewhat resembled the materials department head said to be its offspring, she also felt that he might be the small god. When she woke to rumbling thunder, the sound of the rain was rich. She wondered, "A reference to the coldness of a mountain area?" While the cold was severe she experienced "the curse of a husband not there," and when spring came and it was easier to spend the days, it was "the great god of Ōmiwa of Mount Miwa" who promised to be with her. She had no idea if spring thunder visited Mount Miwa. But she no longer feared the change of the one in charge. Whether the "male gender" looked up at the "great man" above her, found him unreliable, or remained equal, being the same size as herself, the fact remained that any one of them was someone with whom she could associate, and she could only continue to relate to her "male self." This was her thought. Naturally, this interpretation can be laughed off at any moment.

The End.

Notes

1. Earlier in the novel, the author provides the names of three gods: X-rutahiko, X-kunahikona, and O-X-namuchi, each missing one syllable as an indication of the fact that these are her personal versions of Sarutahiko, Sukunahikona, and Ōnamuchi in Japanese mythology. The indigenous god Sarutahiko, large and high nosed,

acted as a guide when Ninigi, grandson of the sun goddess, Amaterasu, descended from heaven. Sukunahikona is a dwarf god who came from the sea. In this novel, Sarutahiko is the central character's original guardian god; Sukunahikona is her new guardian. Ōnamuchi is the principal god of Izumo, now the eastern part of Shimane prefecture. The expression "one in charge" commonly refers to the editor working with the author.

2. An allusion to the Yamato tradition of Japanese mythology found in the *Kojiki* (Records of Ancient Matters, 712) and *Nihon shoki* (Chronicles of Japan, 720).

3. The reference is to the indigenous shining god as separate from the sun goddess, Amaterasu.

4. An oblique reference to a book that characterizes Sukunahikona as a snake-mounted god of sperm (Yoshino Hiroko, *Hebi—Nihon no hebi-shinkō* [Snake: Japanese Snake Worship] [Tokyo: Hōsei University Press, 1979]).

5. Sarutahiko Shrine in Ise city, Mie prefecture.

6. An allusion to *Reviving Heretical Gods* (*Bessatsu rekishi dokuhon* 86, Shin Jinbutsu Ōraisha, 1995).

7. Matsumae Takeshi, *Izumo shin'wa* (Tokyo: Kōdansha, 1976).

8. The author uses an uppercase *S* for the Chinese character corresponding to the syllable "Sa" in the place-name Sakura to indicate that her Sakura is separate from the actual Sakura. Likewise she uses an uppercase *I* for the character for "I" in the place-name Ise.

9. Awashima Shrine in Wakayama city, Wakayama prefecture.

10. A large crow that guided Jimmu, the legendary first emperor, from Kumano to Yamato.

11. The allusion is to the dwarf god Sukunahikona.

12. Ōarai-Isosaki Shrine in Ōarai town in Higashi-Ibaraki county, Ibaraki prefecture, is dedicated to Ōnamuchi and Sukunahikona.

13. Besides the Ōarai-Isomae Shrine, Ōmiwa Shrine, at the foot of Mount Miwa in Sakurai city, Nara prefecture, enshrines Ōnamuchi and Sukunahikona together in addition to its principal god, Ōmononushi, the snake-deity who assisted Ōnamuchi after Sukunahikona had left.

14. As cat-loving females often do, the main character poses as her cats' mother.

15. The award is named after Izumi Kyōka (1873–1939), known for mysterious romanticism. Mori Mari (1903–1987), daughter of Mori Ōgai, was a novelist and essayist with a distinctive aesthetic sensibility.

16. A playful reference to the tasks of critiquing and advising younger authors.

17. The tenth month by the lunar calendar is so called because all gods confer at Izumo at this time, leaving the rest of the country godless.

18. A simple piano piece for children played almost all on the black keys and known in the West as the "Flea Waltz." A child member of the neighboring family plays this piece when Shōno's cats are noisy.

19. The Shirakaba (White Birch) school refers to a group of writers associated with the Peers School and was represented by Mushakōji Saneatsu, Shiga Naoya, and Arishima Takeo. The school, which took its name from a literary journal published between 1910 and 1923, was characterized by libertarianism and individualism. In 1918 Mushakōji Saneatsu established a utopian commune called Atarashiki Mura (New Village) in Hyūga, Kyushu.

20. *Kyōgen*, also known as *nōkyōgen*, is a form of comic drama that developed together with Noh in the fourteenth century and is still performed today.

21. Mori Yoshinobu, *Meruhen no shinsō: Rekishi ga toku dōwa no nazo* (Deep Structure of Märchen: Mysteries of Children's Tales That History Solves) (Tokyo: Kōdansha, 1995).

22. A non-Giants newspaper means any newspaper other than the *Yomiuri*, which owns the Giants.

23. The reference is to Ōmononushi, the god of Mount Miwa, Nara prefecture.

24. Tawada Yōko, a translation of whose "Starlets Scintillating in My Eyes" is included in this volume.

25. These three names stand for Ōkuninushi, Sukunahikona, and Ōmononushi.

26. A 1666 adaptation by Asai Ryōi, and its variants, of an old Chinese story called "A Record of the Peony Lantern." A woman who died of love's longing visits her lover nightly, led by her maid holding a peony lantern. When a neighbor tells him the woman is in fact a skeleton, he takes measures to fend her off, but in the end she kills him.

27. This is a reference to the Mishima Yukio Literary Award. Ichigaya refers to JGSDF Camp Ichigaya, where Mishima committed suicide in 1970. The shrine is the Ise Great Shrine, which is dedicated to the female sun god, Amaterasu Ōmikami.

28. A dispute from the late 1990s lasting several years in which Shōno defended "pure literature," which was criticized by producers of popular literature as inferior to better-selling popular entertainment literature.

29. Yamato Takeru, said to be the second or third son of "emperor" Keikō, was indirectly assisted by his aunt, Yamato-hime, at Ise at the time of his expedition to Kyushu and the northeast. In 1922, a shrine was dedicated to Yamato-hime at Kuratayama in Ise.

30. The main character as it is known in the West of *Ribon no kishi* (The Knight of the Ribbon), from Tezuka Osamu's manga (in installments, 1953–56, revision 1963–66) by that title. It also refers to the entire cycle, including the anime (1967) and musicals based on it. Princess (Prince) Sapphire has both the blue heart of a boy and the pink heart of a girl (http://en.wikipedia.org/wiki/Princess_Knight).

31. Minakata Kumagusu (1867–1941) was a biologist, ethnologist, and folklorist.

32. Yaoi refers to a genre of manga and fiction mostly on young boys' love. The term Yaoi is said to come from the phrase "yamanashi, ochinashi, iminashi" (no climax, no bathos, no meaning).

16

You People's Love Is Near Death

Kawakami Mieko

Now that she has become an adult, she no longer has to consult anyone or read the slight expression on another's face but can choose just what she needs and go anywhere she wants to go, simply according to how her purse, time, and feelings relate.

The woman recalls this when she finds herself at the inner heart of the heart of Shinjuku, gliding along in a happy mood by a cosmetics counter to where more and more people spill out as if from the mouth of an ice machine; walking like that should be neat behavior if anything, but sometimes, by how any two elements floating around her make a small collision, she is discouraged, or somehow even feels as if thrown into terrible anxiety, and stands transfixed. That always lasts only a while, however, so until the spell evaporates with a whirling swish, she tells herself you're okay, you're okay, and, now shutting and now opening her eyes or calming her breath, lets various troubling things escape from within her.

Good fragrances. Good vanity. Good vials. Good bodies. And then, good handbags, and good shapes of all things. Good coloring. Good eyeballs. Good hair and good ambition. Women checking things or looking into mirrors at a cosmetics counter have invariably come here to improve on, or further double, the modest amount, or the large amount that is already becoming impossible to control, of the "good" things within themselves; to take them out and show them to one another, with the corners of their mouths pulled diagonally upward, which, if one looks carefully, turns out to be something called a smiling face.

"Anata-tachi no koi wa hinshi," from Kawakami Mieko, *Chichi to ran* (Breasts and Ova) (Tokyo: Bungei Shunjū, 2008). Copyright 2008 by Mieko Kawasaki. Translated by Kyoko Selden with the permission of the author, arranged through Bungei Shunjū Raitsu Kanribu. Translation copyright 2011 by Kyoko Selden.

Sitting in a chair shaped like white cream that has turned solid, the woman too smiles at a salesperson. Saying uh or something. She pretends to be looking at new products. One new product after another appearing almost every week, when she thought of the number of half-used cosmetics going to waste, she felt her cheeks about to blush just slightly. Do cosmetics, she wondered, properly go bad like other things? The oil passing its time? Because the gleaming light for illuminating the jewelry shines directly from above her head, the woman's face in the mirror looks more romantic than in any other mirror. From within the counter on which she has placed her hand too, pale-blue light is showing a round swell, and she thought, impressed: the way the straight light from above pierces the round light is rather like a numerical figure. The woman's nose looming in the light appears somewhat charming. Yeah yeah, she nods to herself as she looks to the right, looks to the left, and, tensing her eyelids, checks the way her eyelashes are curled.

A young salesperson with her hair drawn back into a bun and wearing a ring with a tiny pink stone on her ring finger fluttered her hand, and saying, Miss, this is pretty incredible, took out a jar of cream from a grandiose case, and, after putting on gloves, also with grandiose gestures, smoothly turned the lid around, removed it fully, and showed the contents to the woman. A mere look at it alone did not tell how soft or cold it was or any trivial thing about the substance. Its fragrance seemed common enough to be found just anywhere, but then it could also be the first fragrance she had ever smelled; it looked extremely good, or perhaps like nothing special. Besides, she didn't know too much about creams. Rather than the nature of this incredible cream, the ring on the salesperson's finger inside the glove was on the woman's mind. Because it was clearly on the left ring finger of all her ten fingers, in eight or nine out of ten cases it would be a gift from her lover; its modest design, which didn't stand in the way, suited very well this salesperson's wearing no makeup, and this combination appeared just slightly distasteful to the woman. It was as if the two unaffected elements, the woman felt, secretly conspired to steal, bit by bit, every night, from something very clever that was within the lover, in ways that would never be noticed by the man himself.

Delicate underwear, a small cotton tank top, an elegant necklace of a slender chain, anything would do, but the presence of something like a sign on the surface of a bare body would be lovely, and such a thing would make the eyes pay attention in bed, in a gloom, or within the reach of body temperature—attention to a piece that could be pulled off, gazed at, or concealed. That would make the lover feel good and excited; and because the deep-colored part of the tough, distasteful temperament of this salesperson, who was able to properly excite her lover for a certain duration of time, daily gobbled those items in that manner, it gave off much fragrance, as if it amplified, leaked, and let the air slowly spread. That's why, the woman thought, the salesperson, whom she had met only once because of the mediation of the effect of such a ridiculous cream, made her imagine this sort of thing.

She walked out of the smooth-surfaced department store while eyeing corners of various brand goods, and looked at her wristwatch to confirm that she had four hours before the appointed time, but this time she was not thrown off anywhere.

She found nothing resembling insecurity no matter how she looked around every part of her mood, so this made her gait light. Shoes with sturdy heels are in fashion these days—as if talking to herself, she called these words to the surface of her mind as she sent her eyes toward the feet of women walking though the streets. I like delicate-looking high heels because they favorably show the shape of my feet from the ankle to the instep, and I can handle this nicely shaped footwear like original parts of my feet. Even if I have no plan for buying shoes, I can enter a shoe store to see my feet in a rectangular mirror meant for feet alone and placed very close to the floor, twirl my body with a polite gesture before a store clerk tries to speak to me, and swing out of the store, leaving a nice impression behind me.

After that, while thinking about what one could do given four hours, the woman involuntarily narrowed her eyes at the evening light of early winter scattering on the road, where people walked, each in a different mind, and tried visualizing a compositional arrangement of herself looking down at herself from somewhere a little higher above.

Then, beyond that point was a cell phone advertisement on a large billboard showing a female face, and while the woman's eyes were being drawn to its outline, her shoulder forcefully collided with that of a female who was walking toward her. The woman, suddenly collided against, barely managed not to fall to one side; but, while not quite landing on her rear, she went into a crouching position despite herself, and the palm supporting her weight, now spotted with white traces from the concrete, looked vague, as if fuzzed up, and part of the skin was also scraped.

Brushing her hand, when the woman looked up at the female who had collided with her, far from apologizing, the latter glared at her, exhaling a sharp, short breath through the slit between her thick lips. The woman could almost see that breath. Large eyes. A short skirt, bare legs, the boot material stretching up to the middle of the calves, full of energy, pale cheeks; she was still very young.

The woman quickly averted her eyes, and with nothing to say, slowly rose, and, unable to stare the young woman in the face, removed, with fingertips, the black, dustlike thing stuck to her palm. There was a scratch of half an inch or so on the heel of one of her high heels. The young woman for a while showed no sign of ever moving, so, with nothing else to do, the woman in the end gave her a glance. The young woman then looked the woman over from head to toe and, without changing the shape of her mouth at all, sniffed just once, seemingly laughing at the woman's whole.

After the young woman spiritedly departed, when the woman was by herself, despite the fact that nobody around her seemed to pay any attention, she loudly heaved a deliberate sigh, as if to exhale all that was within her lungs; she resumed her walking and impatiently waited for the traffic light to turn green, but her heart, which till a few moments ago had controlled things smoothly, ran about inside the skin of her entire body, making an unpleasant noise, so she had to halt a number of times while crossing the carefree, striped intersection.

After managing the traffic lights, as she approached the corner of the shoe store and Kinokuniya bookstore, fingers holding a pack of tissues jumped out before her eyes, and right behind them a male voice said, "Please." Please? For a second, the woman failed to understand what was being offered. Please. Please what? Then, involuntarily she said, "Thanks." Despite the fact that it was a thanks that carried the best part of her reflexes, the man was unable to understand the ambiguous response of the woman, who did not take the pack of tissues, and the soft-edged sound of such an expression as thanks, and, slightly irritated about whether she would take or not take the thing, many times he swiftly repeated the same act of extending the pack of tissues before her eyes as if cutting through the air; but the vacant-minded woman would not take it, further irritating him: what does she mean, this woman? He wanted to ask, "Which is it?" but instead he lazily said "Please" again, until the woman finally saw the pack of tissues, took it, and once again politely responded, "Thanks." This time she looked him in the eyes. There is a frequently used expression, "with the eyes of a person peering into something," but because the woman gazed at him with a feeling of really peering into the slightly moist-looking rims of the black pupils of his eyes, quicker than thought he was filled with liquidlike hatred, as if eyedrops had been forcefully poured into his eyes.

Although he turned his body and extended the next pack of tissues not to the woman but to the next passerby coming his way, the woman swiftly took it and said thanks in a moist voice with a fuller expression than before. Looking uneasy and fed up, the man made no answer to that but moved several steps away from where the woman stood. He thought: how depressing, how long do I have to keep doing this sort of endless, purposeless thing that brings in little money and makes me nervous about the risk of being pestered, a job so dubious, so ordinary; for me there should be something more special, sensible. . . . The man felt like lining up all the curses he knew, but he was in no way equipped with the kind of words that would further excite the feelings experienced on such an occasion. Even as he tried to chase words, all he heard was an empty clatter, as if even the dregs of useless written words were laughing at his life. If this was so, he would cast the dry packs of tissues he held in his hands and litter the ground, kick and scatter right now with determination the contents of the cartons piled up behind the electric pole, then go to the office and continue, to his heart's content, to hit with something hard he might find nearby that ugly, flabby person in charge, younger than he, who speaks like an idiot with dirty spit and orders day laborers about; but somehow the idea of continual hitting did not at all successfully result in a realistic feel on his hand, so after thinking about it a while, he ended in sinking into the depth of a darker, cheaper feeling.

The woman looked fixedly at the man from some distance. If I were a smart foreigner, she fancied, I would cheerfully address him, saying he-e-y; it feels like something just might begin then. She had already reached the cart in front of Kinokuniya that was heaped with books, and, while pretending to be waiting for someone, kept glancing at the man.

As for encountering a totally unknown man and agreeably proceeding to intercourse just like that, she imagined it almost every night; and each time she imagined how it might be, she failed to recognize if her imagination was at all successful or preposterously absurd, so she spent nights that were painful in their own way.

Using cell phones, using computers, or using no other tools but elbows bumping into one another: these may be plenty for not just men or not just women but people—taking an agile, long step over what the woman fancied. In other words, it was something like a ditch that she herself could never jump over, even in her fantasies, as if such a thing never existed from the beginning, while they seemed to her to be quite satisfied with such activities as getting hurt, writing melancholy comments, grieving, and mutually comforting one another. In all aspects of such interaction.

The woman once casually asked a friend—one who had a decent lover and who, however you may look at her, seemed to be almost daily experiencing that satisfaction that women impatiently wish to have a taste of, even if just once—about various things, but every scene the friend talked about somehow formed only a line of flickering words, and the woman didn't know how she should behave if she placed herself in those scenes. There was too big a leap between one act and another for her to understand: for example, how two people, who had been sighing until twenty minutes ago about the cat one of them kept, could go onstage in a scene in which they lick each other's nipples, or how to speak when exiting the stage after finishing various things. If so, she might as well be absentmindedly viewing a film of romantic fiction; even so, using care so as not to be noticed, the woman eagerly took mental notes of the details her friend gave.

"What was the nicest was," the friend said as if it were nothing special, "somehow, many times my eyes met those of a boy standing in front of me on a crowded train, and if I'm asked if he was to my liking or not, he was the kind of boy about whom I might say, 'Let me see, I guess he's so-so'; then it suddenly became much less crowded, that train. So I sat, and the space next to me became empty, so I said please, and the boy sat and asked if I was on my way to work, so I said, 'I'm on my way home,' and then he asked, 'How about something to eat,' so we got off the train and ate dinner, and just like that."

Can that really happen? the woman wished to confirm any number of times, but could only respond, "So that was how it was." She wanted to know in detail the procedure of, and the friend's feelings about, what followed "ate dinner, and just like that"; but, despite the fact that the friend called it "the nicest," she gave it no special treatment at all, so the woman somehow had an irrecoverable setback. Even if she wanted to ask the meaning of "the nicest," the friend looked as if this encounter itself didn't matter, so the woman only said something like, just for the sake of commenting, no joke, and then the topic for some reason or other shifted to their common friend's marriage; to her husband's failure in stocks; to the performance of a camera; to a skillful way of buying a luxury apartment; and last to the latest cure for cavities, and, as always, what the woman wanted to know never clearly appeared before her eyes.

After ruminating on a series of memories, the woman thought to herself by the side of the Kinokuniya cart: but.

Where is the difference between those men or women who can have intercourse just as they meet and those who can't? Once again now, the woman started going around untiringly in circles with this childish question, which she had posed tens of times without having made any progress, and thought of all sorts of possibilities; and so, going around in circles, she asked herself which type she really was—once again in a routine way but feeling quite enfeebled.

When talking about someone you don't know, if you ask what the first thing is that you don't know, it's his name, right? Next, you don't know any part of his so-called background, like his age and basic personality, but then how about the opposite, like having intercourse when the relationship can be described as mutual love, it's not necessarily the case that it's totally satisfactory, and what's crucial is where in that intercourse your independence is, no? As the woman muttered this, she didn't notice how little those words said, but instead became aware that she had been unconsciously counting the motions of the man ably managing his job. While she stood there, he succeeded in handing out nearly a hundred packs of tissues; but if he were holding no packs of tissues in his hands, she thought he would look as though he were performing some kind of odd dance; and while so thinking she tried to find something good about him—within the limits the distance allowed her. The man wore something like a mod-look jacket over a dark-gray parka, black trousers, and black shoes. Uh-huh. The side view of his nose, which showed from time to time from under a hairdo with no character whatsoever, indicated that it was slightly high. After this much observation and saying he-e-y at his back in a small voice in her mind, the woman entered the bookstore because her ankles had started to feel chilly.

As she was moving from bookshelf to bookshelf she had no particular interest in, she remembered that she had another friend who had had intercourse only with a fixed partner.

"I read somewhere," the friend said, looking fully confident, "those who continue to have easygoing intercourse with easygoing partners are very, what shall I say, immature as human beings. I read this somewhere and I agreed vehemently: that's right! Those who often change intercourse partners, you see, are avoiding facing, rather than being unable to face, their partners even at the lowest possible level. They aren't afraid of being hurt but rather they're just plain lazy. So the moment a problem arises, they part, and then they get lonely and go to the next round. That's a peace-at-any-price principle. Of course such people come to a point where they can't even read decent books. Why, because they don't know how to make efforts to relate with anything whatsoever. Honestly, they're like monkeys."

At that time too the woman said, "So that's how it is," and noncommittally let the topic go; but she had a slight sense of something like uneasiness, and that was because of the friend's manner of proudly making an appeal about her own self. While listening to her overly decent story, the woman thought, but I want to try it with a man I don't know. It's because I don't know what sort of thing it really is. I feel like knowing what sort of thing it is not to know. It's hard to go on wanting to test with the use of my body if what's possible is really possible. I don't know how monkeys really are either. Besides, I don't have intercourse with either a fixed partner or an unfixed partner, so in your eyes, I wonder, how do I say it—do I pass? As a human? The woman imagined saying all this with a smile, but stopped herself and, she remembered, gulped the remainder of the tea, which had cooled. She also remembered the bitter dregs on her tongue, the design on the teacup, and the absurd ornament on the spoon of a small, gold hat.

The woman didn't know how valuable her body was, but even so she was fond of buying clothes that covered it. Her hobbies were as good as nonexistent, so on Sundays she invariably went out to Shinjuku and spent her time from morning till night looking at cosmetics and clothes. Even on days when she had nothing to do or no one to see, when she rose in the morning she made herself up. With care. If she happened to skip even one of the routine steps, she started all over again. Sometimes it seemed like she couldn't prepare her skin no matter how many times she tried, and she once had an experience of washing her face three times before going out. Lack of sleep was what she had to avoid more than anything else, and that was not because sleeplessness worsened the condition of her skin, but because her eyes became problematic. No matter how carefully she put on eyeliner, they looked as if they were jumping out of her skin, and her face suggested the claw of an ugly dinosaur, so the thing in the mirror scared her, if just slightly.

Made up carefully and dressed up to a certain extent, the woman thus went into the streets or rode on a crowded train almost every week, but she never encountered an event like the one her friend had, nor was she once addressed by a man. Not once since birth. Although she certainly had many thoughts about this at first, by this time she no longer thought much about it since she had been spending her weekends in this manner for over three years. What was in her mind in perfect form was to make herself up with care daily. To buy any new product that came out. To reflect her face in the well-cared-for, spotlessly clear, high-quality mirror in the light of the wide-open first floor of a department store made her feel as though various feelings were pulled further and further away into the mirror until they changed into things that were elusive even to herself. She stared at them all equally and continued to try to control even the slightest corner of what was visible only from there.

She could not understand why, in comparison, a bookstore was so depressing. As she walked around, no matter how hard she stared at every shelf on every floor, she saw nothing to take in hand. There was a weird smell for one thing, everything was flat with no roundness for another, and somehow people seemed to compulsively gather at such a place and compulsively take books in hand. Not a single person had a happy face; all had an expression of distress as they examined book after book, gesturing as if the books were heavy. Under the cheap fluorescent lights, everyone seemed to be aging at a uniformly high speed, and this gave her a momentary tremor. I've got to get out of this place quickly, she convinced herself. She headed for an exit, making a clatter with her heels; there were ceiling mirrors in places, and when she happened to see her face in one of them, she opened her eyes wide. Look at this, she thought, it's awful. She opened her eyes wider: who would ever wish to have intercourse with a woman of such looks? I can't breathe if I stay in this place. Unless I move fast and demonstrate in the proper light what I have, my weekend will be spoiled. This is a terribly, awfully wrong place. The woman felt her heart move about again in an unpleasant way, and now that Shinjuku, a place she had chosen to come to, seemed an angle of something huge that she failed to understand well, she had no idea where to stand, nor could she any longer stop the fear that rose smokelike to her chest.

When she managed to exit through a door, it was completely dark outside, but she saw the same man by the side of the traffic light a little distance ahead, still handing out tissues. The night was approaching, and through the night's entrance too, more and more people seemed to spill out. The shiny color of the traffic lights looked as if wet, and when she stood watching them she had a sensation that she herself, starting from her eyes, was becoming somewhat moist. And she felt as if many people, who seemed to have faces but didn't really have any, or who gave an impression of the opposite of this, were advancing toward the man, who was not so big, each advocating totally unrelated things, the mass converging to one spot; so, being able to see this without so intending, she suddenly became forlorn and felt as if, amid the tremendously large crowd, the outline of the man alone made this night just slightly special.

The man was exhausted. Tissue is one of those things that never comes to an end no matter how much is handed out, and he often recalls that, when he began this kind of part-time work and when he knew nothing, he burned a boxful of leaflets, not tissue then, along with the box and, when he was caught, got into a terrible situation. That occasion comes back to his mind. Why am I still doing this kind of job, he asks himself. Because it's simple? Because I don't have to talk with people? Because I have no ability? Because anybody can do this? But isn't every job in the world a farce? Take these people who self-importantly throw down the tissues I hand them, I could be their guest on another occasion. Such a thing as this is a ridiculous pretend play, isn't it? Nobody understands this basic thing, and that's why I have to lead such a disagreeable life. So thinking, the man went beyond irritation to anger, what with the hunger and numbness of his legs from standing for over seven hours in a row; and the idea of having to repeat the same motions another hour, or over many more years if things went badly, nearly made hot tears well up in his eyes.

By the side of the automatic door, the woman opened her compact and looked into its mirror with care in order to check how her face looked after escaping from the fluorescent lights, applied some powder to her flat puff, and, after brushing it two or three times with the back of a hand, gently put it on her cheeks and nose. This is magic powder, she thought. Uniformly even color, with a feel of translucence—she was almost completely satisfied by her face in the little round mirror when the face of that young woman she had bumped against in the late afternoon before dark resurfaced, and she was made to think of that skin that was full of life and that soft swell of the cheeks. Around the eyes of the face in the little round mirror the skin was dark and baggy, and the woman felt an impulsive urge to strike her compact against the ground; but she recovered herself and somehow managed to put it back into her handbag.

Exhaling deeply and collecting herself, after one little cough the woman approached where the man was working, with her back terribly straight, and as lightly as possible. Then, tapping him on the shoulder, she said, he-e-y, with a smile. Look, we saw each other a while ago. Do you remember me? Are you still working? Anyway, I swear tissue is important. It helps ve-e-ry much. So, if you have no plans after work, won't you have dinner or something with me?

Suddenly tapped on the shoulder, he turned around and saw the shuddering face of a woman looming gray, an image that seemed to instantly blow off everything into the air, and before he realized it he had knocked her down to the ground. It could be said that, when he swung his arm down from his shoulder with all his might, the woman's face was down there, but anyway he couldn't tell what he had struck at that moment. It was just that his right hand had a sensation of something he had never experienced, and by itself it was not a bad thing at all; it was the first violence he had ever used on another. He was very excited, was desperate to try to suppress his impulse to continue to beat the fallen woman, and attempted to control his breathing by jumping many times in the same place while uttering insensible cries, and this hit onlookers' eyes as something quite creepy. It fared worse with the woman, who fell before she realized what was happening to her, and, with the side of her head badly hit, she was totally immobile. Among the passersby, some stopped walking, compared the man's face and the woman's prone body, and looked restless, but many others behaved with perfect control, as if from the start such an incident had not been seen so there was no need to evade it; and in any case people always managed such situations like geniuses.

The woman's handbag opened wide when it dropped to the ground, and from within a number of cosmetics scattered, each carefully wrapped in thin paper, and a wallet was showing its top. The compact had flown out to a place a little distance away, and the powder and mirror shattered into many pieces so that, viewed from afar, they looked like the dried-out bones of small animals. The fragments of the mirror that were sent further away made a dry, cracking noise under the feet of passersby before even having a chance to glimmer. The woman didn't have a chance to scream but simply lost consciousness, and her cheek, which had hit the ground bearing the entire weight of her body, slowly became bloodstained—and because it was perfectly fitted to the concrete, no smallest light that this night held reached it.

About the Authors

Chiri Yukie 知里幸恵 (1903–1922)

Chiri Yukie was born in Horobetsu, Hokkaido, to Chiri Takakichi and Nami. Nami was the daughter of a Hokkaido Ainu elder, Kannari. Yukie was the older sister of the linguist Chiri Mashiho (1909–1961). When she was five and six years of age, she lived in Horobetsu with her grandmother, the great bard Monasinouk. Yukie grew up listening to recitations in the oral tradition as narrated by Monasinouk and later also by her adoptive mother, Kannari Matsu, Nami's sister. Starting in 1909, she and Monasinouk lived with Matsu at the Episcopal church compound in Chikabumi in the suburbs of Asahikawa. After seven years of schooling, she attended Asahikawa Girls Vocational School for three years, graduating in 1910.

When the linguist Kindaichi Kyōsuke visited Kannari Matsu in 1918 during a research trip to Hokkaido, he learned that Yukie too was versed in the oral tradition. At his encouragement, she began transcription. In 1921 she sent Kindaichi a manuscript that she called "Ainu densetsushū" (A Collection of Ainu Legends). She stayed with the Kindaichis in Tokyo in 1922 to edit the collection for publication. Hours after completing it, she died of heart disease. The work was published in 1923 under the title *Ainu shin'yōshū* (アイヌ神謡集, Ainu Songs of Gods) by Kyōdo Kenkyūsha, presided over by the ethnologist Yanagita Kunio. The book has been included in the Iwanami Library since 1978. In addition to Chiri Yukie's preface, her romanized transcription of the original Ainu songs with Japanese annotations, and her modern Japanese translation, followed by Kindaichi's afterword, the Iwanami edition appends Chiri Mashiho's scholarly essay on these songs. Whereas the first edition stated that the work had been "compiled by Chiri Yukie," the Iwanami editors corrected this to "Compiled and Translated by Chiri Yukie."

The Japanese word *shin'yō* is a translation of *kamuy yukar*, a song in which, in principle, a nature god speaks in the first person. This is distinct from *yukar*, a long epic about human heroes, and *uwepeker*, prose folktales. *Kamuy yukar*, narrated in patterned literary Ainu, as are *yukar*, always contain a refrain, called *sakehe*, that differs from song to song and often ends in a colloquial phrase like *ari . . . kamuy yayeyukar* (thus the so-and-so god sings about himself, or mimics himself in the form of a song of a god) or *ari . . . kamuy isoytak* (thus the so-and-so god tells his tale). *Kamuy yukar* were customarily sung by women, while *yukar* were traditionally sung by men, although female bards had taken over the latter by the mid-twentieth century, when few male bards were left.

Chiri Yukie's book contains thirteen songs of gods such as the owl, fox, rabbit, little wolf, sea, frog, otter, and swamp mussel deities, and the spirit of the damp ground. "Silver Droplets Fall Fall All Around" is the first in her collection and one of the two owl god songs. The owl (or more precisely, in Horobetsu, Blakiston's eagle-owl) is *kotan-kor-kamuy*, the guardian god of the *kotan* (hamlet).

The English translation in this volume is based on Chiri Yukie's Japanese translation in the Iwanami Library edition of *Ainu shin'yōshū*. Her Japanese notes on the romanized Ainu text are also included because they provide useful information. Her spelling is retained wherever she uses Ainu expressions, although the spelling system has changed since then. Her line division is also honored as much as possible, while recent Japanese translation practice is to divide lines to more closely reflect the metrical patterns of the original. Another translation into Japanese of the piece, by Chiri Mashiho, in *Yukar kanshō* (一カラ鑑賞 Appreciation of Yukar [1956]), with his annotations and a commentary by Oda Kunio, is reproduced in Hanasaki Kōhei, *Shimajima wa hanazuna* (The Islands Are a Festoon [Tokyo: Shakai Hyōronsha, 1990]). Chiri Mashiho's version pays closer attention to the metrical pattern and literary devices of the original, such as parallelism and repetition, providing a basis for subsequent translations of *kamuy yukar* and *yukar*. There is a difference in the treatment of the refrain as well. Chiri Yukie interpreted it to mean "silver droplets fall," while Chiri Mashiho took the word "fall" as imperative, thus, "Fall, silver droplets." He also argues that the title means "the song the owl god sang of himself" rather than "the song the owl god himself sang." These and other differences aside, most Japanese readers still refer to Chiri Yukie's version, which has historical weight as the first published transliteration and translation from Ainu oral literature by an Ainu in any language.

Doubts may arise about the logic of transcribing traditional oral performances into a written text, whether romanized or rendered into Japanese. Or, for that matter, into English. Yet such transcriptions and translations have preserved a great Ainu tradition from oblivion. Consider Kayano Shigeru's great cultural preservation project, *Kayano Shigeru no Ainu shin'wa shūsei* (Kayano Shigeru's Collection of Ainu Mythology, 10 vols. [1998]). Based on years of recording recitations by elderly bards, Kayano provides CDs and the romanized text, katakana transcriptions, Japanese translations, and annotations. Kayano's efforts extended to attempts to preserve the Ainu language for future generations. For example, Sapporo Television started an Ainu language lesson program in 1999 with Kayano as the original instructor. It continues today with elderly and younger Ainu lecturers from different areas of Hokkaido representing Ainu local dialects.

Similar attention to the vocal aspects has been paid to Chiri Yukie's thirteen *kamuy yukar* as well in recent years. The Ainu language researcher Katayama Tatsumine (1942–2004) and the Chitose-born bard Nakamoto Mutsuko (1928–), who earlier had collaborated on the text and recording of *Kamuy yukar* (1995), in 2003 published a CD version of Chiri Yukie's *Ainu shin'yōshū* (Sōfūkan). It contains Nakamoto's singing in Ainu, Japanese recitation by Kurotani Masumi, and an English reading by Julie Kaizawa. NHK's widely viewed weekly series *Sono toki rekishi ga ugoita* (History Moved at That Moment) featured Chiri Yukie in October 2008, placing similar importance on her as on the central characters in the other four installments in the same month: the Sengoku warrior Azai Nagamasa, the Chinese heroes of the Three Kingdoms, the late-Tokugawa shogunal wife Atsuhime, and the novelist Murasaki Shikibu. Here too the program included Nakamoto's oral performance of passages from the *Ainu shin'yōshū*.

Direct Ainu-to-English translation by Donald Philippi of the two songs of the owl god from Chiri Yukie's collection appears in his *Songs of Gods, Songs of Humans* (Princeton University Press, 1979). Listening for the original rhythm, he freely divides lines, using even shorter lines than had Chiri Mashiho. He also sets off the refrain from the rest of the text. His translation is from Ainu oral tradition as transcribed by Chiri Yukie. Included in this book is the first English translation from Chiri Yukie's Japanese rendering of the original, which is both a literary product in its own right and a text widely read and recognized in Japan as a landmark of Ainu creativity and Ainu-Japanese cultural relations.

Hayashi Kyōko 林京子 (1930–)

Hayashi Kyōko was born in Nagasaki in 1930. She spent much of her prewar and wartime childhood in Shanghai. Returning to Nagasaki in March 1945, five months before the war had ended, she attended Nagasaki Girls High School. Hayashi was working at a munitions plant in Nagasaki at the time of the atomic bombing on August 9. She was seriously ill for two months, and like the majority of bomb survivors, suffered thereafter from fragile health and fear of the symptoms that affected the offspring of survivors.

Hayashi made her literary debut with the Akutagawa Prize–winning "Matsuri no ba" (祭りの場, Ritual of Death [1975, trans. Kyoko Selden 1984]), which records her exodus from the area of devastation and eventual reunion with her family. Hayashi continued to write of the atomic bomb in a novella "Nanjamonja no men" (なんじゃもんじゃの面, Masks of Whatchamacallit [1976, trans. Kyoko Selden 2004]) and a sequence of twelve short stories called *Giyaman bīdoro* (ギヤマン ビードロ, Cut Glass, Blown Glass [1978]). "Kōsa" (黄砂, Yellow Sand, trans. Kyoko Selden 1982), one of these stories, has a special place in the sequence dealing with the author's experiences in Shanghai. The other eleven stories concern the bombing, with the only reference to Hayashi's Chinese experiences found in a flashback in "Hibiki" (響き, Echo). Hayashi gives a fuller account of her Shanghai experiences in *Missheru no kuchibeni* (ミッシェルの口紅, Michelle Lipstick [1980]), while in *Shanhai* (上海, Shanghai [1985], winner of the Women's Literature Prize), a travelogue, she revisits the city thirty-six years after she had last seen it.

In *Naki ga gotoki* (無きが如き, As If Nothing Had Happened [1981]), her first full-length novel, Hayashi alludes to her determination to be Nagasaki's "chronicler." Her effort as a chronicler in the sixties and seventies led her to recount the bombing, to explore the psychology of survivors, and to write of the fate of her friends and teachers. In the eighties her topics became more diverse: marriage, birth, divorce, her grown son's marriage, the birth of his children, the environment, aging, and death, all of which are nevertheless intricately connected to the bombing and the war. Some stories in *Michi* (道, The Road [1985]) draw on thoughts concerning her son, who is an "A-bomb *nisei*" (second-generation victim of the A-bomb), and her divorced husband. *Sangai no ie* (三界の家, No Abode [1985]), whose title story won the 1983 Kawabata Yasunari Prize, adds depth to Hayashi's study of human psychology through the theme of her father's death and the relationship between her parents. Stories in *Tanima* (谷間, The Valley [1988]) and *Vājinia no aoi sora* (ヴァージニアの青い空, The Blue Skies of Virginia [1988]) draw on her experiences during three years of residence near Washington, DC. *Yasurakani ima wa nemuritamae* (やすらかに今は眠りたまえ, Rest Now in Peace [1990]) is a requiem for a teacher whose journal documenting the lives of mobilized female students was found thirty years after her death, and a farewell to the eleven weeks that ended in the bombing. In *Seishun* (青春, Youth [1994]), a novel about a group called the China Study Group (Chūgoku Kenkyūkai), Hayashi wrote of her postwar youth for the first time.

Nagai jikan o kaketa ningen no keiken (長い時間をかけた人間の経験, Human Experiences Over a Long Time [2000], a Noma Literary Prize winner), consisting of two novellas, concludes Hayashi's A-bomb cycle. The title story traces her pilgrimage to the thirty-three temples on the Miura Peninsula, where she lives. The second, "Toriniti kara Toriniti e" (トリニティからトリニティへ, From Trinity to Trinity, trans. Kyoko Selden 2007), records her trip to Los Alamos, New Mexico, the site of the first atomic bomb experiment, that is, the source of her fifty-five years of experience. Both journeys were taken in an effort to sort out, before the century ended, her August 9 experiences and reflections. The temple pilgrimages fulfilled the promise she had made to a deceased Nagasaki friend that they would be co-pilgrims, while the visit to the Trinity site was motivated by the belief that "what started at Trinity should end at Trinity." Having completed the journey that was at once real and symbolic, Hayashi takes a new direction. Not that she no longer writes about Nagasaki, but she handles the theme differently. In her recent publication *Kibō* (希望, Hope [2005]), the title story (originally published in the July 2004 issue of *Gunzō*) celebrates the process through which a young female *hibakusha* decides to have a child, overcoming, with her husband's support, her fear of transmitting genetic problems to a second generation.

Higuchi Ichiyō 樋口一葉 (1872–1896)

Born in Tokyo the daughter of a minor government official, Higuchi became at the age of fifteen a student at Haginoya, a poetry academy for daughters of local elite families. There she studied *waka* composition as well as classical Japanese literature. Her classmates included Miyake Kaho, whose success as a novelist would later inspire Higuchi to try her own hand at fiction. Around this time, she also began keeping a journal, inspired by the famous poetic diaries of such Heian-period writers as Murasaki Shikibu. When the diary was published posthumously, it became one of her most acclaimed works.

Her father's death in 1889 plunged the family into poverty. It also left her the legal family head, the sole financial support for her mother and siblings. It was in part these economic concerns that drove her to try to become a professional writer. Seeking guidance at first from the newspaper novelist Nakarai Tōsui, she published her debut story in 1892. She began putting her training in classical literature to use as well, writing in a pseudoclassical style that was the fashion of such popular novelists as Kōda Rohan and Ozaki Kōyō. Eventually, she became one of the central figures in the 1890s revival of interest in the writings of the great Edo-period writer Ihara Saikaku.

Financial difficulties led her, in 1892, to open a small store on the fringes of the Yoshiwara licensed quarters in the old central section of Tokyo. Her experiences there, living in a slum district in close company with prostitutes, pimps, and other street-life denizens, would provide the material for many of her later stories. It was also around this time that she came to the attention of the group of young writers and poets attached to the journal *Bungakkai*, who invited her to publish in their magazine.

Over the next several years, she published stories in *Bungakkai* and other literary journals. The most famous, including "Takekurabe" (たけくらべ, Comparing Heights [1895–96]) and "Nigorie" (にごり江, Troubled Waters [1895]), were tragic tales that focused on the everyday struggles of those who lived in and around the licensed quarters. Other stories, such as "Jūsan'ya" (十三夜, Thirteenth Night [1895]) and "Kono ko" (この子, This Child [1895]), depicted the quiet desperation of domestic life, especially the plight of women trapped in unhappy marriages. Her fiction won wide praise from the most respected writers and critics of the day.

Among her works, "This Child" is unusual in that it is written in a colloquial voice, taking the form of a dramatic monologue. The story's reproduction of a modern, educated housewife's spoken language makes it an early harbinger of the *genbun itchi* colloquial writing style that would dominate twentieth-century fiction in Japan.

Higuchi died of tuberculosis at the age of twenty-four, just as she was achieving fame as a writer. Her collected works were published shortly thereafter, sealing her reputation as the greatest female novelist of the Meiji period. Subsequent female writers, including Yosano Akiko, would complain that Higuchi's enormous popularity was owing to her having pandered to male stereotypes about women, but her brilliant stories continue to capture readers' imaginations today, more than a century after her death. The current edition of her collected works comprises seven volumes, including her poetry, diaries, and the twenty-one stories she completed during her short lifetime.

Kawakami Mieko 川上未映子 **(1976–)**

Kawakami Mieko was born in Osaka in 1976. Her mother, Toshie, as the main breadwinner of the family, brought up three children: an aerobic specialist and mother of two, a singer-songwriter, and a well-known rugby player. The musician, known as Mieko without the surname, is the author of "Anata-tachi no koi wa hinshi" (あなたたちの恋は瀕死, You People's Love Is Near Death [2008]), included in this volume. She studied design at the Osaka City Industrial Arts High School and wished to go on to art school, but because of the family situation, she instead worked to help support her brother as a part-time bookstore clerk and a bar hostess while performing as a band member and studying philosophy through Nihon University's correspondence program. She began her professional musical activities in 2002. In 2005 her poems were published in the prestigious poetry magazine

Yuriika (Eureka). She was the 2009 recipient of the Nakahara Chūya Prize for outstanding poetry.

Her first published fiction, "Kanjiru senmonka saiyō shiken" (感じる専門家採用試験, A Feeling Specialist Employment Test [2006]), studies the feel of human existence. The first section, apparently an internal monologue simulating a written test, traces a housewife's feelings about existence, nonexistence, and birth. In the second section, the practical skills test, the housewife meets a pregnant neighbor, the personification of pregnancy in the housewife's imagination, at a food market and tests her thoughts against her neighbor's. The brief concluding paragraph, the test result, introduces a third voice, perhaps of the creator of both the housewife and pregnant woman, that speaks of a desire to return to the place of birth in order to be born. "Watakushi-ritsu in ha—Mata wa sekai" (わたくし率イン歯 —または世界, The Percentage of Myself in the Teeth; or, The World [2007]) concerns the reflections of a pregnant female dental assistant who is obsessed with molars. She thinks in her teeth rather than in the brain or any other part of her body, and experiences life 100 percent in her teeth. It is through her teeth that she ascertains existence, contact with others, or loss thereof.

The main theme of the Akutagawa Prize–winning novella *Chichi to ran* (乳と卵, Breasts and Ova [2007]), published in book form in 2008 along with "You People's Love Is Near Death," is breast enhancement. A woman desiring such surgery and her daughter, who feels uncomfortable about the idea, visit the woman's sister, the first-person narrator. The girl is in the habit of typing her thoughts into her cell phone, refusing to talk to her mother or aunt.

"You People's Love Is Near Death" portrays a lone woman's regular Sunday excursion to Shinjuku. She roams the crowded area in a desolate attempt to relate to other human beings. She singles out a man handing out small packs of tissues for advertising purposes, a common sight near Japanese subway stations since the nineties, but fails to establish any communication. Kawakami has also published a collection of essays (2006) and an anthology of poems (2008).

Kawakami makes abundant use of Osaka dialect, colloquialisms, puns, onomatopoeia, sentence fragments, and long sentences and paragraphs, liberated from the novelistic discipline of coherence and grammar. While reflecting the stylistic preferences of the e-mail and cell-phone generations, she makes conscious efforts to write in a language accessible to young readers of *keitai-shōsetsu* (cell-phone fiction, i.e., twenty-first-century stories published initially through cell phones). At the same time, Kawakami's long sentences and paragraphs can also be seen as a return to premodern narrative styles before the standardization of punctuation and paragraphing. Higuchi Ichiyō, writing in the Meiji period, still resonated with the run-on narrative styles of earlier times. This volume begins with Higuchi Ichiyō and ends with Kawakami Mieko. Interestingly, Higuchi is one author who influenced Kawakami.

Kurahashi Yumiko 倉橋由美子 (1935–2005)

Kurahashi Yumiko began her writing career as a student of French literature at Meiji University with the story "Parutai" (パルタイ, Partei [1960, trans. Yukiko Tanaka 1961]), which appeared in the Meiji University newspaper and was awarded the University President's Prize. Although she had never envisioned a writing career, she continued to publish stories and novellas, and won the Women's Literature Prize in 1961 for *Parutai*, which included the title story, and the Tamura Toshiko Prize in 1962 for her collective literary activities.

Kurahashi's literary output can be chronologically divided by the publication in 1975 of her complete works. Her significant works before 1975 include *Vājinia* (ヴァージニア, Virginia [1968]), a novella featuring a woman she had met in the United States while studying creative writing as a graduate student at the University of Iowa; *Han-higeki* (反悲劇, Anti-Tragedies [1968]), a sequence of stories based on Greek myths; *Sumiyakisuto Q no bōken* (スミヤキストQの冒険, The Adventures of Q the Charcoalist [1969, trans. Dennis Keene 1979]), a parody of revolutionary fiction (*kakumei shōsetsu*); and *Yume no ukihashi* (夢の浮橋, The Floating Bridge of Dreams [1971]). Although publication of her *Complete Works* marked a tentative closure to Kurahashi's literary work, she resumed writing in 1977. Among the best-known works from this later period are *Amanonkoku ōkanki* (アマノン国往還記, Voyage to and Back from Amanon [1987]), *Otona no tame no zankoku dōwa* (大人のための残酷童話, Cruel Fairy Tales for Adults [1984]), and *Mugen no utage* (夢幻の宴, Banquet of Visionary Dreams [1996]).

Kurahashi's interests shifted and expanded from Kafka, Camus, Sartre, and other contemporary European authors, whom she read avidly as a student, to Noh drama and the Greek tragedies, which inspired some of her post-Iowa work. Moreover, her exploration of fairy tales has led her not only to the writing of parodies but also to translation and radio drama. Her work is invariably experimental. She utilizes what she absorbs in the manner of *honkadori* (allusive variation), the traditional poetic device of consciously, creatively twisting and reworking the diction and conception of a well-known source poem. Kurahashi's allusive variations are often bitter and satirical, representing her anger at the foolish and deceitful yet also incorporate moments of discovery of the beautiful in the cruel and poisonous. "Shiroi kami no dōjo" (白い髪の童女, White-Haired Little Girl [1969]), for example, juxtaposes themes from Noh and Greek tragedy, conveying the utmost beauty against the background of cruelty. Along with *Cruel Fairy Tales for Adults*, *Rōjin no tame no zankoku dōwa* (老人のための残酷童話, Cruel Fairy Tales for Elderly People [2003]) exemplifies her interest in fairy tales as potential sources for the dismantling of myths.

"The Strange Story of a Pumpkin" (カボチャ奇譚, Kabocha kitan [1985]) is one of the twenty brief pieces contained in *Kurahashi Yumiko no kaiki shōhen* (倉橋由美子の怪奇掌篇, *Kurahashi Yumiko's Short Tales of the Grotesque* [1985]). Echoing a Roman theme, it likens an insipid prime minister, apparently Japanese, to Emperor Claudius, who at his death was ridiculed by the satirist Seneca, and thereby satirizes not only politicians but the people who elect them and the courts that judge them. Three other stories from the same collection have been translated, by Atsuko Sasaki, in *The Woman with the Flying Head and Other Stories by Kurahashi Yumiko* (M. E. Sharpe, 1998).

Mori Mari 森茉莉 (1903–1987)

Mori Mari was the second child and first daughter born to Ōgai and his second wife, Shige. Mari grew up in the aura of a father who was both a military doctor and a famous scholar-writer, and who, above all, exuded such abundant love and charisma that each of his children felt loved and uniquely favored. Until her death at the age of eighty-four, Mari frequently spoke of her father's love as romantic love. Mari's memory of the aura of her father's love forms the basis of a romantic yearning in her work, a yearning that intensifies with the passage of time since it remains inaccessible. Some have speculated whether her single-minded attachment to her father contributed to her two divorces and her separation from her children as a young mother.

"Toge" (刺, Thorn, included in the collection *Chichi no bōshi* 父の帽子, *My Father's Hat* [1957]) is an autobiographical short story that mirrors Mari's estrangement from her father. Mori married her first husband, Yamada Tamaki, in 1919, when she was sixteen. At the encouragement of Ōgai, Mari joined her husband in Europe in the spring of 1922. Her father died the following summer. Mari captured the bitter regret of their final parting in "Toge," a story replete with chilliness, sorrow, and the subdued tones of brown and gray, in contrast to the verdant green and crimson with which she portrayed her childhood, and the warm lavender and rosy hues with which she creates her world of imagined luxury in her later life (*Zeitaku binbō* 贅沢貧乏, Poverty in Luxury [1963]). The economy of Mari's style in "Thorn" gives the piece an enduring, concentrated power. Its narration is like a steady and silent wail, a classic expression of personal grief.

While many of her mature works are known for their bold and sensual explorations of highly ambiguous relationships, "Thorn," with its classic precision and cold beauty, is one of her finest pieces of writing.

Ogawa Yōko 小川洋子 (1962–)

Since launching her publishing career by winning the 1988 Kaien Prize for new authors for "Agehachō ga kowareru toki" (揚羽蝶が壊れる時, When the Butterfly Disintegrates [1989]), Ogawa Yōko has written numerous short stories, novellas, novels, essays, and literary conversations and has earned almost every major award for fiction offered in Japan. Starting in the mid-1990s, Ogawa's works have been translated into French and German and, increasingly from around 2005, have appeared in English. Born in Okayama prefecture, Ogawa went to Tokyo to attend Waseda University, where she graduated with a degree in creative writing in 1984. To support herself as an author, Ogawa worked for two years as a secretary at Kawasaki Medical University, a job that perhaps informs her literary themes of compassion, empathy, and the resilience of the human spirit in the face of Alzheimer's and other debilitating diseases, the trauma of war, and life-altering change, endured or observed by her female protagonists. In 1990, Ogawa became the youngest woman of the postwar period to win the prestigious Akutagawa Prize. Her award-winning story "Ninshin karendā" (妊娠カレンダー, The Pregnancy Record [1990]) is a younger sister's poignantly humorous report of the trivial events and important bodily and emotional changes her pregnant older sister experiences. Ogawa has also written extensively about travel and memory, including her 1995 book-length investigation of places associated with Anne Frank (*Anne Furanku no kioku* アンネ・フランクの記憶, Memories of Anne Frank), a highly personal work that reflects many of the themes and emotions conveyed in "Transit." Ogawa is perhaps best known for her novel *Hakase no aishita sūshiki* (博士の愛した数式, The Professor and His Beloved Equation [2003, trans. Yosei Sugiwara 2006 as *The Gift of Numbers*]). This story of a friendship between a mathematical genius, who suffers long-term memory loss because of an accident and is unable to remember anything for longer than eighty minutes, and a housekeeper and her son, who share his love for baseball and numbers, was awarded the Yomiuri Prize for Literature and made into a graphic novel and a film in 2006. Ogawa further articulates the aesthetics of numbers and the pleasures of mental journeys in her 2006 *Yo ni mo utsukushii sūgaku nyūmon* (世にも美しい数学入門, An Introduction to the World's Most Beautiful Mathematics), a dialogue with popular essayist and mathematician Fujiwara Masahiko.

"Transit" appears in Ogawa's 1996 short-story collection *Shishū suru shōjo* (刺繍する少女, The Embroidery Girl), which recounts a conversation in a crowded Hong Kong airport waiting area between two strangers—a Japanese woman and a middle-aged Frenchman—both passing the time until their connecting flights home. The first-person narrator shares memories of her grandfather, a French Jew, who was taken from the family that had hid him during the Holocaust to a Nazi concentration camp and helped him to emigrate to Japan after the war. The man, a collector of rocking horses, discusses how these ordinary toys, often disposed of when no longer used, leave traces of childhood innocence on people's memories. The two passengers, who do not ask each other's names, manage to communicate in their shared second language of English (rendered in short, eloquent Japanese sentences by Ogawa), and their talk, framed in the atmosphere of the airport and its diverse passengers, crosses time and space, from the present moment in Hong Kong to wartime France and presumably 1970s and 1980s Japan. "Transit" conveys the notion that such brief encounters, usually quickly forgotten, can reveal the importance of memory, communication, and the human bonds that help us to understand and accept our sometimes painful personal and public histories.

Ogino Anna 荻野アンナ **(1956–)**

Born in 1956 in Yokohama to a French-American father and a Japanese mother, Ogino Anna grew up with an acute sense of what it means to move between languages. She studied French at Keiō University, where she is now professor of French. During her doctoral studies, she traveled to the Sorbonne, where she researched the French comic writer Rabelais. Ogino's peripatetic history with languages and her research on the topsy-turvy world of Rabelais have made her one of the most inventive Japanese writers of her generation, marking her fiction with a constant destabilizing movement between received categories, most notably those of gender and genre. She is a self-styled "destroyer of language" known for her playful puns, often writing in the unconventional genre of "fiction-cum-critique."

Eating and drinking are recurrent themes in both her fiction, *Taberu onna* (食べる女, The Woman Who Eats [1994]), and academic writing, "Kakinagara, kawakinagara" (書きながら、渇きながら, While Writing and Thirsting [1994]). Eating, for Ogino, is a metaphor for reading and writing; for example, the title of her most popular work to date, *Watashi no aidokusho* (私の愛毒書, My Love-Hate Affair with Books [1991]), relies on a playful pun on the Chinese characters for "reading" and "poison." Ogino self-consciously posits her "fiction-cum-critique" within this gastronomic idiom, asking readers to see her as a digestive organ of sorts, mixing, mangling, and absorbing works from different periods, authors, and nations.

"Uchi no okan ga ocha o nomu" (うちのお母んがお茶を飲む, Mama Drinks Her Tea [1989]) was Ogino's first work, garnering the attention of critics and securing her a nomination for the prestigious Akutagawa Prize. She has produced many different kinds of work since then, ranging from parodic fiction, fiction-critiques, and art criticism, and has placed them in a variety of contexts, from literary magazines to more visible popular media. The versatility and breadth of her topics are striking; her 1991 novella *Seoimizu* (背負い水, Water on One's Back [1991]), which got her the Akutagawa Prize, is a meditation on the decline of love in a woman's life, whereas the 2001 Yomiuri Prize for Literature winner *Hora-fuki Anri no bōken* (ホラ吹きアンリの冒険, The Adventures of the Hyperbolic Henri [2001]) reads more like a biography of her father's adventures.

A reading of "Uchi no okan ga ocha o nomu" quickly reveals Ogino's concern with language and food. Though there are two distinct narrators in the story, one speaking in the Kansai dialect and the other in standard Japanese, the reader is left with an enduring impression that they are one voice because their recollections fold into one another. This recounting of the past is explicitly tied to eating, both through the suggestion that food is a way to textualize the past in its sweet and bitter tones and through the poignant remark that one can become happy by getting the heart to shed the excess calorific weight of memories. The reader gets a powerful sense that we gorge ourselves on food and drink both to connect ourselves to the past and to relieve the tedium of the present.

This thematic focus on "idleness" and the loose essayistic structure of the work function to bring into relief another motif of consumption in this work: the author Ogino Anna's incorporation of *Tsurezuregusa* (Essays in Idleness [ca. 1332]). This late Kamakura period masterpiece, in which the poet Yoshida Kenkō reflects back on the happier days of the past, is present in Ogino's text both as stylistic and thematic raw material for her own text. Whereas Yoshida Kenkō embraces the tedium of an isolated life because it offers the tranquillity necessary for reflection and writing, Ogino Anna's two narrators are more ambivalent. Though their ruminations suggest the benefits of solitary meditation, their narrations paradoxically insists on the presence of another, such as a reader or a listener. Thus, in rendering the Kansai dialect of the mother, the translator has focused on the desire of the mother to share her story in the intimate and casual tone afforded by the language of her hometown. The mother's voice, in italics in the translation included in this collection, stands apart from the other narrator, who seems to be writing rather than speaking, the latter demanding a reader rather than a listener.

Ozaki Midori 尾崎翠 (1896–1971)

Ozaki Midori first received recognition as a writer with the publication of her story "Mufūtai kara" (無風帯から, From the Doldrums) in the journal

Shinchō in 1920 while she was a student at Japan Women's University in Tokyo. Over the course of the following twelve years, she published a number of short stories, translations, and critical essays on film, many in the leading feminist literary journal *Nyonin geijutsu* (Women's Art [1928–32]). In 1932, she returned to her home in Tottori and soon gave up writing fiction entirely, severing her ties to the literary world. Although Ozaki has been largely overlooked by literary historians, her writings form a significant contribution to modernist literature in Japan from the end of the Taishō (1912–26) to early Shōwa (1926–89) periods. Incorporating the concepts of psychoanalysis and the techniques of the avant-garde, her works explore the fluid boundaries between consciousness and the unconscious and between the world of everyday reality and the hallucinatory world of the imagination. The work translated in the present volume, "Kōrogi-jō" (こほろぎ嬢, Miss Cricket [1932]), examines the effects of addiction to both drugs and literature, as well as the inner fragmentations of identity. It includes a tribute to another often-overlooked literary figure, the Scottish poet and writer William Sharp (1855–1905), who published a significant number of his writings under the name of his alter ego, Fiona Macleod.

Saegusa Kazuko 三枝和子 **(1929–2003)**

Saegusa Kazuko studied philosophy at Kansai Gakuin University. While a graduate student for one year at Kyoto University, she participated in the Philosophy Club and came to know Morikawa Tatsuya (real name Saegusa Kōichi), whom she married in 1951. They founded the subscription magazines *Bungeijin* (Literary Persons [1956–58]) and *Mushinha bungaku* (Atheist Literature [1958–64]). In 1963, Saegusa's husband inherited the hereditary position of head priest of the Kōmyōji temple, and after moving to Hyōgo prefecture with him, she divided her time between her new home and the home of her deceased mother in the Shakujii area of Tokyo. In 1965 she joined Morikawa's new magazine *Shinbi* (The Aesthetic), which lasted until 1973.

Saegusa began writing fiction at age fifteen during wartime student mobilization work at the Akashi Kawasaki airport. Her first book appeared in 1968, and over the following decades, she yearly published new works that included fiction, stage plays, essays, and critical biographies. In the early days, when she was interested in European philosophy and the antinovel, she sought equality in a male-oriented intellectual world. Later she explored women's literary expression as distinct from men's, among classical Japanese literature and history as well as modern women writers. While doing so, her early interest in Noh also expanded to Greek drama and its tragic heroines. She published literary works about several female historical figures, including the early ruler

Himiko, Kusuko and Sakanoue no Iratsume of the Nara period, Heian-court literati Ono no Komachi and Murasaki Shikibu, and modern authors Higuchi Ichiyō and Okamoto Kanoko. Saegusa received the Tamura Toshiko Prize in 1969 for *Shokei ga okonawarete iru* (処刑が行われている, Punishment in Progress) and the Izumi Kyōka Prize for *Onidomo no yoru wa fukai* (鬼ども の夜は深い, Deep Is the Demons' Night) in 1983.

"Sakura densha" (桜電車, Cherry Blossom Train [1980]) is among the twelve supernatural stories in *Nomori no kagami* (野守の鏡, The Field Guard's Mirror [1980]). It presents the half-real, half-imagined train ride of an unmarried woman, a junior college instructor who has experienced an abortion. Like the train in Friedrich Dürrenmatt's "The Tunnel" (1952) the cherry blossom train enters a tunnel never to leave it. The train carries passengers from this world to another, as does the Milky Way train in Miyazawa Kenji's "Night Train to the Stars" (Ginga tetsudō no yoru [ca. 1927, posthumously published 1941]). The story also resonates with a passage from Ihara Saikaku's *Kōshoku ichidai onna* (The Life of an Amorous Woman [1686]), in which an old woman with an amorous past has a vision one rainy night of her ninety-five or ninety-six aborted fetuses, each wearing something like a hat of lotus leaf, or the placenta, coming near her window coveting her affection. In Saegusa's story, the ride through the tunnel of cherry blossoms is both the endless journey of unborn babies and a merry outing that they would be enjoying had they been born.

Sakiyama Tami 崎山多美 **(1954–)**

Sakiyama Tami was born in 1954 on Iriomote Island, the largest of the Yaeyama island group, to the west of the Miyako Islands, which forms the westernmost portion of Okinawa prefecture. She grew up in a small postwar settlement there until age fourteen, when, because of her father's illness, the family left the island. After moving a number of times, they settled in Koza, present-day Okinawa city, but for some time they continued to travel back and forth between Koza and Naha. Sakiyama graduated from Ryukyu University in Nakagami district.

On Iriomote, settlers spoke different Ryukyuan languages depending upon their origins, while at school children spoke Japanese. Sakiyama's family spoke the dialect of Miyako Island, over 150 miles to the northeast across the sea from Iriomote. On moving to the main island, Sakiyama was exposed to standard Japanese mixed with elements of Okinawan (the Ryukyuan language spoken on mainland Okinawa; the speech of the Miyako Island group and Okinawan are two of the six generally recognized Ryukyuan languages). The linguistic tension she experienced eventually motivated her to write, and to write using Ryukyuan expressions as a conscious strategy. In a piece included in a collection of essays, *Kotoba no umareru basho* (コトバの生まれる場所, The Place Where Words Are Born [2004]), Sakiyama explains that the meaning of writing for her exists in spinning words while envisioning genuine *shimakotoba* (island speech), which is now impossible to directly encounter because it remains only in modified fragments or locked in printed texts and recordings. In her work, the *shimakotoba* of Miyako and elsewhere claims its place in written culture, in defiance of the domination of the master language, standard Japanese.

In 1979 Sakiyama began publishing fiction in Okinawan literary magazines, then, starting in 1988, in literary magazines in mainland Japan. Her stories often depict the lives of islanders in connection with the deep, dark sea that surrounds them, the sound of the wind, the spirit of the water, and voices from the past. "Suijō ōkan" (水上往還, Traveling Across the Water [1988], Kyushu Art Festival Prize for Literature winner and the first of her two Akutagawa Prize nominee stories, published in book form in 1994 with another story), for example, portrays a young woman who accompanies her ailing father across the black sea at night to their old island, readily identifiable as Miyako. The brief, stealthy visit finalizes his disconnection from the island by removing his mother's mortuary tablet in betrayal of her bequest. "Fūsuitan" (風水譚, The Tale of Wind and Water [1997]), included in this volume, is narrated in the voice of a mainland Japanese reporter encountering two local females, one a young woman of Okinawan and American origin by the name of Sato, and the other an enigmatic creature who morphs between being an ageless prostitute and a jellyfish-like sea creature, or a Siren-like spirit of the water, who seems to combine Sato's other self and her deceased grandmother. The male narrator, who first looks at Okinawa with a reporter's prying eye, experiences moments when he feels the situation is reversed: he is being looked at by Okinawa. At the end of the story, when the prostitute-Siren tells him not to turn around, without turning he bends forward and looks through his spread legs to see what is behind him. He cannot fathom whether he is upside down or what he sees is; but the process of reversal seems complete.

Sakiyama's other important work includes *Muiani yuraiki* (ムイアニ由来記, The Origin of Muiani [1999]) and *Yuratiku Yuritiku* (ゆらていく ゆりていく Swaying, Swinging [2003]). The title novella of *The Origin of Muiani* pursues a quest for the unintelligible word *muiani* whispered to the main character, a partial amnesiac, who is gradually led to recognition of what the word, in fact a name, refers to. The title novella of *Swaying, Swinging* concerns an imaginary, legend-ridden lone island called Hotara, where the only residents are now over eighty years of age. A character explains that the name is associated with the Japanese word *hottarakashi* (left alone). That is, the island is abandoned by the world, but not by the islanders, who never leave. Besides the inhabitants' community, there is a secluded dwelling on the beach for outside settlers, who are portrayed as drifters or deranged eccentrics. The area is mostly shunned and the drifters are largely ostracized by the islanders. If this novella problematizes the conventional view of idealized, nostalgic southern islands, the accompanying piece in the book, "Hotara panasu yoteki" (ホタラ綺譚余滴, Gleanings from Hotara's Strange Legends), even more clearly rejects the view of the Okinawan islands as a utopian matriarchal and sea-bound land of bright sun. Here, the islanders share a legend about the gradual disappearance of little children during a severe famine. As if to solve the pain associated with this mostly suppressed story, another legend develops, ascribing the disappearance to a female drifter in the cave. Responding to this legend, the islanders ritualistically kill her to comfort the spirits of the wronged children and to stop more such wrongs.

Shōno Yoriko 笙野頼子 (1956–)

Shōno Yoriko was born into a pearl-trading family in Ise, Mie prefecture. Her maternal grandmother was haiku poet Iwamoto Akiko. At age thirteen Shōno was already reading such authors as Saikaku, Tanizaki Jun'ichirō, and Mishima Yukio. While enrolled in the Law Department at Ritsumeikan University in Kyoto, she wrote fiction at home with greater enthusiasm than that for attending classes. She received the Gunzō Literary Prize for new authors in 1980. During the following decade she published several magazine pieces but remained largely unrecognized. She won literary acclaim in 1991 with the publication of her first collection of stories, titled *Nani mo shite inai* (なにもしていない, I'm Not Doing Anything, recipient of the Noma Literary Prize). This and her second book, *Ibasho mo nakatta* (1993, There Wasn't Even a Place to Live [居場所もなかった]), chronicle her struggles as a single woman. In 1994 she won the Mishima Yukio Prize for "Nihyakkaiki" (二百回忌, The Two Hundredth Anniversary of Death [1993]) and the Akutagawa Prize for "Taimu surippu konbināto (タイムスリップ・コンビナート, The Time Slip Complex [1994]). Other major works include *Haha no hattatsu* (母の発達, A Mother's Development [1996]), *Yūkai Mori-musume ibun* (幽界森娘異聞, Unauthentic Accounts of the Mori Daughter from the Other World [2001]), and *Konpira* (金毘羅, Kumbhīra [2004]). More recently, the *Dainihhon* trilogy called attention for its fierce satirization of today's society: "Dainihhon Ontako meiwaku-shi" (だいにっぽん、おんたこめいわく史, Annoying History of Ontako in Dainihhon [2006]), "Dainihhon Ronchiku ogeretu-ki" (だいにっぽん、ろんちくおげれつ記, Vulgar Record of Ronchiku in Dainihhon [2006]), and "Dainihhon Roriribe shindeke-roku"

(だいにっぽん、ろりりべしんでけ録, Death to the Lolita Complex and Liberalism in Dainihhon [2007]). Dainihhon is the author's creative variant of Dai Nippon (Great Japan).

Shōno characteristically writes colloquially and loquaciously, often with biting sarcasm, about human relations, worldly prejudices, mythology, and gender-based literary and social issues, moving back and forth between dream and reality, fantasy and daily life. "Shōsetsu-nai shōsetsu: 'Shōno Yoriko, shōsetsu' " (小説内小説、「小説笙野頼子」, Fiction Within Fiction: "Shōno Yoriko, Fiction"), included in this volume, is an independent segment of "S-kura meikyū kanketsu" (S-倉迷宮完結, S-kura Labyrinth, Completed), a novella constituting part 3 of a three-part novel, *S-kura meimō tsūshin* (S-倉迷妄通信, Illusory Communication from S-kura [2002]). The novel's first-person narrator is Sawano Senbon, the alter ego of the author Shōno. Sawano, a creation of the author-character Shōno, writes a piece of fiction on her creator. The novel as a whole has multiple narrative layers involving the author-character Shōno, the first-person narrator Sawano as created by Shōno, and Shōno as described by Sawano in third-person narration, which make the interpolated story in fact a story within a story within a story. The chapters are preceded by photos of the cats the narrator has protected, including the four that live with her. It also comes with Shōno Yoriko's small note in the back matter saying that all feline and human characters in the novel, including Shōno Yoriko therein, are fictitious. Shōno Yoriko skillfully lures the reader using layers of words and themes, dreams and realities, earnestness and playfulness.

Tamura Toshiko 田村俊子 (1884–1945)

Tamura Toshiko was born in Asakusa, Tokyo, the daughter of Satō Ryōken and Kinu. She attended what is today's Japan Women's University for one semester before leaving because of illness. She began studying writing with the novelist Kōda Rohan, and while doing so fell in love with another of Rohan's students, Tamura Shōgyo, whom she married in 1909 following his seven years of study abroad. After writing several pieces in literary Japanese, the results of which did not satisfy her, she left Rohan and pursued acting for two or so years, returning to writing in 1911. Her full-length novel *Akirame* (あきらめ, Giving Up [1911]), which she wrote with the encouragement and urging of Tamura Shōgyo, won the first prize in the Osaka Asahi's literary competition. Subsequently she published nearly every month in leading magazines, winning attention for her characteristic aestheticism as well as persistent exploration of male-female conflicts. As she became famous, however, she grew economically stressed because of her pleasure-seeking way of life, which also coincided with difficulties in her marriage. Eventually she had an affair with a married Asahi reporter, Suzuki Etsu, and in 1918 she followed him to Vancouver, where they lived as a married couple. She lived there for eighteen years until after his death. During that time, she hardly wrote fiction and instead devoted her time to supporting Suzuki's social movement and to enlightening Japanese women living in Canada. In 1936 she returned to Japan, and two years later she fell in love with Kubokawa Tsurujirō, nineteen years younger than she and the leftist writer husband of her close friend and novelist Sata Ineko. In order to end the relationship, in 1939 Tamura left for China, where she remained until she died, four months before the war ended. While in Shanghai, as a part-time embassy employee, she edited a literary journal addressed to Chinese women, *Nüsheng* (女声, Female Voices). The Tamura Toshiko Prize was established in 1960 with the use of her posthumous royalties. It lasted until 1976. Among its recipients are Mori Mari, Kurahashi Yumiko, Saegusa Kazuko, and Tsushima Yūko, authors represented in this volume.

"Kanojo no seikatsu" (彼女の生活, Her Daily Life [1915]) is a study of a young, aspiring woman writer's unsteady psychology as she periodically swings back and forth between housework and professional work, respect for family life and desire to establish her own identity, devotion and independence. An intelligent woman, she knows how to find a theoretical solution, but in real life her perfectionist efforts gradually drain her energy, partly because she belongs to an age when family demanded greater self-sacrifice from women than after the war. This story has recently been freshly reevaluated from the viewpoint of gender issues, along with her other well-known pieces, such as "Ikichi" (生き血, Blood of Living Beings [1911]), "Onna sakusha" (女作者, A Woman Writer [1913]), "Hōraku no kei" (焙烙の刑, Punishment at the Stake [1914]), and especially "Miira no kuchibeni" (木乃伊の口紅, A Mummy's Lipstick [1913]).

Tawada Yōko 多和田葉子 **(1960–)**

Tawada Yōko is among the first Japanese fiction writers to publish successfully both in Japanese and a European language. While studying Russian literature at Waseda University, at age nineteen, she toured Moscow, Warsaw, Berlin, Hamburg, and Frankfurt, experiencing alienation amid foreign languages. She subsequently worked in Hamburg for several years at an export book company and elsewhere, and in 2000 earned a PhD in German literature from the University of Zürich. After having lived in Hamburg for many years beginning in 1982, she now lives in Berlin.

A writer from early youth, Tawada began publishing professionally in 1987.

Nur da wo du bist da ist nichts (Only Where You Are There Is Nothing [1987]) consists of one short story and nineteen poems with the original Japanese alternating with German translations by Peter Pörtner. Her Japanese works include *Kitsunetsuki* (きつね月, Fox-Possessed Moon [1997]) (a collection of eighteen poetic prose pieces); "Kakato o nakushite" (かかとを失くして, recipient of the 1991 Gunzō Literary Prize, translated by Margaret Mitsutani as "Missing Heels" [1998]); "Inumukoiri" (犬婿入り, winner of the 1993 Akutagawa Prize, translated by Margaret Mitsutani as "The Bridegroom Was a Dog" [1998]); *Arufabetto no kizuguchi* (アルファベットの傷口, An Open Wound in the Alphabet [1993]) (essays); *Gottoharuto tetsudō* (ゴットハルト鉄道, The Gotthard Railway [1997]) (novellas); *Seijo densetsu* (聖女伝説, The Life of a Saintly Woman [1996]) (a novel); *Hikon* (飛魂 The Flying Spirit, 1998) (a novel); *Hikari to zerachin no raipuchihhi* (光とゼラチンのライプチッヒ, Leipzig of Light and Gelatin [2000]) (short stories). Tawada received the twenty-eighth Izumi Kyōka Prize for *Hinagiku no ocha no baai* (When It's Chamomile [2000]). The original Japanese of "Das Bad" (The Bath [1989], translated into German by Peter Pörtner]) remains deliberately unpublished, whereas an English translation was included in *Where Europe Begins* (trans. Susan Bernofsky and Yumi Selden [2002]), a work reflecting Tawada's characteristic play with language.

Among Tawada's original German works are *Das Fremde aus der Dose* (Canned Foreign [1992]) (two stories translated by Susan Bernofsky as "Canned Foreign" and "The Talisman"); *Die Kranichmaske, die bei Nacht strahlt* (The Crane Mask, Which Radiates at Night [1993]) (a stage play); *Ein Gast* (A Guest [1993]) (a collection of short stories); *Aber die Mandrainen müssen heute abend noch geraubt werden* (But the Mandarins Must Still Be Stolen This Evening [1996]) (a collection of prose poems); and *Wie der Wind im Ei* (As the Wind in the Egg [1996]) (a play).

In 1996 Tawada became the first Japanese recipient of the Adelbert von Chamisso Prize, awarded for German-language writings by an author whose mother tongue is not German. She was a 1997 recipient of the Förderpreis für Literatur der Hansestadt Hamburg (Hamburg City Prize for Encouraging Literature) for her "Wo Europa anfängt" (Where Europe Begins [1998], trans. Susan Bernofsky) and other pieces. Tadawa's more recent work includes *Ekusofonī* (エクソフォニー, Exophony [2003]) (essays); *Umi ni otoshita namae* (海に落とした名前, The Name That Dropped to the Sea [2006]) (novellas); and *Sōru-Berurin tamatsuki shokan* (ソウル―ベルリン玉突き書簡, Seoul–Berlin Billiard Letters [2007]) (correspondence with the ethnic Korean Japan-based writer Suh Kyungsik). Since 1987, Tawada has given numerous readings in cultural halls, theaters, and universities in and out of Germany, most notably in Japan and the United States.

Tawada's central theme is often language, or alienation from language. Turning that alienation and ambiguity to her advantage, she plays with words and creates new meanings. She also brings back to life old expressions from earlier Japanese literature, as in "Stars Scintillating in My Eyes," a tetralogy originally published in the *Asahi shimbun* in 1999 and published in 2000 in *Hinagiku no ocha no baai* (ヒナギクのお茶の場合) along with four other pieces. The title of this tetralogy, a quotation from the fourth story, not only plays with the name of the station and the scars on the eyes of the central character but also hints at Edo Japanese. The titles of the four stories employ archaisms from even earlier days; indeed, these stories of contemporary Hamburg are strewn with Japanese archaisms, including humorous echoes from Sei Shōnagon's diction, and this seemingly effortless combination of widely different elements is part of the charm of the work.

Tsushima Yūko 津島佑子 **(1947–)**

Tsushima Yūko was born in Tokyo to the famous novelist Dazai Osamu. Taking up writing herself while still at college, she made her debut with the publication of "Requiemu: Inu to otona no tame ni" (レクイエム—犬と大人のために, Requiem for a Dog and an Adult [1969]) in the journal *Mita bungaku* in 1969, the same year she graduated with a degree in English literature. Since her debut, her writing has received acclaim in Japan, and she has captured many prestigious literary awards, including the Women's Literature Prize for *Chōji* (寵児, Beloved Child [1978]) in 1978, the Kawabata Yasunari Prize for *Danmari ichi* (黙市, Silent Traders [1984]) in 1984, the Yomiuri Prize for Literature in 1986 for *Yoru no hikari ni owarete* (夜の光に追われて, Driven by the Light of Night [1986]), the Tanizaki and Noma Prizes for *Hi no yama: Yamazaru-ki* (火の山—山猿記, Mountain of Fire: An Account of a Wild Monkey [1998]), and the Murasaki Shikibu Prize for *Nara repōto* (ナラ・レポート, Nara Report [2005]).

Themes commonly explored in Tsushima's works are family relations, parenthood, sexuality, and the meaning of life and death, the universal nature of which make her works particularly accessible to non-Japanese readers. In Japan, they are especially popular among women readers for their strong heroines and positive treatment of female experience.

A distinctive feature of Tsushima's writing is her use of strikingly vivid natural imagery and minute detail to develop her themes and evoke the inner worlds of her characters. This technique, traditionally used by Japanese poets, dates back to the eleventh century. *Hikari no ryōbun* (光の領分, The Territory of Light [1979]), the collection from which the translation included in the present volume was taken, is one of the best examples to date of her use of the technique.

Yū Miri 柳美里 (1968–)

Yū Miri is one of Japan's most prominent contemporary writers. Born to Korean parents in Yokohama, her home life was frequently violent, and she encountered discrimination in school. After dropping out of high school in 1984, she joined the theater troupe Tokyo Kid Brothers. Several years later she founded her own drama troupe, Young May Party, and began writing plays. In the mid-1990s she turned to writing novels. Her breakthrough came in 1997 with the publication of the Akutagawa Prize–winning *Kazoku shinema* (家族シネマ, Family Cinema), in which a young career woman returns from work one day to find a film crew in her home making a movie about her troubled family life. Yū's 1998 novel *Gōrudo rasshu* (ゴールドラッシュ, Gold Rush) was inspired by a true story about a violent teenager who murders his father in order to take control of his pachinko business. It has been translated into English by Stephen Snyder. Beginning in the late nineties, Yū published a series of memoirs about her difficult life. *Inochi* (命, Life), published in 2000, is about her experiences as the single mother of the son she bore with a married man. The book became a runaway best seller and was later made into a movie. Yū has achieved a degree of popularity unprecedented for a writer of Korean descent. She appears frequently on television and is followed by the mainstream media. Although a Korean citizen, she resists defining herself as a minority writer, saying that she views herself as "neither Japanese nor Korean."

About the Editors and Translators

Michael K. Bourdaghs teaches modern Japanese literature at the University of Chicago. He is the author of *The Dawn That Never Comes: Shimazaki Tōson and Japanese Nationalism* and the translation editor of Kamei Hideo's *Transformations of Sensibility: The Phenomenology of Meiji Literature*, and coeditor of Natsume Sōseki's *Theory of Literature and Other Critical Writings*.

Susan Bouterey is currently the head of the School of Languages, Cultures and Linguistics at the University of Canterbury, Christchurch, New Zealand, where she lectures on Japanese literature and language. Her area of specialization is modern Japanese literature with a special emphasis on postwar Japanese women writers and Okinawan novelists.

Alisa Freedman is an assistant professor of Japanese literature and film at the University of Oregon. Her work investigates how the city shapes culture and psychology, giving rise to gender roles that characterize Japan. She is preparing two books: the first, *Tokyo in Transit: Japanese Culture on the Road and Rails* (forthcoming from Stanford University Press), explores the ways mass transportation have changed Japan's social fabric; the second analyzes images of working women on Japanese television. She is also editing a volume on *Modern Girls on the Go: Gender, Mobility, and Labor in Japan*. Freedman has published articles about Japanese youth culture, humor as social critique, the gender politics of "otaku" culture, the intersection of literature and new media, and has published translations of Japanese fiction, including Kawabata Yasunari's *The Scarlet Gang of Asakusa* (University of California Press, 2005).

Gillian Kinjo has been working as a freelance translator since graduating with a master of arts degree from the University of Canterbury in New Zealand.

246 ABOUT THE EDITORS AND TRANSLATORS

Based in Tokyo for the past ten years, she combines her work as a translator with raising her four children.

Seiji M. Lippit is associate professor of modern Japanese literature at the University of California, Los Angeles. He is the author of *Topographies of Japanese Modernism* and the editor of *The Essential Akutagawa*. He is currently working on a study of memory and urban space in postwar literature.

Noriko Mizuta is professor and chancellor of Josai University. Her research interests include American literature, comparative women's literature, and gender culture. She is the author of *Nijusseiki no josei hyōgen—Jendā bunka no gaibu* (Women's Self-Expression in the Twentieth Century: Toward the Externality of Gender Culture [2003]); *Joseigaku to no deai* (Encounters with Women's Studies [2004]); *Ozaki midori: Dai-nana kankai hōkō no sekai* (Midori Ozaki: The World of the Questing Seventh Sense [2005]); *Kanryū sabukarucha to josei* (Recent Trends in Women and the "Korean Wave" Culture in Gender Perspective [2006]); *Kiro* (Homebound Road, a collection of poems [2008]). She is also the editor-translator, with Kyoko Selden, of *Stories by Contemporary Japanese Women Writers* (1982), *Japanese Women Writers: Twentieth Century Short Fiction* (1991), and *The Funeral of a Giraffe: Seven Stories by Tomioka Taeko* (2000).

Kyoko Selden is editor and translator, with Noriko Mizuta, of *Stories by Contemporary Japanese Women Writers* (1982), *Japanese Women Writers: Twentieth Century Short Fiction* (1991), and *The Funeral of a Giraffe: Seven Stories by Tomioka Taeko* (2000). She is also the editor of *Annotated Japanese Literary Gems* (Cornell East Asia series), of which two volumes have appeared. Her other translations include *The Atomic Bomb: Voices from Hiroshima and Nagasaki* (1989), Kayano Shigeru's *Our Land Was a Forest* (1994), and Honda Katsuichi's *Harukor: An Ainu Woman's Tale* (2000).

Vyjayanthi Ratnam Selinger is assistant professor of Asian studies at Bowdoin College, where she teaches Japanese language and literature. Her primary research areas are medieval warrior literature and intellectual history. Her research has recently appeared in a special issue on the *Heike monogatari* in the journal *Kokubungaku* and in the spring 2009 issue of *Japanese Language and Literature*.

Robert Steen is an associate professor of Japanese language and literature at Oglethorpe University in Atlanta, Georgia. His research is on the postwar writer Sakaguchi Ango. His article on literary representations of Niigata in

Ango's fiction recently appeared in *Literary Mischief: Sakaguchi Ango, Culture, and the War*, edited by James Dorsey and Doug Slaymaker.

Angela Yiu is a professor at Sophia University, Tokyo, specializing in modern Japanese literature. Her current research interests include literature and urban space, utopian studies, and postwar literature. Recent publications include "Beautiful Town: The Discovery of the Suburbs and the Vision of the Garden City in Late Meiji and Taishō Literature," *Japan Forum* 18, no. 3 (2006); "Atarashikimura—The Literary Context of a Taishō Communal Village," *Japan Review*, no. 20 (2008); and "Okuizumi Hikaru and the Mystery of War Memory," in *Imag(in)ing the War in Japan: Representing and Responding to Trauma in Postwar Literature and Film*. Edited by David Stahl and Mark Williams. Leiden: Brill, 2010. She is the author of *Chaos and Order in the Works of Natsume Sōseki* (1998).